컴팩트 오픽 Compact OPIc IH-AL

북플레이트

컴팩트 오픽

초판 1쇄 발행 2025년 8월 29일
지은이 이보람, (주)지알케이에듀케이션
펴낸곳 (주)에스제이더블유인터내셔널
펴낸이 양홍걸 이시원

주소 서울시 영등포구 영신로 166 시원스쿨
구입 문의 02)2014-8151
고객센터 02)6409-0878

ISBN 979-11-7550-001-3 13740

이 책은 저작권법에 따라 보호받는 저작물이므로 무단복제와 무단전재를 금합니다.
이 책 내용의 전부 또는 일부를 이용하려면 반드시
저작권자와 (주)에스제이더블유인터내셔널의 서면 동의를 받아야 합니다.

서문 Preface

안녕하세요! 저는 이 책의 원고 집필에 참여한 오픽 강사 이보람입니다. 지금 이 자리에서 오픽 시험 준비를 위한 〈Compact OPIc 컴팩트 오픽〉을 소개하게 되어 매우 기쁘고 감사한 마음입니다. 오픽 강사로 활동하면서 많은 수험생이 시험에 대한 어려움과 불안을 겪는다는 사실에 공감하게 되었습니다. 저 또한 영어를 배울 때 그랬듯이, 수험생 여러분이 영어라는 큰 벽 앞에 놓여 있을 것이라는 생각으로 이 책을 집필했습니다.

영어 실력을 향상시키는 것은 쉬운 일이 아닙니다. 하지만, 올바른 학습 방법으로 꾸준히 노력한다면 누구나 유창한 영어 실력을 갖출 수 있다고 믿습니다. 이 책이 오픽 시험을 준비하는 수험생 여러분뿐만 아니라 궁극적으로 영어 실력을 키우고 싶은 많은 학습자에게 친절한 길잡이가 되기를 희망합니다.

〈Compact OPIc 컴팩트 오픽〉은 저만이 아니라 많은 전문가의 검토를 거쳐 가장 신뢰할 수 있는 정보를 제공하려고 노력했습니다. 이 책에서는 실제 오픽 시험에서 자주 출제되는 주제와 문제 유형, 그리고 효과적인 답변을 준비하는 방법과 학습 전략을 최대한 상세하게 다루었습니다. 또한 실전 모의고사를 포함하여 오픽 시험을 준비하는 학습자들이 필요로 하는 모든 정보를 최대한으로 제공하고 있습니다.

저는 이 책이 시험을 준비하는 수험생 여러분에게 큰 격려와 도움이 되기를 바랍니다. 포기하지 않고 노력한다면, 반드시 좋은 결과가 있을 것입니다. 오픽 시험을 준비하는 모든 수험생이 꿈꾸는 결과를 얻을 수 있도록 진심으로 응원합니다.

Hello! I am Lee Boram, an OPIc instructor who participated in the writing of this book. I am writing this with great joy and gratitude as I introduce <Compact OPIc: A Textbook for OPIc Test Preparation>. As an OPIc instructor, I empathize with the difficulties and anxieties many students face when preparing for the test. Just like when I was learning English, the thought that test-takers would face a significant barrier called English motivated me to write this book.

Improving English proficiency is not an easy task. However, I firmly believe that with consistent effort and the right learning approach, anyone can attain fluent English proficiency. I hope this book not only serves as a guide for test-takers preparing for the OPIc test but also as a friendly roadmap for many learners who aspire to enhance their English skills.

<Compact OPIc> has strived to provide the most reliable information, not only from my perspective but also through the review of many experts. In this book, we have covered frequently asked topics and question types in the actual OPIc test, along with effective ways to prepare responses and learning strategies, in as much detail as possible. Furthermore, we have included practical mock tests to provide learners preparing for the OPIc test with all the necessary information they need.

I genuinely hope this book serves as a source of encouragement and assistance to the students preparing for the OPIc test. If you persist and work hard, you will undoubtedly achieve favorable results. I sincerely cheer for all students preparing for the OPIc test to achieve the results they dream of.

목차 Contents

 교재 활용 가이드

- <컴팩트 오픽> 미리 보기
  Preview of this book
- 맞춤 완성 학습 플랜
  Learning plan

 OPIc 공략 가이드

- 시험 소개
  All About OPIc
- 시험 진행 순서
  The order of exam
- 백그라운드 서베이 응답 전략
  Strategy for the background survey
- 난이도 선택 전략
  Strategy for the self-assessment
- 자기 소개 답변 연습
  How to respond to the first question

Section 1 설문 주제 Survey-based Questions

Chapter 1 Job 신분
Unit 1   Combo Set (1)   22
Unit 2   Combo Set (2)   31

Chapter 2 Residence 거주
Unit 3   Combo Set (1)   42
Unit 4   Combo Set (2)   51

Chapter 3 Watching 관람·시청
Unit 5   Combo Set (1)   62
Unit 6   Combo Set (2)   71

Chapter 4 Listening to Music 음악 감상
Unit 7   Combo Set (1)   82
Unit 8   Combo Set (2)   91

Chapter 5 Reading·Cooking 독서·요리
Unit 9   Combo Set (1)   102
Unit 10 Combo Set (2)   111

Chapter 6 Exercise 운동
Unit 11 Combo Set (1)   122
Unit 12 Combo Set (2)   131

Chapter 7 Travel·Business Trip 여행·출장
Unit 13 Combo Set (1)   142
Unit 14 Combo Set (2)   151

Section 2 | 돌발 주제 Random Questions

Chapter 8 Weather·Season 날씨·계절
    Unit 15   Combo Set (1)   164
    Unit 16   Combo Set (2)   173

Chapter 9 Recycling 재활용
    Unit 17   Combo Set (1)   184
    Unit 18   Combo Set (2)   193

Chapter 10 Fashion·Industry 패션·산업
    Unit 19   Combo Set (1)   204
    Unit 20   Combo Set (2)   213

Chapter 11 Geography·Environmental Issues
지형·환경 문제
    Unit 21   Combo Set (1)   224
    Unit 22   Combo Set (2)   233

Chapter 12 Transportation·Health 교통·건강
    Unit 23   Combo Set (1)   244
    Unit 24   Combo Set (2)   253

Chapter 13 Bank 은행
    Unit 25   Combo Set (1)   264
    Unit 26   Combo Set (2)   273

Chapter 14 Technology·Internet 기술·인터넷
    Unit 27   Combo Set (1)   284
    Unit 28   Combo Set (2)   293

Chapter 15 Holiday·Gathering 명절·모임
    Unit 29   Combo Set (1)   304
    Unit 30   Combo Set (2)   313

부록 Appendix

Actual Test 01   324
Actual Test 02   325

〈컴팩트 오픽〉 미리 보기 Preview of this book

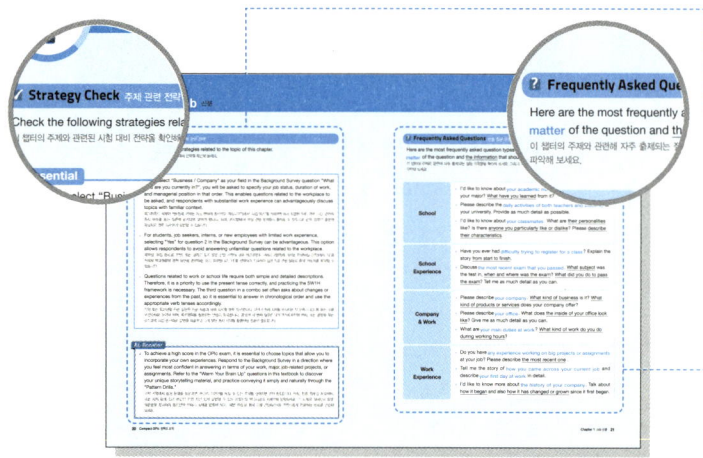

Strategy Check 주제 관련 전략

이 챕터의 주제와 관련된 시험 대비 전략을 확인해 보세요. AL을 목표로 하고 있다면 AL Booster에서 다루는 내용까지 학습할 것을 권장합니다.

Frequently Asked Questions 기출 질문

다음은 이 챕터의 주제와 관련해 가장 자주 출제되는 질문들입니다. 각 질문의 중심 소재와 질문이 요구하는 정보가 무엇인지 파악해 보세요.

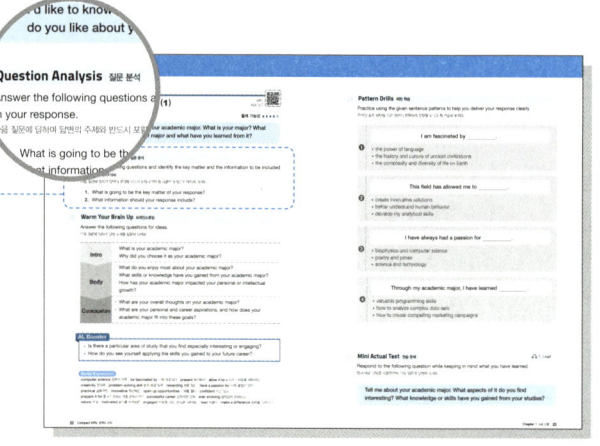

Question Analysis 질문 분석

문제를 잘못 이해하여 동문서답하지 않도록, 질문 내용을 정확하게 파악하는 연습을 합니다.

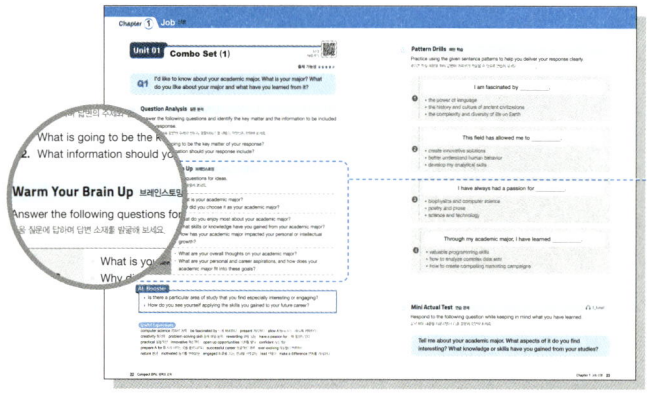

Warm Your Brain Up 브레인스토밍

제공되는 질문들을 통해 본인이 가장 자신 있게 말할 수 있는 답변 소재를 브레인스토밍 합니다.

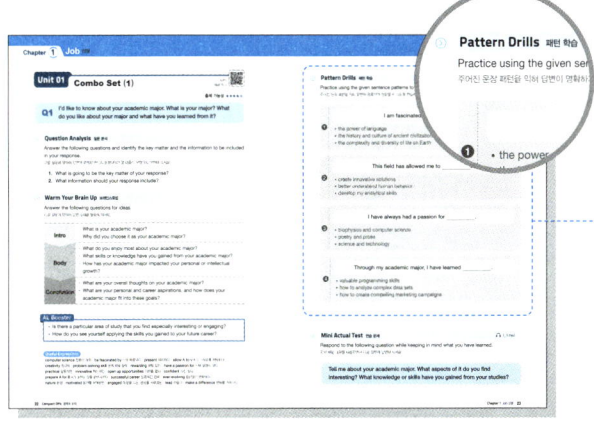

Pattern Drills 패턴 학습

브레인스토밍 한 소재들을 효과적이고 조리 있게 말할 수 있도록, 문장 패턴을 익혀 본인만의 문장을 만들어 봅니다.

Mini Actual Test 연습 문제

앞서 학습한 내용을 바탕으로 실제 시험에 임하는 것처럼 질문에 답변하는 연습을 합니다.

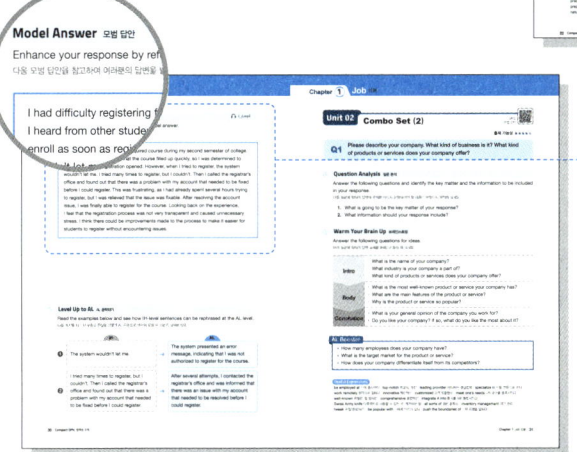

Model Answer 모범 답안

AL 득점자의 답변을 확인한 후 본인의 답변과 비교하여 어떤 점을 개선할 수 있는지 확인합니다.

Level Up to AL AL 공략하기

IH 수준의 문장을 AL 득점자는 어떻게 말하는지 살펴보고, 본인의 문장을 개선하여 완벽한 AL 등급을 받을 수 있도록 대비합니다.

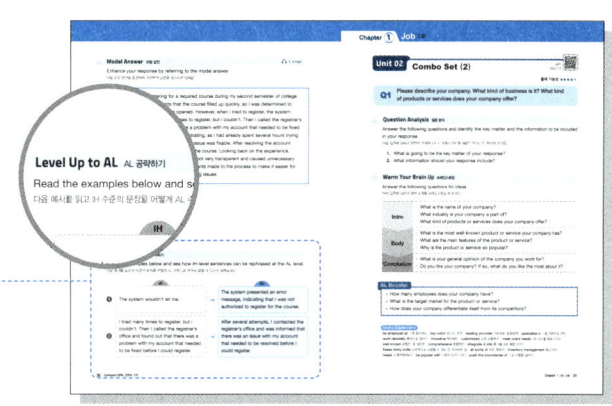

맞춤 완성 학습 플랜 Learning Plan

2주 완성

#단기 완성 #12일 #하루3단원

1. 단기간의 본 교재를 최대한 효과적으로 활용하는 방법은 〈모범 답안〉부터 역순으로 학습하는 것입니다.
2. 〈모범 답안〉에서 주요 아이디어를 차용하고, 〈패턴 학습〉을 통해 아이디어를 본인만의 문장으로 바꾸어 말해 봅시다. 답안 내용이 충분하지 않다고 생각한다면, 〈브레인스토밍〉의 질문들을 참고하여 소재를 추가해 보세요.
3. 하루에 많게는 3가지 주제를 다루게 되므로, 학습한 내용이 휘발되지 않도록 아이디어나 기억해야 할 포인트들을 필기해 두세요. 또한, 일일이 스크립트를 작성하기보다 〈연습 문제〉를 통해 답변을 녹음하고, 녹음본을 들으며 개선점을 정리하길 권장합니다.

Day 1	Day 2	Day 3	Day 4	Day 5	Day 6
년 월 일	년 월 일	년 월 일	년 월 일	년 월 일	년 월 일
☐ Unit 1(2) ☐ Unit 3 ☐ Unit 4	☐ Unit 5 ☐ Unit 6 ☐ Unit 7	☐ Unit 8 ☐ Unit 9 ☐ Unit 10	☐ Unit 11 ☐ Unit 12 ☐ Unit 13	☐ Unit 14 ☐ Unit 15 ☐ Unit 16	☐ Unit 17 ☐ Unit 18 ☐ Unit 19
Day 7	**Day 8**	**Day 9**	**Day 10**	**Day 11**	**Day 12**
년 월 일	년 월 일	년 월 일	년 월 일	년 월 일	년 월 일
☐ Unit 20 ☐ Unit 21 ☐ Unit 22	☐ Unit 23 ☐ Unit 24 ☐ Unit 25	☐ Unit 26 ☐ Unit 27 ☐ Unit 28	☐ Unit 29 ☐ Unit 30 ☐ Final Review	☐ Actual Test 01	☐ Actual Test 02

4주 완성

#꼼꼼 대비 #20일 #하루2단원

1. 빈출 유형에 꼼꼼하게 대비하고 싶다면, 교재 구성을 순서대로 차근차근 학습할 것을 권장합니다.
2. 〈브레인스토밍〉에서 발굴한 아이디어에 〈패턴 학습〉의 문장 패턴을 접목시켜 본인만의 답변을 구성한 뒤, 〈모범 답안〉 및 〈AL 공략하기〉와 비교하여 본인의 문장 구성력을 발전시켜 보세요.
3. 각 섹션을 학습한 후 배운 내용을 복습하며 어려웠던 점과 유념해야 할 점을 정리해 보세요. 정리한 내용을 응시 당일, 시험이 시작되기 직전 복기하며 실수 없이 본시험을 치를 수 있도록 해 보세요.

Day 1	Day 2	Day 3	Day 4	Day 5
년 월 일	년 월 일	년 월 일	년 월 일	년 월 일
☐ 자기소개연습 ☐ Unit 1(2)	☐ Unit 3 ☐ Unit 4	☐ Unit 5 ☐ Unit 6	☐ Unit 7 ☐ Unit 8	☐ Unit 9 ☐ Unit 10
Day 6	**Day 7**	**Day 8**	**Day 9**	**Day 10**
년 월 일	년 월 일	년 월 일	년 월 일	년 월 일
☐ Unit 11 ☐ Unit 12	☐ Unit 13 ☐ Unit 14	☐ 섹션 복습	☐ Unit 15 ☐ Unit 16	☐ Unit 17 ☐ Unit 18

Day 11	Day 12	Day 13	Day 14	Day 15
년 월 일	년 월 일	년 월 일	년 월 일	년 월 일
☐ Unit 19 ☐ Unit 20	☐ Unit 21 ☐ Unit 22	☐ Unit 23 ☐ Unit 24	☐ Unit 25 ☐ Unit 26	☐ Unit 27 ☐ Unit 28
Day 16	**Day 17**	**Day 18**	**Day 19**	**Day 20**
년 월 일	년 월 일	년 월 일	년 월 일	년 월 일
☐ Unit 29 ☐ Unit 30	☐ 섹션 복습	☐ Actual Test 01	☐ Actual Test 02	☐ 최종 정리

6주 완성 #부담 제로 #30일 #하루1단원

1. 일일 한 개 단원을 완벽하게 소화한다고 생각하며, 교재 구성을 순서대로 꼼꼼하게 학습할 것을 권장합니다.
2. 〈브레인스토밍〉을 통해 얻은 아이디어와 그 외 학습 단계에서 배운 표현 및 문장 패턴 중 꼭 기억해야 할 것들을 정리해 놓으세요.
3. 〈연습 문제〉 단계에서 본인의 답변을 녹음해 보고, 녹음한 내용을 들으며 〈모범 답안〉 및 〈AL 공략하기〉의 문장들과 비교해 보세요. 이를 통해 본인의 답변을 개선할 수 있는 방향을 분석해 보고, 개선점을 정리해 보세요.

Day 1	Day 2	Day 3	Day 4	Day 5
년 월 일	년 월 일	년 월 일	년 월 일	년 월 일
☐ 자기소개연습 ☐ Unit 1(2)	☐ Unit 3	☐ Unit 4	☐ Unit 5	☐ Unit 6
Day 6	**Day 7**	**Day 8**	**Day 9**	**Day 10**
년 월 일	년 월 일	년 월 일	년 월 일	년 월 일
☐ Unit 7	☐ Unit 8	☐ Unit 9	☐ Unit 10	☐ Unit 11
Day 11	**Day 12**	**Day 13**	**Day 14**	**Day 15**
년 월 일	년 월 일	년 월 일	년 월 일	년 월 일
☐ Unit 12	☐ Unit 13	☐ Unit 14	☐ Unit 15	☐ Unit 16
Day 16	**Day 17**	**Day 18**	**Day 19**	**Day 20**
년 월 일	년 월 일	년 월 일	년 월 일	년 월 일
☐ Unit 17	☐ Unit 18	☐ Unit 19	☐ Unit 20	☐ Unit 21
Day 21	**Day 22**	**Day 23**	**Day 24**	**Day 25**
년 월 일	년 월 일	년 월 일	년 월 일	년 월 일
☐ Unit 22	☐ Unit 23	☐ Unit 24	☐ Unit 25	☐ Unit 26
Day 26	**Day 27**	**Day 28**	**Day 29**	**Day 30**
년 월 일	년 월 일	년 월 일	년 월 일	년 월 일
☐ Unit 27	☐ Unit 28	☐ Unit 29	☐ Unit 30	☐ Actual Test 01 ☐ Actual Test 02

OPIc 시험 소개 All about OPIc

• OPIc이란?

OPIc(Oral Proficiency Interview – computer)은 컴퓨터를 통해 진행되는 외국어 말하기 시험입니다. 시험 당일, 응시자는 배정받은 자리의 컴퓨터 헤드셋을 착용하고 화면 및 음성 지시에 따라 시험을 진행하게 됩니다. 컴퓨터 화면에는 가상의 시험 진행자가 나타나며, 이 인물과 질문을 주고 받는 형식으로 시험이 진행됩니다.

OPIc은 어휘나 문법 같이 응시자의 단편적인 지식을 평가하지 않습니다. 이 시험의 평가 기준은 '실제 상황에서 얼마나 효과적이고 적절하게 언어를 구사하는지'이므로, 응시자는 다방면으로 영어 실력을 향상시킬 필요가 있습니다.

2007년부터 국내에서 시행되어 현재 약 1,700여 개 기업 및 기관에서 채용과 인사 고과를 위해 활용되고 있으며, 최근에는 회화 실력에 대한 기업의 수요가 높아져 필기 시험보다 OPIc에서 높은 레벨을 취득하고자 하는 응시자들이 증가하는 추세입니다.

• OPIc 한 눈에 보기

시험 시간	• 총 약 60분 • 오리엔테이션 20분 + 본시험 40분 ※ 문항 청취 시간 제외 약 30~35분 간 답변
문제 개수	• 난이도 1~2 : 12문항　　　• 난이도 3~6 : 15문항
시험 특징	• 백그라운드 서베이 응답 기반 개인 맞춤형 주제 + 교통, 환경, 산업 등 무작위로 출제되는 일반 주제 • 하나의 주제에 2~3개 문제가 연이어 출제
평가 기준	• 응시자의 회화 역량을 4가지 영역으로 평가 • 과제 수행 기능: 특정 과제를 수행하기 위한 언어 능력 • 문맥 및 내용: 과제를 수행하기 위해 사용하는 언어적 문맥 및 내용 • 정확도 및 의사 전달 능력: 답변의 보편적 이해도, 정확성 • 문장 구성 능력: 답변의 길이와 구성 능력
평가 등급	• 총 9개 등급(NL, NM, NH, IL, IM1, IM2, IM3, IH, AL) • 인문계열 대졸자 취업 시 평균적으로 IH/AL 등급을 요구 • 이공계열 대졸자 취업 시 평균적으로 IM2 이상의 등급을 요구
평가 방식	• 절대 평가 • 응시자의 답변 녹음본을 시험 개발사 ACTFL 공식 채점인에게 전달 • 공식 채점인은 ACTFL의 평가 기준에 따라 응시자에게 등급 부여
접수 방법	• 온라인 접수만 가능 • 오픽 공식 웹사이트(www.opic.or.kr)에서 시험 일정 확인 및 접수 가능 • 접수 시 세부 진단서를 신청하고 추가 금액을 지불할 시, 세부 영역에 대한 진단표와 채점인의 코멘트 제공
결과 발표	• 응시일로부터 5일 후 온라인 발표
시험 규정	• 준비물: 규정 신분증, 수험표 • 유의 사항: 　① 시험 도중 필기 금지 　② 시험 도중 휴대 전화 음성(진동)이 울리거나 전자 기기 소지 적발 시 당회 시험 무효 처리 및 1년간 응시 제한 　③ 25일 규정으로 인해 OPIc 시험 응시자는 최근 응시일로부터 25일 간 재응시 제한 　④ 단, 응시자별 1회에 한하여 25일 내 재응시할 수 있는 웨이버(Waiver) 제도 존재 　⑤ 성적 유효 기간은 시험 시행일로부터 2년

• OPIc 등급 체계

등급	등급별 요약 설명	
AL (Advanced Low)	사건을 서술할 때 일관적으로 동사 시제를 관리하고, 사람과 사물을 묘사할 때 다양한 형용사를 사용한다. 적절한 위치에서 접속사를 사용하기 때문에 문장간의 결속력도 높고 문단의 구조를 능숙하게 구성할 수 있다. 익숙하지 않은 복잡한 상황에서도 문제를 설명하고 해결할 수 있는 수준의 능숙도다.	취업/승진시 평균적으로 요구되는 등급
IH (Intermediate High)	개인에게 익숙하지 않거나 예측하지 못한 복잡한 상황을 만날 때, 대부분의 상황에서 사건을 설명하고 문제를 효과적으로 해결할 수 있다. 발화량이 많고, 다양한 어휘를 사용한다.	
IM (Intermediate Mid)	일상적인 소재 뿐 아니라 개인적으로 익숙한 상황에서는 문장을 나열하며 자연스럽게 말할 수 있다. 다양한 문장형식이나 어휘를 실험적으로 사용하려고 하며, 상대방이 조금만 배려해주면 오랜 시간 대화가 가능하다. ※ IM 등급은 IM1(하), IM2(중), IM3(상)으로 세분화하여 제공된다.	
IL (Intermediate Low)	일상적인 소재에서는 문장으로 말할 수 있다. 대화에 참여하고 선호하는 소재에서는 자신감을 가지고 말할 수 있다.	
NH (Novice High)	일상적인 대부분의 소재에 대해서 문장으로 말할 수 있다. 개인정보에 대해 질문을 하고 응답을 할 수 있다.	
NM (Novice Mid)	이미 암기한 단어나 문장으로 말하기를 할 수 있다.	
NL (Novice Low)	제한적인 수준이지만 영어 단어를 나열하며 말할 수 있다.	

시험 진행 순서 The order of exam

• ORIENTATION 오리엔테이션(약 20분)

오리엔테이션은 본격적인 시험을 시작하기 전 진행됩니다. 4단계로 진행되며, 이 중 첫 순서인 백그라운드 서베이와 두 번째 순서인 자가 평가는 본시험에 어떤 문항이 출제될지 결정짓는 설문이므로 신중하게 응답할 것을 권장합니다.

Background Survey 사전 설문 조사

− 4개의 파트로 구분하여 7개 주제에 대해 설문
− 응시자가 선택한 항목 중 일부가 본시험의 주제로 출제

Tips! 본 교재의 〈백그라운드 서베이 응답 전략(p.00)〉을 확인하여 효율적인 시험 대비를 위해 어떤 전략을 세워야 하는지 파악해 보세요.

Self Assessment 시험 난이도 선택

− 1~6단계의 난이도 중 택1
− 레벨6이 가장 어려운 수준
− 각 난이도별 말하기 수준에 대한 설명과 샘플 음원이 제공

Tips! 본 교재의 〈난이도 선택 전략(p.00)〉을 확인하여 시험장에서 선택할 난이도를 미리 정해두고 시험 대비 계획을 세워 보세요.

Pre-Test Setup 사전 점검

− 기술 점검 단계
− 화면이 제대로 작동하는지, 음량이 본인에게 맞는지, 녹음이 정상적으로 되는지 확인
− 직접 녹음한 뒤 들어보는 단계에서 목소리 크기를 어느 정도로 해야 하는지 가늠할 수 있음

Sample Question 시험 미리 보기

− 화면 조작 안내
− 화면 구성, 질문 재청취 방법, 시험 진행 방식을 미리 파악할 수 있음

• **TEST** 본 시험 (약 40분)

본 시험은 두 개의 세션으로 구성되어 있으며, 첫 번째 세션이 끝나고 난 뒤에는 시험의 난이도를 다시 설정할 수 있는 기회가 주어집니다.

1st Session 첫 번째 세션
- 약 7문제 출제
- 자기 소개를 해달라는 질문으로 시작
- 문제를 듣고 5초 이내 Replay 누르면 한 번 더 청취 가능
- 준비 및 답변 시간 제한 없음

Difficulty Level Adjustment 난이도 재조정
- 시험 난이도를 다시 설정할 수 있음
- 기존 난이도와 비교하여 '쉽게,' '비슷하게,' '어렵게' 3개의 선택지 중 택1
- 응답 결과에 따라 두 번째 세션의 난이도가 조정

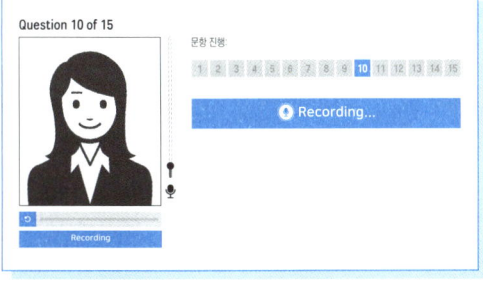

2nd Session 두 번째 세션
- 난이도가 조정된 상태에서 문제 출제
- 1~2단계 수준이면 5문제, 3~6단계 수준이면 8문제 출제

백그라운드 서베이 응답 전략
Strategy for the background survey

- 백그라운드 서베이는 4개의 파트로 구분되어 있으며, 응시자는 8~12개의 문항에 응답하게 됩니다. 문항 개수가 가변적인 이유는, 직업 유무를 묻는 파트 1에서 응시자의 응답에 따라 추가 질문의 개수가 달라지기 때문입니다.
- 백그라운드 서베이 응답에 따라 본시험에 출제되는 문제가 달라지므로, 시험에 응시하기 전 백그라운드 서베이에서 어떤 항목을 선택할 것인지 미리 정해 놓을 것을 권장합니다. 이때, 본인이 직접 경험하였거나 잘 알고 있으며, 말하기 쉬운 주제를 선택하는 것이 중요합니다. 잘 알고 있는 주제이더라도, 영어로 설명하기 복잡하다면 선택을 피해 출제 가능성을 차단하는 것이 좋습니다.
- 1번부터 3번까지의 문항에서는 선택지를 1개만 고르면 됩니다. 단, 4번부터 7번까지는 4개 문항 합산 12개 이상의 선택지를 골라야 하며 4번은 최소 2개 이상, 나머지 문항은 최소 1개 이상의 항목을 선택해야 한다는 제한이 있습니다.
- 시험 범위를 최소화하려면, 백그라운드 서베이의 항목을 전략적으로 선택하는 것이 중요하며 연계하여 대비할 수 있는 주제들을 고르는 것이 좋습니다. 아래 백그라운드 서베이 화면을 참고하여 시험 대비 계획을 세워 보세요.

백그라운드 서베이 응답 예시

Part 1 of 4

1. 현재 귀하는 어느 분야에 종사하고 계십니까?
   - ☐ 사업/회사
   - ☐ 재택근무/재택사업
   - ☐ 교사/교육자
   - ☐ 일 경험 없음

("교사/교육자"를 선택한 경우) 현재 귀하는 어디에서 학생을 가르치십니까?
   - ☐ 대학 이상
   - ☐ 초등/중/고등학교
   - ☐ 평생교육

1.1. 현재 귀하는 직업이 있으십니까?
   - ☐ 예
   - ☐ 아니오

1.2. 귀하의 근무 기간은 얼마나 되십니까?
   - ☐ 첫직장- 2개월 미만
   - ☐ 첫직장- 2개월 이상
   - ☐ 첫직장 아님 – 경험 많음

("교사/교육자"를 선택한 경우) 귀하의 근무 기간은 얼마나 되십니까?
   - ☐ 2개월 미만 – 첫직장
   - ☐ 2개월 미만 – 교직은 처음이지만 이전에 다른 직업을 가진 적이 있음
   - ☐ 2개월 이상

1.3. 귀하는 부하직원을 관리하는 관리직을 맡고 있습니까?
   - ☐ 예
   - ☐ 아니요

Part 2 of 4

2. 현재 당신은 학생입니까?
   - ☐ 예
   - ☐ 아니요

> 1~2번에서는 본인이 가장 잘 대답할 수 있는 항목으로 응답하는 것이 좋습니다. 다만, 1번에서 '일 경험 없음'을 선택하고 2번에서 '아니오'와 '수강 후 5년이 지남'을 선택하는 경우 신분 관련 주제가 출제되지 않을 확률이 높아집니다.

2.1. ("예"를 선택한 경우) 현재 어떤 강의를 듣고 있습니까?
- ☐ 학위 과정 수업
- ☐ 전문 기술 향상을 위한 평생 학습
- ☐ 어학수업

2.2. ("아니오"를 선택한 경우) 현재 어떤 강의를 듣고 있습니까?
- ☐ 학위 과정 수업
- ☐ 전문 기술 향상을 위한 평생 학습
- ☐ 어학수업
- ☐ 수강 후 5년 이상 지남

Part 3 of 4

3. 현재 귀하는 어디에 살고 계십니까?
- ☑ 개인주택이나 아파트에 홀로 거주
- ☐ 친구나 룸메이트와 함께 주택이나 아파트에 거주
- ☐ 가족(배우자/자녀/기타 가족 일원)과 함께 주택이나 아파트에 거주
- ☐ 학교 기숙사
- ☐ 군대 막사

Part 4 of 4

4. 아래의 설문에서 총 12개 이상의 항목을 선택하십시오. 귀하는 여가 활동으로 주로 무엇을 하십니까? (두 개 이상 선택)
- ☑ 영화 보기
- ☐ 클럽/나이트클럽 가기
- ☑ 공연 보기
- ☑ 콘서트 보기
- ☐ 박물관 가기
- ☐ 공원 가기
- ☑ TV 시청
- ☐ 쇼핑하기
- ☐ 캠핑 가기
- ☐ 해변 가기
- ☐ 스포츠 관람
- ☐ 게임하기
- ☐ 리얼리티 방송 시청
- ☐ 주거 개선
- ☐ 자원 봉사 하기
- ☐ SNS에 글 올리기
- ☐ 요리 관련 프로 시청
- ☐ 구직 활동
- ☐ 술집/바에 가기
- ☐ 친구들과 문자하기
- ☐ 당구 치기
- ☐ 시험 대비 과정 수강
- ☐ 차로 드라이브 하기
- ☐ 뉴스 보거나 듣기
- ☐ 카페/커피 전문점 가기
- ☐ 체스하

5. 귀하의 취미나 관심사는 무엇입니까? (한 개 이상 선택)
- ☐ 아이에게 책 읽어주기
- ☐ 그림 그리기
- ☑ 음악 감상하기
- ☐ 악기 연주하기
- ☐ 춤 추기
- ☐ 애완 동물 기르기
- ☑ 독서
- ☐ 혼자 노래 부르거나 합창하기
- ☐ 글쓰기(편지, 단문, 시 등)
- ☑ 요리하기
- ☐ 여행 관련 잡지나 블로그 글 읽기
- ☐ 사진 촬영하기
- ☐ 주식 투자하기
- ☐ 신문 읽기

6. 귀하는 주로 어떤 운동을 즐기십니까? (한 개 이상 선택)
- ☐ 농구
- ☐ 야구/소프트볼
- ☐ 축구
- ☐ 미식 축구
- ☐ 하키
- ☐ 크리켓
- ☐ 골프
- ☐ 배구
- ☐ 테니스
- ☐ 배드민턴
- ☐ 탁구
- ☐ 수영
- ☐ 자전거
- ☐ 스키/스노우보드
- ☐ 아이스 스케이트
- ☑ 조깅
- ☑ 걷기
- ☐ 요가
- ☑ 하이킹/트레킹
- ☐ 낚시
- ☐ 헬스
- ☐ 태권도
- ☐ 운동 수업 수강하기
- ☑ 운동을 전혀 하지 않음

> 6번에서는 답변을 연계하여 준비하기 쉬운 '조깅,' '걷기,' '하이킹/트레킹'을 선택하고 추가로 '운동을 전혀 하지 않음'을 선택하면 운동 관련 주제의 출제 확률을 낮출 수 있습니다.

7. 귀하는 어떤 휴가나 출장을 다녀온 경험이 있습니까? (한 개 이상 선택)
- ☐ 국내출장
- ☐ 해외출장
- ☑ 집에서 보내는 휴가
- ☐ 국내 여행
- ☐ 해외 여행

난이도 선택 전략
Strategy for the self-assessment

1. **난이도 선택이란?**

   오픽은 다른 시험과는 다르게 응시자가 직접 출제 난이도를 선택할 수 있습니다. 응시자에게는 시험 시작 전과 중간, 2회의 난이도 선택 기회가 주어집니다. 이때, 응시자가 선택한 난이도에 따라 출제 문항 개수와 획득 가능한 등급의 상한선이 달라질 수 있습니다. 오픽 난이도는 1부터 6까지 총 여섯 가지 단계로 나누어지며, 시험 출제 형식이 동일함을 기준으로 1과 2를 낮은 수준, 3과 4를 중간 수준, 5와 6을 높은 수준으로 구분합니다.

2. **난이도 1~2 선택 시**

   난이도 1 또는 2를 선택할 경우, 학생들은 총 12개의 질문을 받게 되며 이 난이도를 선택한 응시자는 평균적으로 IL 등급을 받을 수 있습니다.

3. **난이도 3 이상 선택 시**

   난이도 3 이상을 선택하면 총 15개의 질문을 받게 되는데, 이때 난이도 3, 4와 난이도 5, 6의 가장 큰 차이는 14번과 15번 문제 유형에 있습니다. 난이도 3 또는 4를 선택하면 14번 문제는 일반 서술형 문항이 출제되고, 15번 문제는 역할극 문항이 출제됩니다. 반면, 난이도 5 또는 6을 선택하는 경우, 14번 문항은 비교/대조를 요구하는 질문이 출제되고, 15번 문항은 사회 이슈와 관련한 질문이 출제되는 경향이 있습니다.

4. **난이도 선택 전략**

   14번과 15번의 문제 형식을 고려하여 자신 있게 답변할 수 있는 난이도를 선택하세요. 통계적으로 5 또는 6단계를 선택하면 IH, AL을 획득할 수 있는 가능성이 높아집니다. 다만, 난이도 선택은 부수적인 전략일뿐, 가장 중요한 것은 본인의 답변 수준임을 유념하도록 합시다.

시험 당일 꿀팁
What to do on the day of the test

1. **시험 전, 자기 소개를 위한 간단한 대본이나 핵심 문장을 준비해 보세요.**

   자기 소개는 오픽 시험의 첫 질문이자, 고정으로 출제되는 문제입니다. 자기 소개는 채점 범위에 포함되지 않는다고 하지만, 채점에 영향을 줄 수는 있습니다. 오픽은 사람이 채점하는 시험이므로 자기 소개에서 좋은 인상을 남길 수 있도록 합니다.

2. **시험 중 집중력을 유지하세요.**

   시험 질문이 화면에 표시되지 않으므로 질문을 정확하게 듣고 이해하는 것이 중요합니다. 만약 질문을 듣지 못했다면, 재청취 기회를 최대한 활용하세요.

3. **일상 생활에서 지인과 대화하듯 편하게 말하세요.**

   오픽은 유창성을 평가하는 시험이므로 자연스럽게 말하는 것이 무엇보다 중요합니다. 본인의 답변이 잘 들릴 수 있도록 적절한 속도와 억양을 유지하는 데 신경 써 보세요. 또한 답변 중 실수했다면, 말을 멈추는 대신 "which means"나 "What I am trying to say is" 등의 표현을 사용해 정적을 메워 보세요.

4. **답변 시간을 잘 분배하세요.**

   모든 질문에 충분한 시간을 할애할 수 있도록 하세요. 본시험은 총 40분으로 제한되어 있으므로 각 질문에 적절한 시간을 분배하여 대답하는 것이 중요합니다.

자기 소개 답변 연습
How to respond to the first question

1. **미리 준비하기**
   시험 전, 어떤 주요 내용을 언급할지 미리 준비해 보세요.

2. **인사로 시작하기**
   "Hello," "Nice to talk to you" 등 가벼운 인사말로 자기 소개를 시작해 보세요. 인사말로 시작하는 자기 소개는 친근한 분위기를 조성할 뿐만 아니라, 긴장을 풀어주고 자신감을 불어넣어 줄 수 있습니다.

3. **간결하게 소개하기**
   이름, 출신 지역, 학력이나 직업에 관한 간단한 정보를 이야기해 보세요. 길고 장황하게 설명하지 않고 간결하고 명료하게 표현하세요.

4. **자신감 있게 말하기**
   발화 시 자신감 있는 태도가 중요합니다. 명확한 목소리로 말하고, 긍정적이고 적극적인 어조와 톤을 유지하여 채점관에게 좋은 인상을 심어 줍시다.

1. **Prepare in advance**
   Take some time before the exam to prepare what key points you want to mention.

2. **Start with a greeting**
   Begin your self-introduction with a light greeting such as "Hello" or "Nice to talk to you." Starting with a greeting sets a friendly tone and helps to ease tension while instilling confidence.

3. **Keep it concise**
   Provide brief information including your name, hometown, education, or occupation. Avoid being long-winded and express yourself in a concise and clear manner.

4. **Speak confidently**
   Show confidence when speaking. Use a clear voice, maintain a positive and proactive tone, and create a favorable impression.

Basic Sentence Patterns

- **Hello, my name is [Your Name].** 안녕하세요. 제 이름은 [이름]입니다.
- **Nice to meet you.** 만나서 반갑습니다.
- **I'm from [Your City/Country].** 저는 [도시/나라] 출신입니다.
- **I'm currently studying [Your Major/Subject].** 저는 현재 [전공/과목]을 공부하고 있습니다.
- **I have [number] years of experience in [Your Field/Industry].** 저는 [숫자]년간 [분야/산업]에서 경험을 쌓았습니다.
- **I'm interested in [Your Hobbies/Interests].** 저는 [취미/관심사]에 관심이 있습니다.
- **I speak [Languages]. My proficiency level in English is [Proficiency Level].** [언어]를 구사합니다. 영어의 숙련도는 [숙련도 수준]입니다.
- **In my free time, I enjoy [Your Activities/Hobbies].** 여가 시간에는 [활동/취미]를 즐깁니다.

Section

01

Survey-based Questions

선택 주제

- **Chapter 1** 신분 Job
- **Chapter 2** 거주 Residence
- **Chapter 3** 관람·시청 Watching
- **Chapter 4** 음악 감상 Listening to Music
- **Chapter 5** 독서·요리 Reading·Cooking
- **Chapter 6** 운동 Exercise
- **Chapter 7** 여행·출장 Travel·Business Trip

Chapter 1

Job 신분

✓ Strategy Check 주제 관련 전략

Check the following strategies related to the topic of this chapter.
이 챕터의 주제와 관련된 시험 대비 전략을 확인해 보세요.

IH Essential

- If you select "Business / Company" as your field in the Background Survey question "What field are you currently in?", you will be asked to specify your job status, duration of work, and managerial position in that order. This enables questions related to the workplace to be asked, and respondents with substantial work experience can advantageously discuss topics with familiar context.
  백그라운드 서베이 1번(현재 귀하는 어느 분야에 종사하고 계십니까?)에서 '사업/회사'를 선택하면 이어 직업의 유무, 근무 기간, 관리직 종사 여부를 묻는 질문에 순서대로 답하게 됩니다. 이때, 본시험에서 직장 관련 문제들이 출제될 수 있으므로 근무 경력이 충분한 응답자의 경우 익숙하게 답변할 수 있습니다.

- For students, job seekers, interns, or new employees with limited work experience, selecting "Yes" for question 2 in the Background Survey can be advantageous. This option allows respondents to avoid answering unfamiliar questions related to the workplace.
  재학생, 취업 준비생, 인턴, 또는 경력이 길지 않은 신입 사원의 경우 백그라운드 서베이 2번(현재 귀하는 학생이십니까?)에서 '네'를 선택해 학교생활에 관한 답변을 준비하는 것이 유리합니다. '네'를 선택하여 익숙하지 않은 직장 관련 질문의 출제 가능성을 배제할 수 있습니다.

- Questions related to work or school life require both simple and detailed descriptions. Therefore, it is a priority to use the present tense correctly, and practicing the 5W1H framework is necessary. The third question in a combo set often asks about changes or experiences from the past, so it is essential to answer in chronological order and use the appropriate verb tenses accordingly.
  직장 또는 학교생활 관련 질문은 단순 서술과 상세 묘사를 모두 요구합니다. 따라서 현재 시제를 구사하는 데 오류가 없도록 하는 것을 우선순위로 두어야 하며, 육하원칙을 활용하는 연습이 필요합니다. 콤보의 세 번째 질문은 대개 과거로부터의 변화, 또는 경험을 묻는 것이므로 시간 순서대로 답변을 서술하고 그에 맞는 동사 시제를 활용하는 연습이 중요합니다.

AL Booster

- To achieve a high score in the OPIc exam, it is essential to choose topics that allow you to incorporate your own experiences. Respond to the Background Survey in a direction where you feel most confident in answering in terms of your work, major, job-related projects, or assignments. Refer to the "Warm Your Brain Up" questions in this textbook to discover your unique storytelling material, and practice conveying it simply and naturally through the "Pattern Drills."
  오픽 시험에서 높은 등급을 받으려면, 본인의 이야기를 녹일 수 있는 주제를 선택하는 것이 중요합니다. 직장, 전공, 업무상 프로젝트, 또는 과제 등에 있어 본인이 가장 자신 있게 답변할 수 있는 방향으로 백그라운드 서베이에 응답하세요. 이 교재의 '브레인스토밍' 질문들을 참고하여 본인만의 이야기 소재를 발굴해 보고, '패턴 학습'을 통해 이를 간단하면서도 자연스럽게 전달하는 방법을 연습해 보세요.

❓ Frequently Asked Questions 빈출 질문 유형

Here are the most frequently asked question types related to the topic. Try to identify the key matter of the question and the information that should be included in your response.
이 챕터의 주제와 관련해 자주 출제되는 질문 유형들을 확인해 보세요. 그리고 각 질문의 중심 소재와 답변에 어떤 정보를 포함시켜야 하는지 파악해 보세요.

School	• I'd like to know about your academic major. What do you like about your major? What have you learned from it? • Please describe the daily activities of both teachers and students at your university. Provide as much detail as possible. • I'd like to know about your classmates. What are their personalities like? Is there anyone you particularly like or dislike? Please describe their characteristics.
School Experience	• Have you ever had difficulty trying to register for a class? Explain the story from start to finish. • Discuss the most recent exam that you passed. What subject was the test in, when and where was the exam? What did you do to pass the exam? Tell me as much detail as you can.
Company & Work	• Please describe your company. What kind of business is it? What kind of products or services does your company offer? • Please describe your office. What does the inside of your office look like? Give me as much detail as you can. • What are your main duties at work? What kind of work do you do during working hours?
Work Experience	• Do you have any experience working on big projects or assignments at your job? Please describe the most recent one . • Tell me the story of how you came across your current job and describe your first day at work in detail. • I'd like to know more about the history of your company. Talk about how it began and also how it has changed or grown since it first began.

Chapter 1 Job 신분

Unit 01 Combo Set (1)

출제 가능성 ★★★★☆

Q1 I'd like to know about your academic major. What is your major? What do you like about your major and what have you learned from it?

Question Analysis 질문 분석

Answer the following questions and identify the key matter and the information to be included in your response.
다음 질문에 답하며 답변의 주제와 반드시 포함되어야 할 내용이 무엇인지 파악해 보세요.

1. What is going to be the key matter of your response?
2. What information should your response include?

Warm Your Brain Up 브레인스토밍

Answer the following questions for ideas.
다음 질문에 답하며 답변 소재를 발굴해 보세요.

Intro	• What is your academic major? • Why did you choose it as your academic major?
Body	• What do you enjoy most about your academic major? • What skills or knowledge have you gained from your academic major? • How has your academic major impacted your personal or intellectual growth?
Conclusion	• What are your overall thoughts on your academic major? • What are your personal and career aspirations, and how does your academic major fit into these goals?

AL Booster

- Is there a particular area of study that you find especially interesting or engaging?
- How do you see yourself applying the skills you gained to your future career?

Useful Expressions

computer science 컴퓨터 과학　be fascinated by ~에 매료되다　present 제시하다　allow A to-v A가 ~하도록 허락하다
creativity 창의력　problem-solving skill 문제 해결 능력　rewarding 보람 있는　have a passion for ~에 열정이 있다
practical 실용적인　innovative 혁신적인　open up opportunities 기회를 열다　confident 자신 있는
prepare A for B A가 B하는 것을 준비시키다　successful career 성공적인 경력　ever-evolving 끊임없이 변화하는
nature 본성　motivated 동기를 부여받은　engaged 마음을 끄는, 관심을 사로잡는　lead 이끌다　make a difference 변화를 가져오다

Pattern Drills 패턴 학습

Practice using the given sentence patterns to help you deliver your response clearly.
주어진 문장 패턴을 익혀 답변이 명확하게 전달될 수 있도록 연습해 보세요.

❶ I am fascinated by _____.
- the power of language
- the history and culture of ancient civilizations
- the complexity and diversity of life on Earth

❷ This field has allowed me to _____.
- create innovative solutions
- better understand human behavior
- develop my analytical skills

❸ I have always had a passion for _____.
- biophysics and computer science
- poetry and prose
- science and technology

❹ Through my academic major, I have learned _____.
- valuable programming skills
- how to analyze complex data sets
- how to create compelling marketing campaigns

Mini Actual Test 연습 문제   🎧 1_1.mp3

Respond to the following question while keeping in mind what you have learned.
앞서 배운 내용을 떠올리면서 다음 질문에 답변해 보세요.

> Tell me about your academic major. What aspects of it do you find interesting? What knowledge or skills have you gained from your studies?

Model Answer 모범 답안

 1_2.mp3

Enhance your response by referring to the model answer.
다음 모범 답안을 참고하여 여러분의 답변을 발전시켜 보세요.

> As a computer science major, I am fascinated by the limitless possibilities technology presents. This field has allowed me to explore my creativity and problem-solving skills, which I find incredibly rewarding. I have always had a passion for mathematics and logic, and computer science has given me a way to apply these interests in practical and innovative ways. Through my academic major, I have learned valuable skills such as programming, database management, and systems analysis. These skills have opened up opportunities for me in various industries, from software development to data analysis. I am confident that the knowledge and experience I have gained from my academic major will prepare me for a successful career in the tech industry. One of the most exciting aspects of computer science is the ever-evolving nature of the field. There is always something new to learn, which keeps me motivated and engaged. I'm excited to see where my studies lead me and how I can make a difference in the technology field.

Level Up to AL AL 공략하기

Read the examples below and see how IH-level sentences can be rephrased at the AL level.
다음 예시를 읽고 IH 수준의 문장을 어떻게 AL 수준으로 바꾸어 말할 수 있는지 살펴보세요.

	IH	→	AL
❶	I am fascinated by the limitless possibilities technology presents.	→	I am deeply intrigued by the boundless potential that technology offers.
❷	I have learned valuable skills such as programming, database management, and systems analysis.	→	I have been trained in the fundamental practices of programming, database management, and systems analysis.
❸	I'm excited to see where my studies lead me and how I can make a difference in the technology field.	→	I am excited to see where my academic major takes me in the future and to contribute to the ongoing innovation in the tech industry.

출제 가능성 ★★★☆☆

Q2 Please describe the daily activities of both professors and students at your university. Please provide as much detail as possible.

Question Analysis 질문 분석

Answer the following questions and identify the key matter and the information to be included in your response.
다음 질문에 답하며 답변의 주제와 반드시 포함되어야 할 내용이 무엇인지 파악해 보세요.

1. What is going to be the key matter of your response?
2. What information should your response include?

Warm Your Brain Up 브레인스토밍

Answer the following questions for ideas.
아래 질문에 답하며 답변 소재를 브레인스토밍 해 보세요.

Intro	• How do students spend their time during a regular day on campus? • How do you think professors spend their time during a regular day on campus?
Body	• How do you think professors prepare for their lectures? • How do students spend their time during / between classes? • What kind of assignments, projects, or exams do students typically complete, and how much time do they spend on them?
Conclusion	• What are the most important aspects of the daily activities of both professors and students at your university? • How do these daily routines contribute to the learning and academic success of students?

AL Booster

- What are some facilities where students can study, relax, or socialize?
- Are there any extracurricular activities or events that take place on campus during the day, and how do they involve professors and students?

Useful Expressions

task 일, 업무   depend on ~에 달려 있다   be involved in ~에 관여하다   in general 대체로   participate in ~에 참여하다
between classes 수업 사이에   review 복습하다   socialize with ~와 어울리다   grab a quick meal 간단히 식사를 하다
deliver a lecture 강의를 하다   grade 채점하다   hold office hours 근무 시간에 자리를 지키다   provide support 도움을 주다
extracurricular 정규 과목 이외에, 과외의   overall 전반적으로   professional development 전문성 개발
be designed to ~하도록 설계되다   dynamic 역동적인   enriching 풍요로운

Pattern Drills 패턴 학습

Practice using the given sentence patterns to help you deliver your response clearly.
주어진 문장 패턴을 익혀 답변이 명확하게 전달될 수 있도록 연습해 보세요.

❶ It depends on _____.
- how well the team works together
- the professors' availability
- the benefits that they will get

❷ Between classes, students _____.
- prepare for their next lecture
- drink coffee at the campus cafe
- meet with their professors to ask questions

❸ Some students may use this time to _____.
- study for upcoming exams
- finish up their assignments or projects
- relax and recharge before their next class

❹ The daily activities are designed to _____.
- enhance students' learning experience
- help students acquire practical skills
- cultivate students' leadership skills

Mini Actual Test 연습 문제 🎧 1_3.mp3

Respond to the following question while keeping in mind what you have learned.
앞서 배운 내용을 떠올리면서 다음 질문에 답변해 보세요.

> **Please describe the typical activities and schedules of both professors and students on a daily basis at your university.**

Model Answer 모범 답안

 1_4.mp3

Enhance your response by referring to the model answer.
다음 모범 답안을 참고하여 여러분의 답변을 발전시켜 보세요.

> At my university, students and professors have different tasks to do every day. It depends on the program or course they are involved in. In general, students attend lectures, participate in discussions, work on assignments and projects, and take exams. Between classes, they engage in various activities such as reviewing lecture notes, participating in study groups, or socializing with peers. Some students may also use this time to rest or grab a quick meal before their next class. Many students also work part-time jobs or have internships, which can affect their daily schedules. Professors, on the other hand, prepare and deliver lectures, grade assignments and exams, or hold office hours, providing support to students. In addition, there are extracurricular activities such as clubs, sports, and cultural events that students can participate in. Overall, the daily activities are designed to help students learn and succeed in their chosen fields while also providing opportunities for personal and professional development. Both professors and students are actively engaged in creating a dynamic and enriching learning environment.

Level Up to AL AL 공략하기

Read the examples below and see how IH-level sentences can be rephrased at the AL level.
다음 예시를 읽고 IH 수준의 문장을 어떻게 AL 수준으로 바꾸어 말할 수 있는지 살펴보세요.

IH	AL
❶ At my university, students and professors have different tasks to do every day. It depends on the program or course they are involved in.	At my university, the daily activities of both professors and students vary depending on the specific program or course.
❷ In general, students attend lectures, participate in discussions, work on assignments and projects, and take exams.	Typically, students engage in a variety of academic pursuits, such as attending lectures, participating in discussions, diligently working on assignments and projects, and taking exams.

Chapter 1 Job 신분 **27**

출제 가능성 ★★★★☆

Q3 Have you ever had difficulty trying to register for a class? Explain this story from start to finish.

Question Analysis 질문 분석

Answer the following questions and identify the key matter and the information to be included in your response.
다음 질문에 답하며 답변의 주제와 반드시 포함되어야 할 내용이 무엇인지 파악해 보세요.

1. What is going to be the key matter of your response?
2. What information should your response include?

Warm Your Brain Up 브레인스토밍

Answer the following questions for ideas.
다음 질문에 답하며 답변 소재를 발굴해 보세요.

Intro	• Did you encounter any issues during registration? • What class did you try to register for? • What was the registration process like?
Body	• What difficulties did you experience during registration? • Did you seek help from anyone, such as academic advisors or instructors? • What steps did you take to try to resolve these issues?
Conclusion	• What did you learn from this experience? • Do you have any suggestions for how the registration process could be improved?

AL Booster

- Did you encounter any technical issues, such as website crashes or error messages, while registering?
- Did you encounter any logistical issues, such as conflicting schedules or full classes?
- How did you feel when you encountered these issues?

Useful Expressions

have difficulty -ing ~하는 데 곤란을 겪다   second semester 2학기   fill up quickly 금방 차다   determined 단호한, 굳은 결심의   as soon as ~하자마자   registration 등록   registrar's office 등록 문의처   find out 알아내다   account 계정   be fixed 고쳐지다   spend (time) -ing ~하는 데 시간을 보내다   relieved 안도하는   fixable 고칠 수 있는   resolve 해결하다   looking back on ~을 돌아보면   registration process 등록 절차   transparent 투명한   cause 야기하다   unnecessary stress 불필요한 스트레스   encounter (문제에) 봉착하다, 부딪히다

Pattern Drills 패턴 학습

Practice using the given sentence patterns to help you deliver your response clearly.
주어진 문장 패턴을 익혀 답변이 명확하게 전달될 수 있도록 연습해 보세요.

I had difficulty _____.

❶
- remembering all the details
- meeting the deadline
- understanding the complex instructions

I tried many times to _____, but I couldn't.

❷
- connect to the Wi-Fi
- access the online portal
- reach the professor by email

This was _____, as I had already spent several hours _____.

❸
- frustrating / preparing for the course
- disappointing / researching the topic
- annoying / planning for the entire semester

Looking back on the experience, I feel that _____.

❹
- I could have asked for help earlier
- I should have double-checked the registration deadline
- the university could have communicated better about the registration process

Mini Actual Test 연습 문제   🎧 1_5.mp3

Respond to the following question while keeping in mind what you have learned.
앞서 배운 내용을 떠올리면서 다음 질문에 답변해 보세요.

> **Describe your experience of trying to register for a class, including the challenges you faced and how you overcame them.**

Model Answer 모범 답안

Enhance your response by referring to the model answer.
다음 모범 답안을 참고하여 여러분의 답변을 발전시켜 보세요.

> I had difficulty registering for a required course during my second semester of college. I heard from other students that the course filled up quickly, so I was determined to enroll as soon as registration opened. However, when I tried to register, the system wouldn't let me. I tried many times to register, but I couldn't. Then I called the registrar's office and found out that there was a problem with my account that needed to be fixed before I could register. This was frustrating, as I had already spent several hours trying to register, but I was relieved that the issue was fixable. After resolving the account issue, I was finally able to register for the course. Looking back on the experience, I feel that the registration process was not very transparent and caused unnecessary stress. I think there could be improvements made to the process to make it easier for students to register without encountering issues.

Level Up to AL AL 공략하기

Read the examples below and see how IH-level sentences can be rephrased at the AL level.
다음 예시를 읽고 IH 수준의 문장을 어떻게 AL 수준으로 바꾸어 말할 수 있는지 살펴보세요.

IH → **AL**

❶ The system wouldn't let me. → The system presented an error message, indicating that I was not authorized to register for the course.

❷ I tried many times to register, but I couldn't. Then I called the registrar's office and found out that there was a problem with my account that needed to be fixed before I could register. → After several attempts, I contacted the registrar's office and was informed that there was an issue with my account that needed to be resolved before I could register.

Chapter 1 Job 신분

Unit 02 Combo Set (2)

MP3 바로가기

출제 가능성 ★★★★☆

Q1 Please describe your company. What kind of business is it? What kind of products or services does your company offer?

Question Analysis 질문 분석

Answer the following questions and identify the key matter and the information to be included in your response.
다음 질문에 답하며 답변의 주제와 반드시 포함되어야 할 내용이 무엇인지 파악해 보세요.

1. What is going to be the key matter of your response?
2. What information should your response include?

Warm Your Brain Up 브레인스토밍

Answer the following questions for ideas.
아래 질문에 답하며 답변 소재를 브레인스토밍 해 보세요.

Intro	What is the name of your company? What industry is your company a part of? What kind of products or services does your company offer?
Body	• What is the most well-known product or service your company has? • What are the main features of the product or service? • Why is the product or service so popular?
Conclusion	• What is your general opinion of the company you work for? • Do you like your company? If so, what do you like the most about it?

AL Booster

- How many employees does your company have?
- What is the target market for the product or service?
- How does your company differentiate itself from its competitors?

Useful Expressions

be employed at ~에 종사하다   top-notch 최고의, 멋진   leading provider 선도하는 공급업체   specialize in ~을 전문으로 하다
work remotely 원격으로 일하다   innovative 혁신적인   customized 고객 맞춤형의   meet one's needs ~의 요구를 충족시키다
well-known 유명한, 잘 알려진   comprehensive 종합적인   integrate A into B A를 B로 통합시키다
Swiss Army knife 다목적으로 사용될 수 있는 것, 맥가이버 칼   all sorts of 모든 종류의   inventory management 재고 관리
tweak 수정(변경)하다   be popular with ~에게 인기가 있다   push the boundaries of ~의 지평을 넓히다

Pattern Drills 패턴 학습

Practice using the given sentence patterns to help you deliver your response clearly.
주어진 문장 패턴을 익혀 답변이 명확하게 전달될 수 있도록 연습해 보세요.

❶
> My company is a _____ that specializes in _____.

- fashion brand / clothing
- marketing agency / advertising campaigns

❷
> We develop _____ designed to meet the needs of _____.

- training programs / diverse workforces
- mobile applications / our clients

❸
> One of our well-known products is our _____.

- software
- handbag line
- financial planning service

❹
> My company is very popular with _____.

- investors
- job seekers
- local businesses

Mini Actual Test 연습 문제

🎧 2_1.mp3

Respond to the following question while keeping in mind what you have learned.
앞서 배운 내용을 떠올리면서 다음 질문에 답변해 보세요.

> You have indicated that you work. Tell me about the company you currently work for. What kind of business is it? Also, talk about one particular product or service that your company specializes in.

Model Answer 모범 답안  2_2.mp3

Enhance your response by referring to the model answer.
다음 모범 답안을 참고하여 여러분의 답변을 발전시켜 보세요.

> I work at ABC Corporation. It is a top-notch tech company that specializes in creating advanced solutions for businesses. Currently, we have around 130 employees who work remotely across different time zones. We develop highly innovative and customized software solutions designed to meet our clients' unique business needs. One of our well-known products is our ABC software. It is a comprehensive business management solution that integrates various functions into one system. It's like a Swiss Army knife for businesses in that it can do all sorts of things like accounting, inventory management, and so forth. And the best part? It's totally customizable, so we can tweak it to fit any business perfectly. Our ABC software is very popular with businesses of all kinds, from hospitals to car dealerships. People love it because it helps them run their businesses more efficiently and effectively. I'm really proud to work for a company that's always pushing the boundaries of what's possible with technology.

Level Up to AL AL 공략하기

Read the examples below and see how IH-level sentences can be rephrased at the AL level.
다음 예시를 읽고 IH 수준의 문장을 어떻게 AL 수준으로 바꾸어 말할 수 있는지 살펴보세요.

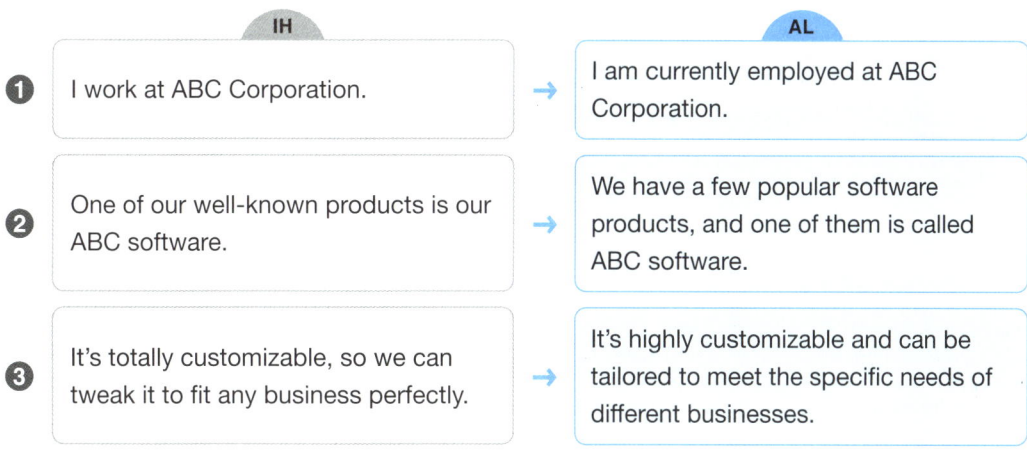

Q2 What are your main duties at work? What kind of tasks do you do during working hours?

Question Analysis 질문 분석

Answer the following questions and identify the key matter and the information to be included in your response.
다음 질문에 답하며 답변의 주제와 반드시 포함되어야 할 내용이 무엇인지 파악해 보세요.

1. What is going to be the key matter of your response?
2. What information should your response include?

Warm Your Brain Up 브레인스토밍

Answer the following questions for ideas.
다음 질문에 답하며 답변 소재를 발굴해 보세요.

Intro
- What is your job title, and what duties do you perform at work?
- What is(are) the first thing(s) you do when you start work?

Body
- How do you prioritize your work for the day?
- How do you spend your afternoon at work?
- How often do you have meetings? Who do you have meetings with?

Conclusion
- What do you do before leaving work?
- How do you prepare for the next day?

AL Booster

- What kind of projects and tasks are on your current to-do list?
- What kind of discussions take place in the meetings?
- What do you think is the core value of your work?

Useful Expressions

typical workday 일반적인 근무일   urgent 긴급한   priority 우선순위   tackle 문제를 다루다   conduct research 연구(조사)를 진행하다
analyze data 데이터를 분석하다   write a report 보고서를 쓰다   collaborate with ~와 협동하다   ongoing project 진행 중인 프로젝트
department 부서   initiative 계획   come up with ~을 제시(제안)하다   call it a day 하루 업무를 마치다   skim through ~을 대충 훑어보다
figure out 이해하다, 계산하다   prioritize 우선순위를 매기다   be ready to roll 시작할 준비가 되다   organized 정리된(계획된)
focused 집중한   collaborative 협력적인   meet a goal 목표를 달성하다

Pattern Drills 패턴 학습

Practice using the given sentence patterns to help you deliver your response clearly.
주어진 문장 패턴을 익혀 답변이 명확하게 전달될 수 있도록 연습해 보세요.

❶
My typical workday starts with _____.
- checking my email
- reviewing my schedule
- prioritizing my tasks for the day

❷
I have a quick team meeting to _____.
- discuss our progress on the project
- brainstorm new ideas
- plan the details of an upcoming event

❸
During these meetings, I often _____.
- present my work or ideas
- share updates on our progress
- go over the feedback

❹
Before calling it a day, I usually _____.
- clean up my workspace
- review my to-do list
- send any last-minute emails or messages

Mini Actual Test 연습 문제

🎧 2_3.mp3

Respond to the following question while keeping in mind what you have learned.
앞서 배운 내용을 떠올리면서 다음 질문에 답변해 보세요.

> How do you spend your day at work? Describe your typical routine in as much detail as possible.

Model Answer 모범 답안

🎧 2_4.mp3

Enhance your response by referring to the model answer.
다음 모범 답안을 참고하여 여러분의 답변을 발전시켜 보세요.

> I am a team leader on the marketing team. My typical workday starts with checking my emails and responding to any urgent messages or requests. Then I have a quick team meeting to discuss priorities and goals for the day. Most of my day is spent tackling different projects and tasks on my to-do list. This includes conducting research, analyzing data, writing reports, or collaborating with other team members. In the afternoon, I attend meetings with clients or other departments to discuss ongoing projects or new initiatives. During these meetings, I often present my work or ideas and collaborate with others to come up with effective solutions. Before wrapping up for the day, I review my to-do list and prioritize tasks for the following day. I also check in with my team members to offer assistance or support. I believe that staying organized, focused, and collaborative is essential to meeting goals and delivering high-quality work.

Level Up to AL AL 공략하기

Read the examples below and see how IH-level sentences can be rephrased at the AL level.
다음 예시를 읽고 IH 수준의 문장을 어떻게 AL 수준으로 바꾸어 말할 수 있는지 살펴보세요.

	IH		AL
❶	I am a team leader on the marketing team.	→	I hold the position of team leader, and my team specializes in marketing.
❷	Most of my day is spent tackling different projects and tasks on my to-do list.	→	The bulk of my day is spent working on various projects and tasks that are on my to-do list.
❸	Before wrapping up for the day, I review my to-do list and prioritize tasks for the following day.	→	Before calling it a day, I usually skim through my to-do list and figure out what needs to get done tomorrow. Then I prioritize things so I'm ready to roll when I start up again.

출제 가능성 ★★★★☆

Q3 Do you have any experience working on big projects or assignments at your job? Talk about the last big project or assignment that you worked on.

Question Analysis 질문 분석

Answer the following questions and identify the key matter and the information to be included in your response.
다음 질문에 답하며 답변의 주제와 반드시 포함되어야 할 내용이 무엇인지 파악해 보세요.

1. What is going to be the key matter of your response?
2. What information should your response include?

Warm Your Brain Up 브레인스토밍

Answer the following questions for ideas.
다음 질문에 답하며 답변 소재를 발굴해 보세요.

Intro	• What was your most recent significant project or assignment? • What were your responsibilities and contributions to it?
Body	• What were the biggest challenges you faced while working on the project? • How did you get through the challenges? • With whom did you collaborate on the project? What were your collective responsibilities or tasks?
Conclusion	• Was the project successful? If so, what factors contributed to its success? • How did you feel upon completing the project?

AL Booster

- What were the objectives or goals of the project?
- What did you learn from the project?

Useful Expressions

develop 개발하다 mobile application 모바일 앱 keep track of ~을 기록하다, 끊임없이 정보를 얻어내다 personalized 개인 맞춤의 make sure 확실하게 하다 healthcare provider 의료인 strict rule 엄격한 규칙 privacy 사생활 legal team 법률팀 feature 특징 protect 보호하다 private information 개인 정보 mix A with B A를 B와 섞다 solve 해결하다 work well 잘 운영되다 get better 호전되다

Chapter 1 Job 신분 | 37

Pattern Drills 패턴 학습

Practice using the given sentence patterns to help you deliver your response clearly.
주어진 문장 패턴을 익혀 답변이 명확하게 전달될 수 있도록 연습해 보세요.

❶
One of the biggest work projects I had was _____.
- developing a marketing campaign
- designing a website
- implementing a new management system

❷
The hardest part was _____.
- staying motivated
- overcoming technical issues
- accommodating the diverse needs of the clients

❸
This project was great because _____.
- it had a significant impact on education
- it allowed us to collaborate with experts in diverse fields

❹
It was amazing to see _____.
- the performance of the team members
- the great work that resulted in so much profit
- the level of innovation and creativity

Mini Actual Test 연습 문제

🎧 2_5.mp3

Respond to the following question while keeping in mind what you have learned.
앞서 배운 내용을 떠올리면서 다음 질문에 답변해 보세요.

> What is the biggest work project you have ever had? Explain what the project was, identify a few of the particular challenges you had during the project, and talk about how you solved those challenges.

Model Answer 모범 답안

 2_6.mp3

Enhance your response by referring to the model answer.
다음 모범 답안을 참고하여 여러분의 답변을 발전시켜 보세요.

> One of the biggest work projects I had was developing a mobile application for a healthcare client. The application helps patients to keep track of their symptoms, get personalized health advice, and talk with their healthcare provider. The hardest part of the project was making sure the application was easy for everyone to use, even if they weren't good with technology. We did lots of testing and listened to feedback to make sure the application was simple and easy to use. We also had to make sure the application adhered to the strict rules about patient privacy in healthcare. To do this, we worked with the client's legal team and added strong security features to protect people's private information. This project was great because we got to mix technology with healthcare. It also gave us some really interesting problems to solve. It was amazing to see the application work so well and help patients get better medical information.

Level Up to AL AL 공략하기

Read the examples below and see how IH-level sentences can be rephrased at the AL level.
다음 예시를 읽고 IH 수준의 문장을 어떻게 AL 수준으로 바꾸어 말할 수 있는지 살펴보세요.

IH → **AL**

① The hardest part of the project was making sure the application was easy for everyone to use. → The most challenging aspect of the project was ensuring the mobile application was universally accessible and user-friendly.

② This project was great because we got to mix technology with healthcare. → This project was exceptional since it allowed us to blend technology and healthcare.

③ It was amazing to see the application work so well and help patients get better medical information. → It was fulfilling to see the application successfully launched and help patients have easy access to medical information.

Chapter 2

Residence 거주

✓ Strategy Check 주제 관련 전략

Check the following strategies related to the topic of this chapter.
이 챕터의 주제와 관련된 시험 대비 전략을 확인해 보세요.

IH Essential

- If you choose "Living alone in a personal house or apartment" in Background Survey question 3(Where do you currently live?), the scope of the question narrows down to your own home or neighborhood, making the difficulty level of the questions relatively easy.
  백그라운드 서베이 3번(현재 귀하는 어디에 살고 계십니까?)에서 '개인 주택이나 아파트에 홀로 거주'를 선택하면 출제 범위가 본인의 집이나 이웃 정도로 축소되기 때문에 문제의 난이도가 비교적 쉬워집니다.

- If you choose "School dormitory," it may lead to complex questions that require detailed descriptions about your experiences related to the dormitory. Therefore, even if you are currently a student, it is not recommended to select "School dormitory" in question 3.
  '학교 기숙사'를 선택하면 기숙사와 관련된 본인의 경험을 묻는 등 복잡한 서술을 요하는 문제가 출제될 수 있으므로 현재 신분이 학생이더라도 3번 문항에서 '학교 기숙사'를 선택하는 것은 추천하지 않습니다.

- The most frequently asked question types regarding your residence are simple descriptions of your home or neighborhood, or detailed descriptions of activities at home and interactions with neighbors. Additionally, there is a high probability of questions that require comparing past experiences with current facts in a combo set, so it's essential to familiarize yourself with expressions used for comparison and practice using verb tenses correctly to avoid grammatical errors.
  거주지와 관련해 가장 빈번하게 출제되는 문제 유형은 집이나 이웃에 대한 단순 묘사, 또는 집에서 하는 일이나 이웃과의 교류에 관한 세부 묘사를 요하는 유형입니다. 또한 과거 경험과 현재 사실을 비교해야 하는 문제가 콤보에 포함될 확률이 높으므로, 비교에 활용할 수 있는 표현들을 알아두고 동사 시제를 헷갈리지 않도록 연습해야 합니다.

AL Booster

- In questions that require descriptions, the more specific your answers are, the higher the probability of obtaining a good score. To effectively demonstrate your communication skills, you should provide as much detailed information as possible about your place of residence, such as its location, the atmosphere in the neighborhood, nearby facilities, and the environment. Therefore, it is necessary to familiarize yourself with suitable adjectives and adverbs for descriptions and practice using them fluently.
  묘사를 요하는 문제에서는 그 답변이 구체적일수록 좋은 점수를 얻게 될 확률이 높습니다. 자신의 의사소통 능력을 충분히 보여줄 수 있도록 거주지의 위치, 주변 분위기, 시설, 환경 등 최대한 자세한 정보들을 제공해야 합니다. 이를 위해 묘사에 적합한 형용사, 부사들을 알아두고 입에 붙이는 연습이 필요합니다.

❓ Frequently Asked Questions 빈출 질문 유형

Here are the most frequently asked question types related to the topic. Try to identify the key matter of the question and the information that should be included in your response.
이 챕터의 주제와 관련해 자주 출제되는 질문 유형들을 확인해 보세요. 그리고 각 질문의 중심 소재와 답변에 어떤 정보를 포함시켜야 하는지 파악해 보세요.

House	• I'd like to talk about where you live. Can you describe your house to me? What does it look like, and how many rooms does it have? • Tell me about the house or apartment you lived in when you were a child. How was it different from the one you live in now? What are the differences and the similarities?
Furniture	• What kind of furniture do you have at home? Tell me about each piece of furniture. Plus, what is your favorite piece of furniture? Why do you like it? • Can you tell me about a piece of furniture you bought recently? Why did you buy it? What was it? Where did you buy it? • Have you ever had some problem with the furniture you bought? What happened and how did you handle it?
Neighbor & Neighborhood	• Describe your neighbors or people who live near your home. • Describe the interactions that you have with your neighbors. How often do you see one another, what do you discuss with them, and what types of activities do you do with them? • Tell me about the area where you live. What does it look like? And what is it like to live there? • Can you describe for me some of the most memorable events that have taken place in the area where you live? What kinds of things have happened since you lived there?
Routine	• Describe your daily routine at home, including the activities you typically do during the week and on weekends. • Tell me about the housework responsibilities you have. Can you provide a detailed description of the chores you do?

Chapter 2 Residence 거주

Unit 03 Combo Set (1)

출제 가능성 ★★★★★

Q1 Can you describe your house to me? What does it look like, and how many rooms does it have?

Question Analysis 질문 분석

Answer the following questions and identify the key matter and the information to be included in your response.
다음 질문에 답하며 답변의 주제와 반드시 포함되어야 할 내용이 무엇인지 파악해 보세요.

1. What is going to be the key matter of your response?
2. What information should your response include?

Warm Your Brain Up 브레인스토밍

Answer the following questions for ideas.
다음 질문에 답하며 답변 소재를 발굴해 보세요.

Intro	• What is your living situation? • How long have you been living in your current home? • What do you enjoy about your living space?
Body	• Can you provide a detailed description of your house's appearance? • What is the layout of your home? • How many rooms does your home have, and what are they used for? • What is your favorite room in your home, and why?
Conclusion	• What are your overall feelings about your living situation? • In your opinion, what makes your house special or unique?

AL Booster

- How have you personalized your living space to make it feel like home?
- How does your living space contribute to your daily life and well-being?

Useful Expressions

apartment 아파트 cozy 아늑한 location 위치 access 접근; 접근하다 necessities 필수품 spacious 널찍한 plenty of 많은 brightly lit 밝은 빛을 띤 natural light 자연광 relaxing 편안한 atmosphere 분위기 comfortable 편안한 coffee table 커피 테이블 tiny 아주 작은 functional 기능적인 electric stove 전기스토브 convenient 편리한 without any hassle 어떠한 번거로움 없이

Pattern Drills 패턴 학습

Practice using the given sentence patterns to help you deliver your response clearly.
주어진 문장 패턴을 익혀 답변이 명확하게 전달될 수 있도록 연습해 보세요.

①
It's a _____ place with _____.
- charming / a great view of the city
- spacious / high ceilings and an open floor plan
- peaceful / lush greenery surroundings

②
_____ is the first thing you see when you enter _____.
- The spacious living room / the apartment
- The beautiful garden / my yard

③
My apartment is a _____ but _____ place that I call home.
- modest / welcoming
- humble / cozy
- unpretentious / charming

④
It's not _____, but it has everything I need to _____.
- luxurious / live comfortably
- high-end / be content
- lavish / relax

Mini Actual Test 연습 문제

🎧 3_1.mp3

Respond to the following question while keeping in mind what you have learned.
앞서 배운 내용을 떠올리면서 다음 질문에 답변해 보세요.

> I'd like to talk about where you live. Describe your house to me. What do the inside and outside of your house look like? How many rooms are there?

Model Answer 모범 답안  3_2.mp3

Enhance your response by referring to the model answer.
다음 모범 답안을 참고하여 여러분의 답변을 발전시켜 보세요.

> I live in a small apartment in the city center. I have lived in this place for over 10 years. It's a cozy place in a great location that allows me to conveniently access all the necessities of life. My apartment has two rooms, a bedroom, and a living room. It also has a small kitchen and a bathroom. The living room is spacious, and it's the first thing you see when you enter the apartment. It's brightly lit and has a large window that allows plenty of natural light to come in. The walls are painted light blue, which creates a relaxing atmosphere. In the corner, there's a comfortable sofa and a coffee table, where I spend most of my time watching TV or reading books. My favorite space in the house is the kitchen. The kitchen is tiny but functional. It has a refrigerator, an electric stove, and a sink. I love cooking, and the kitchen allows me to do so without any difficulty. Overall, my apartment is a small but great place that I call home. It's not luxurious, but it has everything I need to live a comfortable life. I'm grateful for the location, which allows me to access all the necessities of life without any hassle.

Level Up to AL AL 공략하기

Read the examples below and see how IH-level sentences can be rephrased at the AL level.
다음 예시를 읽고 IH 수준의 문장을 어떻게 AL 수준으로 바꾸어 말할 수 있는지 살펴보세요.

	IH	→	AL
❶	I live in a small apartment in the city center. I have lived in this place for over 10 years.	→	The place I call home is a small apartment located in the city center, which I've lived in for over a decade.
❷	My apartment has two rooms, a bedroom and a living room. It also has a small kitchen and a bathroom.	→	My apartment has two rooms, a living room and a bedroom as well as a small kitchen and a bathroom.
❸	The walls are painted light blue, which creates a relaxing atmosphere.	→	The walls are painted in a calming light blue color, creating a peaceful atmosphere.

출제 가능성 ★★★★☆

Q2 Describe the interactions that you have with your neighbors. How often do you see one another, what do you discuss with them, and what types of activities do you do with them?

Question Analysis 질문 분석

Answer the following questions and identify the key matter and the information to be included in your response.
다음 질문에 답하며 답변의 주제와 반드시 포함되어야 할 내용이 무엇인지 파악해 보세요.

1. What is going to be the key matter of your response?
2. What information should your response include?

Warm Your Brain Up 브레인스토밍

Answer the following questions for ideas.
다음 질문에 답하며 답변 소재를 발굴해 보세요.

Intro	• Have you ever talked to your neighbors? • When and how did you first meet your neighbors?
Body	• How often and in what context do you see your neighbors? • What kinds of conversations do you have with your neighbors? • Do you share any common interests or hobbies with your neighbors? • What activities have you engaged in with your neighbors, for instance, parties, sports, or community events?
Conclusion	• What are the key points of your relationship with your neighbors?

AL Booster

- Do you think it is important to maintain good relationships with your neighbors? Why?
- Has your experience with neighbors impacted your overall view of community and social connections? How?

Useful Expressions

essential 필수적인   apartment complex 아파트 단지   tenant 세입자   common area 공용 구역   move-in day 입주일
maintain 유지하다   interact 소통하다   hallway 복도   latest news 최신 소식   occasionally 때때로   encounter 맞닥뜨리다
late-night 심야의   resolve 해결하다   amicably 우호적으로   be engaged in ~에 참여하다   foster 조성하다
sense of belonging 소속감   strengthened 강화된   social connection 사회적 유대

Pattern Drills 패턴 학습

Practice using the given sentence patterns to help you deliver your response clearly.
주어진 문장 패턴을 익혀 답변이 명확하게 전달될 수 있도록 연습해 보세요.

❶ In my case, I live in a ＿＿＿＿ with ＿＿＿＿.
- small town / a close-knit community
- bustling city / people from different cities
- high-rise apartment complex / many other tenants

❷ We have maintained a ＿＿＿＿ relationship since ＿＿＿＿.
- friendly / we met at the park
- distant / we had a disagreement about an issue
- close / resolving our issue

❸ Occasionally, we encounter issues like ＿＿＿＿.
- parking conflicts
- disagreements over property lines
- barking dogs at night

❹ It has strengthened my belief in ＿＿＿＿.
- the importance of community
- the power of communication
- the need for compromise

Mini Actual Test 연습 문제 🎧 3_3.mp3

Respond to the following question while keeping in mind what you have learned.
앞서 배운 내용을 떠올리면서 다음 질문에 답변해 보세요.

> Tell me about your relationship with your neighbors. How often do you run into each other? Discuss what topics you usually talk about and what activities you engage in together.

Model Answer 모범 답안

 3_4.mp3

Enhance your response by referring to the model answer.
다음 모범 답안을 참고하여 여러분의 답변을 발전시켜 보세요.

> Having good relationships with neighbors is essential, especially when living in an apartment complex. In my case, I live in a four-story building with several tenants, and we all share common areas. I met my neighbors for the first time on move-in day, and we have maintained a good relationship since then. We interact with each other daily in the hallways and discuss topics like our work, hobbies, and the latest news. Occasionally, we encounter issues like noise or late-night parties, but we always find a way to resolve them amicably. Unfortunately, we haven't engaged in any activities together, but I believe it would help foster a sense of belonging in the complex. Overall, having a good relationship with my neighbors has made living here more enjoyable, and it has strengthened my belief in the importance of community and social connections.

Level Up to AL AL 공략하기

Read the examples below and see how IH-level sentences can be rephrased at the AL level.
다음 예시를 읽고 IH 수준의 문장을 어떻게 AL 수준으로 바꾸어 말할 수 있는지 살펴보세요.

IH → **AL**

❶ I live in a four-story building with several tenants, and we all share common areas. → I live in a four-story building with other tenants, and we all share common areas like hallways, staircases, and possibly a laundry room.

❷ …, but we always find a way to resolve them amicably. → …, but we always manage to find an amicable solution to the issues.

❸ Overall, having a good relationship with my neighbors has made living here more enjoyable. → Overall, cultivating positive relationships with my apartment neighbors has greatly enhanced my living experience.

출제 가능성 ★★★★☆

Q3 Can you describe for me one of the most memorable events that has taken place in the area where you live? What has happened since you lived there?

> **Question Analysis** 질문 분석

Answer the following questions and identify the key matter and the information to be included in your response.
다음 질문에 답하며 답변의 주제와 반드시 포함되어야 할 내용이 무엇인지 파악해 보세요.

1. What is going to be the key matter of your response?
2. What information should your response include?

> **Warm Your Brain Up** 브레인스토밍

Answer the following questions for ideas.
다음 질문에 답하며 답변 소재를 발굴해 보세요.

Intro	• What is the area that you live in, and how long have you lived there? • Why did you choose this particular event?
Body	• What was the event, and when did it happen? • What were the causes and effects of the event? • What were the reactions of the community to the event?
Conclusion	• What have you learned from reflecting on this memorable event?

AL Booster
- How did this event impact the area and its residents at the time?
- Does the event still have an effect on you and your community? How?

Useful Expressions

memorable 기억에 남는   incident 사건   heavy rainfall 폭우   lead to ~로 이어지다   overflowing 범람   substantial damage 상당한 손해   unforgettable 잊을 수 없는   impact on ~에 대한 영향   community 지역 사회   emergency services 응급 구조대   keep + (sb) + (adj.) ~가 …하도록 유지하다   safety 안전   underline 강조하다   robust 탄탄한   infrastructure 사회 기반 시설   resistant 강한, 저항력이 있는   confront 닥치다   challenge 어려움, 도전

Pattern Drills 패턴 학습

Practice using the given sentence patterns to help you deliver your response clearly.
주어진 문장 패턴을 익혀 답변이 명확하게 전달될 수 있도록 연습해 보세요.

① One of the most memorable incidents was _____.
- the street fair in 2020
- the community clean-up day last year
- the 2019 music festival

② This event was unforgettable because (of) _____.
- it was the first time I witnessed a natural disaster
- the incredible display of fireworks that lit up the night sky

③ It underlined the importance of _____.
- community service and its impact
- taking action to protect our planet
- understanding cultural diversity

④ This event taught me _____.
- the value of teamwork
- the power of forgiveness
- the significance of empathy

Mini Actual Test 연습 문제

🎧 3_5.mp3

Respond to the following question while keeping in mind what you have learned.
앞서 배운 내용을 떠올리면서 다음 질문에 답변해 보세요.

> Tell me about the most memorable event in your neighborhood in as much detail as possible.

Chapter 2 Residence 거주 49

Model Answer 모범 답안

Enhance your response by referring to the model answer.
다음 모범 답안을 참고하여 여러분의 답변을 발전시켜 보세요.

> I have lived in the same area for almost ten years, and one of the most memorable incidents that has taken place in this area was the 2015 flood. Heavy rain for several days led to the overflowing of the river, resulting in substantial damage to residences and businesses. The event was unforgettable because of its impact on the community, which came together to help those affected. Also, emergency services worked hard to keep everyone safe. The flood underlined the significance of having a robust support system during crises and reminded us how quickly our lives can change. Since then, the community has focused on enhancing its infrastructure and preventing future flooding, making the area more resilient. This event taught me the importance of teamwork in confronting challenges.

Level Up to AL AL 공략하기

Read the examples below and see how IH-level sentences can be rephrased at the AL level.
다음 예시를 읽고 IH 수준의 문장을 어떻게 AL 수준으로 바꾸어 말할 수 있는지 살펴보세요.

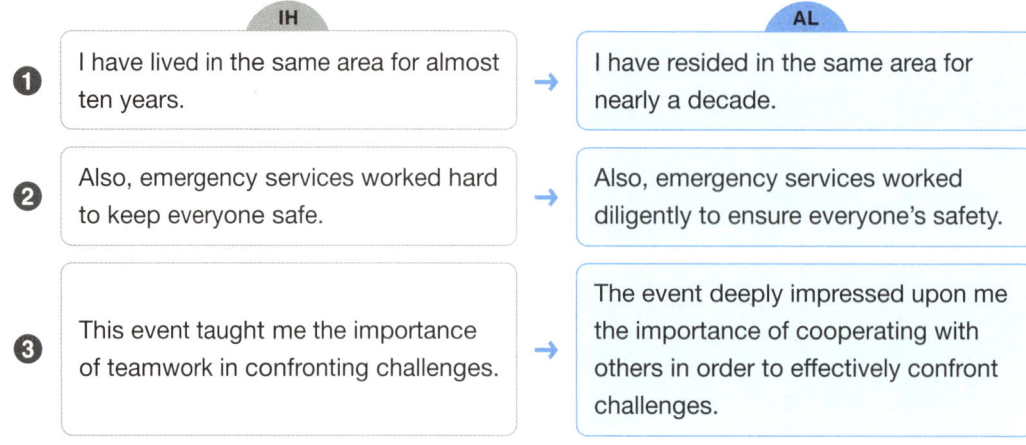

Chapter 2 Residence 거주

Unit 04 Combo Set (2)

출제 가능성 ★★★★★

Q1 What kind of furniture do you have at home? Tell me about each piece of furniture. Plus, what is your favorite piece of furniture? Why do you like it?

Question Analysis 질문 분석

Answer the following questions and identify the key matter and the information to be included in your response.
다음 질문에 답하며 답변의 주제와 반드시 포함되어야 할 내용이 무엇인지 파악해 보세요.

1. What is going to be the key matter of your response?
2. What information should your response include?

Warm Your Brain Up 브레인스토밍

Answer the following questions for ideas.
다음 질문에 답하며 답변 소재를 발굴해 보세요.

Intro	• What pieces of furniture do you have at home? • What is your favorite piece of furniture? • Why is it your favorite?
Body	• What materials is the piece of furniture made of? • What is the design and style of this piece of furniture? How does it fit in with the overall decor of your home?
Conclusion	• Do you agree that it is important to fill your house with the pieces of furniture you like?

AL Booster

- What kind of emotional or sentimental value does this piece of furniture hold for you?
- What would you like to tell people who consider investing in similar pieces of furniture for their own homes?

Useful Expressions

vintage 고전적인, 예스러운   armchair 안락의자   belong to ~에 속하다   be made of ~으로 만들어지다   wooden 나무로 된
remind A of B A에게 B를 상기시키다   spend time with ~와 시간을 보내다   match ~와 어울리다   classic design 고전적인 디자인
take care of ~을 돌보다   dust 먼지를 털다   clean 청소하다   regularly 정기적으로   treasure 보물   plan 계획하다
keep 계속 가지고 있다   so that ~하도록   grandchildren 손주   fond memory 좋은 기억

Pattern Drills 패턴 학습

Practice using the given sentence patterns to help you deliver your response clearly.
주어진 문장 패턴을 익혀 답변이 명확하게 전달될 수 있도록 연습해 보세요.

❶ My favorite piece of furniture in my home is _____.
- a leather sofa
- a wooden dining table
- a bookshelf that holds all of my favorite novels

❷ This piece of furniture is special to me because _____.
- it was the first item I bought for my home
- it was a gift from my parents
- it's where I spent countless hours studying during my school years

❸ It looks great in my home because _____.
- its bold pattern stands out against my solid-colored walls
- its natural wood finish adds warmth and texture to my space

❹ I plan to keep it in my family for a long time so that _____.
- my children can enjoy its beauty
- it can continue to hold memories
- it can be a reminder of my grandparents

Mini Actual Test 연습 문제   🎧 4_1.mp3

Respond to the following question while keeping in mind what you have learned.
앞서 배운 내용을 떠올리면서 다음 질문에 답변해 보세요.

> What is your favorite piece of furniture in your house? Describe it in as much detail as possible.

Model Answer 모범 답안

 4_2.mp3

Enhance your response by referring to the model answer.
다음 모범 답안을 참고하여 여러분의 답변을 발전시켜 보세요.

> My favorite piece of furniture in my home is a vintage armchair that belonged to my grandmother. It's made of wood and has a soft cushion that feels like a hug when I sit in it. This chair is special to me because it reminds me of my grandmother, who I loved spending time with. Whenever I sit in the chair, I feel like she's still with me. The chair looks great in my home because it has a classic design that matches my other furniture. I take care of it by dusting and cleaning it regularly. This chair is a treasure to me, and I plan to keep it in my family for a long time so that my children and grandchildren can enjoy it too.

Level Up to AL AL 공략하기

Read the examples below and see how IH-level sentences can be rephrased at the AL level.
다음 예시를 읽고 IH 수준의 문장을 어떻게 AL 수준으로 바꾸어 말할 수 있는지 살펴보세요.

IH → **AL**

❶ My favorite piece of furniture in my home is a vintage armchair that belonged to my grandmother. → Among all the pieces of furniture in my home, the one I treasure the most is a vintage armchair that was once owned by my grandmother.

❷ This chair is special to me because it reminds me of my grandmother. → The reason why this chair is of great importance to me is that it brings back fond memories of my grandmother.

❸ This chair is a treasure to me. → This chair holds precious memories and has sentimental value to me.

Chapter 2 Residence 거주   53

출제 가능성 ★★★★☆

Q2 Can you tell me about a piece of furniture you bought recently? What was it? Where and why did you buy it?

Question Analysis 질문 분석

Answer the following questions and identify the key matter and the information to be included in your response.
다음 질문에 답하며 답변의 주제와 반드시 포함되어야 할 내용이 무엇인지 파악해 보세요.

1. What is going to be the key matter of your response?
2. What information should your response include?

Warm Your Brain Up 브레인스토밍

Answer the following questions for ideas.
다음 질문에 답하며 답변 소재를 발굴해 보세요.

Intro	• What piece of furniture did you purchase recently? • Why did you choose it?
Body	• What makes this piece of furniture special or unique? • How does this piece of furniture fit into your home or living space? • Did you have any difficulties or challenges when buying or setting up this piece of furniture?
Conclusion	• Are you happy with your purchase, and would you recommend this piece of furniture to others? • What have you learned from this experience?

AL Booster

- Did you have any specific requirements or preferences in mind when shopping for furniture?
- How has the experience impacted your relationship with your home and living space?

Useful Expressions

work from home 재택근무를 하다   comfortable 편안한   aesthetically pleasing 미적으로 기분 좋게 하는   essential 필수적인   purchase 구매하다   vintage desk 빈티지 책상   home office 집에서 일하기 위한 공간   search 찾아보다   furniture store 가구점   local 동네의, (해당) 지역의   solid 단단한   intricate 정교한   carved into ~에 새겨진   leg (가구의) 다리   drawer 서랍   have the perfect size for ~에 딱 맞는 크기이다   ample storage 넉넉한 저장 공간   work supplies 사무용품   character 특징   transform A into B A를 B로 바꾸다

Pattern Drills 패턴 학습

Practice using the given sentence patterns to help you deliver your response clearly.
주어진 문장 패턴을 익혀 답변이 명확하게 전달될 수 있도록 연습해 보세요.

①

After searching through multiple furniture stores, I found _____.

- a beautiful wooden desk with a matching chair
- a comfortable recliner with a built-in massager and heating pad

②

It was the perfect size for _____.

- my small apartment
- my living room
- my collection of books

③

What made it special to me was _____.

- the unique design
- the clean and minimalist design
- the convenience of having it

④

It added _____ to my home office.

- warmth and charm
- a relaxing and inviting vibe
- a touch of elegance and sophistication

Mini Actual Test 연습 문제

🎧 4_3.mp3

Respond to the following question while keeping in mind what you have learned.
앞서 배운 내용을 떠올리면서 다음 질문에 답변해 보세요.

> Tell me about a piece of furniture you recently purchased. Describe it in detail.

Model Answer 모범 답안

 4_4.mp3

Enhance your response by referring to the model answer.
다음 모범 답안을 참고하여 여러분의 답변을 발전시켜 보세요.

> As someone who works from home, having a comfortable and aesthetically pleasing workspace is essential. Recently I purchased a vintage desk for my home office. After searching through multiple furniture stores, I found the perfect desk at a local vintage shop. This desk is made of solid wood and has intricate details carved into the legs and drawers. It is the perfect size for my office space and has ample storage for all of my work supplies. What makes it special to me is its history and character. I can imagine the previous owner sitting at this desk, writing letters or completing important work tasks. It adds personality to my home office and makes it a space I enjoy being in. I recommend searching for unique pieces with character to transform your workspace into a place you love being in.

Level Up to AL AL 공략하기

Read the examples below and see how IH-level sentences can be rephrased at the AL level.
다음 예시를 읽고 IH 수준의 문장을 어떻게 AL 수준으로 바꾸어 말할 수 있는지 살펴보세요.

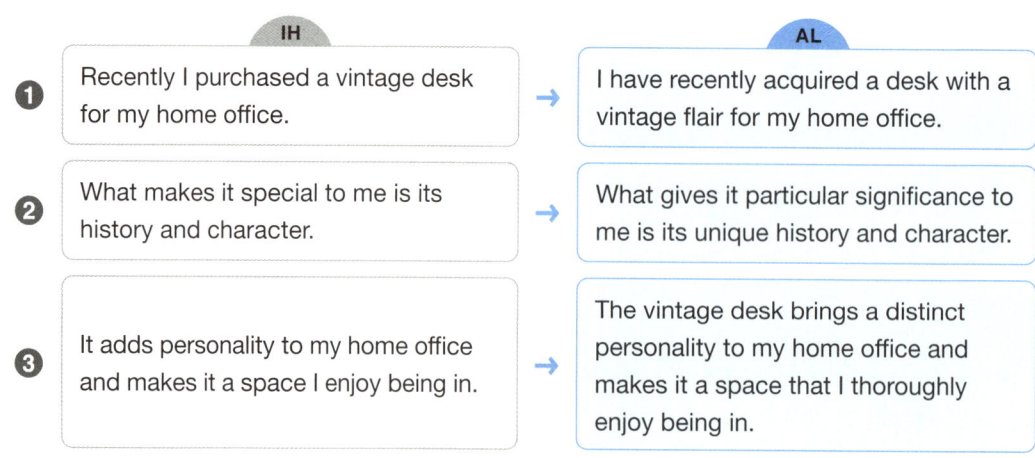

	IH	AL
❶	Recently I purchased a vintage desk for my home office.	I have recently acquired a desk with a vintage flair for my home office.
❷	What makes it special to me is its history and character.	What gives it particular significance to me is its unique history and character.
❸	It adds personality to my home office and makes it a space I enjoy being in.	The vintage desk brings a distinct personality to my home office and makes it a space that I thoroughly enjoy being in.

출제 가능성 ★★★★★

Q3 Have you ever had some problem with the furniture you bought? What happened and how did you handle it?

Question Analysis 질문 분석

Answer the following questions and identify the key matter and the information to be included in your response.
다음 질문에 답하며 답변의 주제와 반드시 포함되어야 할 내용이 무엇인지 파악해 보세요.

1. What is going to be the key matter of your response?
2. What information should your response include?

Warm Your Brain Up 브레인스토밍

Answer the following questions for ideas.
다음 질문에 답하며 답변 소재를 발굴해 보세요.

Intro	• Have you ever experienced a problem with your furniture? • Did you ever have a piece of furniture that got damaged or broken?
Body	• What happened to the furniture? How did it get damaged or broken? • How did you feel when you noticed the problem with your furniture? • Did you try to fix it yourself or did you seek professional help? • How long did it take to resolve the problem?
Conclusion	• Looking back on this experience, what lessons did you learn about maintaining furniture? • How did this experience change the way you think about taking care of your furniture?

AL Booster

- What steps did you take to ensure that your furniture was repaired or replaced in a timely and effective manner?
- Were there any challenges you faced during the repair process?

Useful Expressions

unfortunate 불행한   incident 사건   break off 부러져 떨어지다   collapse 무너지다   frustrated 좌절한   upset 속상한
good night's sleep 숙면   check the damage 손상된 부분을 살피다   beyond repair 고칠 수 없는   replace 교체하다
perfect match 완벽하게 잘 어울림   bed frame 침대 틀   install 설치하다   reinforce 보강하다   additional support 추가 지원
prevent 막다   unexpected problem 예기치 않은 문제   problem-solving skills 문제 해결 능력   overcome 극복하다
mishap 작은 사고

Pattern Drills 패턴 학습

Practice using the given sentence patterns to help you deliver your response clearly.
주어진 문장 패턴을 익혀 답변이 명확하게 전달될 수 있도록 연습해 보세요.

1
I woke up one morning to find that _____.
- the bed had been damaged by my cat
- my laptop screen was cracked
- my refrigerator had stopped working

2
I was initially _____ and _____.
- disappointed / frustrated
- surprised / amazed
- skeptical / hesitant

3
_____ is so important to me for the next day.
- Getting enough sleep
- Completing my to-do list
- Doing meal prep

4
Overall, it was an unexpected problem, but _____.
- I was able to overcome it by thinking logically
- I used it as an opportunity to learn and grow

Mini Actual Test 연습 문제

🎧 4_5.mp3

Respond to the following question while keeping in mind what you have learned.
앞서 배운 내용을 떠올리면서 다음 질문에 답변해 보세요.

> Tell me about a time when you had problems with your furniture. Perhaps it got damaged for some reason, or it could have broken. Tell me exactly what happened and how you solved the problem.

Model Answer 모범 답안

 4_6.mp3

Enhance your response by referring to the model answer.
다음 모범 답안을 참고하여 여러분의 답변을 발전시켜 보세요.

> Last year, I had an unfortunate incident with my bed. I woke up one morning to find that one of the bed legs had broken off during the night, and it caused the entire bed frame to collapse. I was initially frustrated and upset. However, I quickly realized that I needed to find a solution to this problem because a good night's sleep is so important to me for the next day. I checked the damage and found that the bed leg was beyond repair, so I decided to replace it. I visited a local furniture store and found a replacement bed leg that was a perfect match for my bed frame. I installed the new leg and reinforced the other legs with additional support to prevent a similar incident from happening in the future. Overall, it was an unexpected problem, but I learned that with a bit of effort and problem-solving skills, it is possible to overcome furniture mishaps.

Level Up to AL AL 공략하기

Read the examples below and see how IH-level sentences can be rephrased at the AL level.
다음 예시를 읽고 IH 수준의 문장을 어떻게 AL 수준으로 바꾸어 말할 수 있는지 살펴보세요.

IH → **AL**

1 I woke up one morning to find that one of the bed legs had broken off during the night, and it caused the entire bed frame to collapse. → Upon awakening one morning, I discovered that during the night one of the bed legs had snapped off, resulting in the complete collapse of the bed frame.

2 … because a good night's sleep is so important to me for the next day. → … because I rely on a good night's sleep to function properly during the day.

Chapter 3

Watching 관람·시청

✓ Strategy Check 주제 관련 전략

Check the following strategies related to the topic of this chapter.
이 챕터의 주제와 관련된 시험 대비 전략을 확인해 보세요.

IH Essential

- In Background Survey question 4(What do you mainly do for leisure activities?), you must select at least two out of over 20 options. Questions related to the chosen leisure activities will be asked, so it is recommended to choose three or four topics that are easy to talk about. Including options such as "Watching movies," "Watching performances," and "Going to concerts" is highly recommended.
  백그라운드 서베이 4번(귀하는 여가 활동으로 주로 무엇을 하십니까?)에서는 총 20개 이상의 선택지 중 최소 2가지 이상을 선택해야 합니다. 선택한 여가 활동과 관련된 문제가 출제되기 때문에 말하기 쉬운 주제들로 최대 4가지 정도 선택하는 것을 권장합니다. 특히, '영화 보기, 공연 보기, 콘서트 보기'를 포함하여 선택할 것을 추천합니다.

- If you have chosen options related to watching, you can create just a few storylines to prepare for various questions. For example, if you recently watched a performance, you could answer that you "watched it on TV," or you could change your response to "watched it at a movie theater" or "watched it at a concert hall."
  시청 및 관람과 관련된 선택지를 고른 경우, 몇 가지 스토리 라인을 만들어 여러 문제에 대비할 수 있습니다. 예를 들어, 최근 어떤 공연을 보았는데, 그것을 'TV로 시청했다'고 답변할 수도 있고, '영화관에서 봤다'거나 '콘서트장에 직접 가서 봤다'고 바꾸어 답변할 수도 있습니다.

- Regarding watching, common topics that are frequently asked include "what you recently watched," "people you watched it with," "what you did before and after watching," and "the atmosphere of the place." It is essential to prepare your response regarding these matters with as much detail as possible.
  시청 및 관람 관련하여 자주 출제되는 소재로는 '최근에 관람한 것, 함께 관람한 사람, 관람 전후에 한 일, 관람 장소의 분위기' 등이 있습니다. 이와 관련하여 최대한 자세하게 답변을 할 수 있도록 준비하는 것이 중요합니다.

AL Booster

- A question where you have to perform a role-play based on the leisure activity you have chosen may be asked. Familiarize yourself with common question types that are frequently asked and sentence patterns that can be used to respond to such questions.
  선택한 여가 활동과 관련하여, 상황을 주고 역할극을 하라는 문제가 출제될 수 있습니다. 자주 출제되는 문제 유형 및 해당 질문에 답변할 때 사용할 수 있는 문장 패턴 등을 익혀 상황극을 요구하는 문제에 당황하지 않고 답변할 수 있도록 준비합니다.

- If the test difficulty is set to level 5, questions about social issues related to the selected topics may be asked. If your goal is to achieve an AL level, it is advantageous to focus on frequently asked questions and prepare responses related to social issues as well.
  오리엔테이션에서 시험 난이도를 5로 설정한 경우, 선택한 항목과 관련된 사회 이슈를 묻는 문제가 출제될 수 있습니다. AL을 목표로 하고 있다면, 빈출 문제를 중심으로 사회 이슈에 관한 답변까지 준비하는 것이 유리합니다.

❓ Frequently Asked Questions 빈출 질문 유형

Here are the most frequently asked question types related to the topic. Try to identify the key matter of the question and the information that should be included in your response.
이 챕터의 주제와 관련해 자주 출제되는 질문 유형들을 확인해 보세요. 그리고 각 질문의 중심 소재와 답변에 어떤 정보를 포함시켜야 하는지 파악해 보세요.

TV	• I'd like to know about your favorite TV show. Pick the one you like most and tell me about it in detail. • Tell me how you first became interested in watching TV or movies. • TV shows have definitely changed over time. Describe for me a TV show that you remember from your childhood. How was it different from the TV shows that are popular today?
Movies	• You indicated in the survey that you like to see movies. What types of movies do you enjoy seeing? • I'd like you to tell me about your favorite actor / actress. What do you like most about him / her? What movies has he / she starred in? • Reflect on the last movie you went to. Discuss all of the things that happened on that particular day—before, during, and after the movie. • Compare the movies today to the movies that you watched when you were young. How have movies changed over the years? • What are some issues that the movie industry is facing these days? What makes them so important?
Concerts & Performances	• Talk about the last concert you attended. Describe the concert hall in as much detail as you can. Who did you go to the concert with? Tell me about it in detail. • I'll give you a situation and ask you to act it out. You want to watch a performance with your friends. Call the ticket office and ask 3~4 questions about buying tickets. • Unfortunately, you have a problem which you need to resolve. You are ill on the day of the performance. Call one of your friends and explain your situation. Then offer two alternatives for this situation. • Have you ever had tickets for a performance or other event, but you couldn't go? If so, why couldn't you attend? How did this affect your plan?

Chapter 3 — Watching 관람·시청

Unit 05 Combo Set (1)

MP3 바로가기

출제 가능성 ★★★★★

Q1 You indicated in the survey that you like to see movies. What types of movies do you enjoy seeing?

Question Analysis 질문 분석

Answer the following questions and identify the key matter and the information to be included in your response.
다음 질문에 답하며 답변의 주제와 반드시 포함되어야 할 내용이 무엇인지 파악해 보세요.

1. What is going to be the key matter of your response?
2. What information should your response include?

Warm Your Brain Up 브레인스토밍

Answer the following questions for ideas.
다음 질문에 답하며 답변 소재를 발굴해 보세요.

Intro	• Why do you like movies? • Why do movies matter to you?
Body	• What are the types of movies that you enjoy seeing? • What draws you to those types of movies? • Are there any directors or actors that you particularly admire? • Why do you like them?
Conclusion	• What impact do movies have on your life? • Do you see any trends in the types of movies that you enjoy?

AL Booster

- How do the themes or messages in the movies you enjoy relate to your life or experiences?
- How do the movies you enjoy reflect your personality or values?

Useful Expressions

pastime 취미   allow A to-V ···A가 ~하도록 (허락)하다   escape from ~에서 탈출하다   reality 현실   immerse 몰두하게 만들다
action movie 액션 영화   adventure movie 모험 영화   special effect 특수 효과   drama 극적인 사건
suspense (미스터리와 같은 장르에서의) 긴장감   unique 독특한   imaginative 상상력이 풍부한   have a lot of respect for ~를 많이 존경하다
talented 재능이 있는   see different perspectives on ~에 대해 다른 견해를 갖다   inspired 영감을 받은
entertainment 오락, 엔터테인먼트   bring together 합치다, 묶다   shared experience 함께한 경험

Pattern Drills 패턴 학습

Practice using the given sentence patterns to help you deliver your response clearly.
주어진 문장 패턴을 익혀 답변이 명확하게 전달될 수 있도록 연습해 보세요.

1
_____ is one of my favorite pastimes.
- Reading books
- Playing video games
- Watching movies

2
I particularly enjoy _____ because they have _____.
- comedy movies / funny jokes
- superhero movies / incredible special effects and action-packed scenes
- horror movies / suspenseful plots

3
Movies are a great way to _____.
- make yourself feel warm and fuzzy inside
- spend time with friends and family
- learn about different cultures

4
Movies can also make you feel _____.
- inspired to achieve your goals
- a wide range of emotions such as happy, sad, excited, scared, nostalgic, or inspired
- entertained and uplifted

Mini Actual Test 연습 문제

🎧 5_1.mp3

Respond to the following question while keeping in mind what you have learned.
앞서 배운 내용을 떠올리면서 다음 질문에 답변해 보세요.

> You indicated in the survey that you like to see movies. What particular genres do you find enjoyable and why? Explain in detail.

Model Answer 모범 답안

Enhance your response by referring to the model answer.
다음 모범 답안을 참고하여 여러분의 답변을 발전시켜 보세요.

> Watching movies is one of my favorite pastimes because it allows me to escape from reality and immerse myself in different worlds and stories. I particularly enjoy action and adventure movies because they have impressive special effects and exciting scenes. Dramas and thrillers are also fun to watch because they have interesting stories and characters. One director that I really like is Christopher Nolan because he makes movies that are unique and imaginative. I also have a lot of respect for actors and actresses like Tom Hardy and Emma Stone because they are very talented. Movies are a fun way to learn new things and gain different perspectives on the world. They can also make you feel happy or inspired. I think movies are a great form of entertainment that can bring people together and create shared experiences.

Level Up to AL AL 공략하기

Read the examples below and see how IH-level sentences can be rephrased at the AL level.
다음 예시를 읽고 IH 수준의 문장을 어떻게 AL 수준으로 바꾸어 말할 수 있는지 살펴보세요.

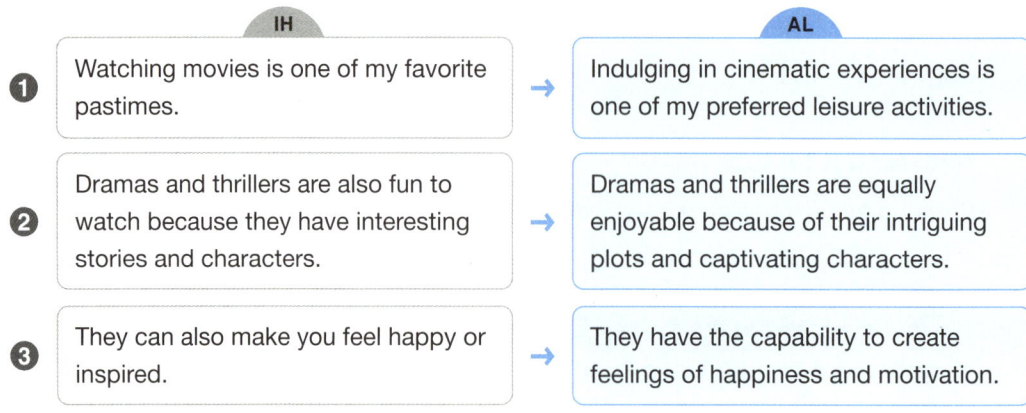

출제 가능성 ★★★★★

> **Q2** Reflect on the last movie you went to. Describe all of the things that happened on that particular day—before, during, and after the movie.

Question Analysis 질문 분석

Answer the following questions and identify the key matter and the information to be included in your response.
다음 질문에 답하며 답변의 주제와 반드시 포함되어야 할 내용이 무엇인지 파악해 보세요.

1. What is going to be the key matter of your response?
2. What information should your response include?

Warm Your Brain Up 브레인스토밍

Answer the following questions for ideas.
다음 질문에 답하며 답변 소재를 발굴해 보세요.

Intro	• What was the last movie that you saw? • Did you see the movie alone or with friends?
Body	• Did you have any expectations before watching the movie? If so, what were they? • How did you feel during the movie? • What did you do after the movie ended?
Conclusion	• Did the experience of watching this movie change your perception of movies in general? • Would you recommend this movie to others? Why or why not?

AL Booster

- How did you hear about the movie?
- Were there any particular scenes that stood out to you? Why?
- Did the movie meet your expectations? Why or why not?

Useful Expressions

hear a lot of buzz 떠들썩한 소리를 듣다   intrigued 호기심이 있는   high expectations 높은 기대   nervous 긴장한   intense 격렬한
be engrossed in ~에 열중하다   a wide range of 넓은 범위의   do one's routine ~의 본분을 다하다   theme 주제, 테마
pick up on 이해하다, 알아차리다   leave a lasting impact 오래가는 영향(여운)을 남기다   think deeply about ~에 관하여 깊이 생각하다
social issue 사회 문제   mental health 정신 건강   violence 폭력   highly 대단히   recommend 추천하다   caution 경고하다
faint of heart 겁쟁이

Pattern Drills 패턴 학습

Practice using the given sentence patterns to help you deliver your response clearly.
주어진 문장 패턴을 익혀 답변이 명확하게 전달될 수 있도록 연습해 보세요.

❶ I recently went to see a movie with _____.
- my friends
- my significant other
- a group of classmates

❷ During the movie, I _____.
- laughed at the funny scenes
- cried during the emotional parts
- enjoyed the soundtrack

❸ After the movie ended, my friends and I spent some time _____.
- discussing the plot and characters
- taking photos outside the theater
- sharing our favorite parts of the movie
- debating whether or not it was worth the ticket price

❹ The movie made me _____.
- feel like I was part of the story
- question my beliefs
- think about life

Mini Actual Test 연습 문제   🎧 5_3.mp3

Respond to the following question while keeping in mind what you have learned.
앞서 배운 내용을 떠올리면서 다음 질문에 답변해 보세요.

> **Tell me about the most recent movie you watched and describe what happened before, during, and after the film.**

Model Answer 모범 답안

 5_4.mp3

Enhance your response by referring to the model answer.
다음 모범 답안을 참고하여 여러분의 답변을 발전시켜 보세요.

> I recently went to see the movie *The Joker* with a few friends. We had heard a lot of things about the movie and were intrigued to see what it was all about. I had high expectations going in but was also a bit nervous because I had heard that the movie was quite intense. During the movie, I was completely engrossed in the story and felt a range of emotions from sadness to anger. The scene where the Joker does his first stand-up comedy routine was particularly memorable to me. After the movie ended, my friends and I spent some time discussing the different themes and messages that we had picked up on throughout the movie. The movie left a lasting impact on me and made me think more deeply about societal issues, such as mental health and the impact of violence. Overall, I would highly recommend this movie to others, although I would caution that it is not for the faint of heart.

Level Up to AL AL 공략하기

Read the examples below and see how IH-level sentences can be rephrased at the AL level.
다음 예시를 읽고 IH 수준의 문장을 어떻게 AL 수준으로 바꾸어 말할 수 있는지 살펴보세요.

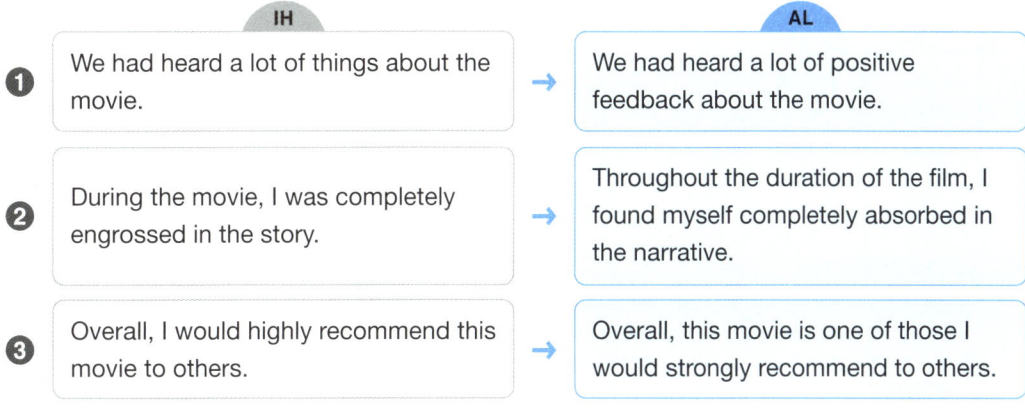

출제 가능성 ★★★☆☆

Q3 What are some issues that the movie industry is facing these days? What makes them so important? Tell me about some recent issues in the movie industry.

Question Analysis 질문 분석

Answer the following questions and identify the key matter and the information to be included in your response.
다음 질문에 답하며 답변의 주제와 반드시 포함되어야 할 내용이 무엇인지 파악해 보세요.

1. What is going to be the key matter of your response?
2. What information should your response include?

Warm Your Brain Up 브레인스토밍

Answer the following questions for ideas.
다음 질문에 답하며 답변 소재를 발굴해 보세요.

Intro	• What are some of the current issues the movie industry is facing? • Why is it important to address these issues?
Body	• What is the most significant issue the movie industry is facing? • Why are fewer people going to movie theaters to watch movies? • What is one issue related to diversity in the movie industry?
Conclusion	• What is required to deal with these problems? • Who needs to make continuous efforts to overcome these challenges?

AL Booster
- How are people's media consumption habits changing?
- What mindset is necessary to tackle these challenges?

Useful Expressions

movie industry 영화 산업   significant 중대한   media consumption 미디어 소비   streaming service 스트리밍 서비스   decline 감소   revenue 수익   concerning 우려되는   diversity 다양성   representation 표상   a limited range of 한정된 범위의   social group 사회 집단   scandal 추문   controversy 논쟁   harassment 괴롭힘   abuse 학대, 남용   workplace safety 직장 내 안전   accountability 설명(해명)할 책임   diverse 다양한   come up with 찾아내다   keep up with ~을 따라잡다, 따라가다   find out 알아내다

Pattern Drills 패턴 학습

Practice using the given sentence patterns to help you deliver your response clearly.
주어진 문장 패턴을 익혀 답변이 명확하게 전달될 수 있도록 연습해 보세요.

❶
One of the biggest problems is that _____.
- income inequality is growing at an alarming rate
- racial discrimination and prejudice continue to exist in society

❷
This has caused a decline in _____.
- traditional media outlets, such as movie theaters
- face-to-face communication and human connection
- cultural preservation and heritage

❸
Another issue is _____.
- the spread of misinformation and fake news in the digital age
- the inequality and injustice faced by marginalized communities

❹
To solve these problems, they should prioritize _____.
- empathy and social justice
- education and public awareness
- sustainable development and environmental protection

Mini Actual Test 연습 문제 🎧 5_5.mp3

Respond to the following question while keeping in mind what you have learned.
앞서 배운 내용을 떠올리면서 다음 질문에 답변해 보세요.

> Discuss the current challenges faced by the movie industry and talk about why they are significant. What recent incidents or concerns are affecting the industry? Explain in detail.

Model Answer 모범 답안

 5_6.mp3

Enhance your response by referring to the model answer.
다음 모범 답안을 참고하여 여러분의 답변을 발전시켜 보세요.

> The movie industry is facing significant challenges today. One of the biggest problems is that people's media consumption habits are changing. Due to the rise of streaming services like Netflix, fewer people are going to theaters to watch movies. This has caused a decline in box office revenues, which is concerning for the theater business. Another issue is the lack of diversity and representation. Some people are concerned that Hollywood tends to show a limited range of social groups. In addition, there have been recent scandals and controversies related to harassment and abuse in the movie industry, making workplace safety and accountability more important than ever. To solve these problems, the movie industry should include more diverse types of people in movies and TV shows and come up with new and interesting ideas. They also need to keep up with new technology and find out what people want to see.

Level Up to AL AL 공략하기

Read the examples below and see how IH-level sentences can be rephrased at the AL level.
다음 예시를 읽고 IH 수준의 문장을 어떻게 AL 수준으로 바꾸어 말할 수 있는지 살펴보세요.

IH → **AL**

① Some people are concerned that Hollywood tends to show a limited range of social groups. → There is a growing concern that the film industry tends to portray certain types of people more frequently, while other social groups remain comparatively underrepresented.

② ···, the movie industry should include more diverse types of people in movies and TV shows. → ···, the film industry should make a conscious effort to cast a wider range of individuals in movies and TV shows to better represent and reflect the diverse makeup of society.

Chapter 3 Watching 관람·시청

Unit 06 Combo Set (2)

출제 가능성 ★★★★☆

Q1 Discuss the last concert that you attended. Describe the concert hall in as much detail as you can. Who did you go to concerts with? Tell me about it in detail.

Question Analysis 질문 분석

Answer the following questions and identify the key matter and the information to be included in your response.
다음 질문에 답하며 답변의 주제와 반드시 포함되어야 할 내용이 무엇인지 파악해 보세요.

1. What is going to be the key matter of your response?
2. What information should your response include?

Warm Your Brain Up 브레인스토밍

Answer the following questions for ideas.
다음 질문에 답하며 답변 소재를 발굴해 보세요.

Intro	Have you attended many concerts before, or was this a relatively new experience for you? What made you decide to attend this concert?
Body	• When and where did the concert take place? What was the venue like? • Who was the performer, or who were the performers? • What was the audience like? Did you go with anyone, or were you there alone? • How did you feel during the concert? Did any particular moments stand out to you?
Conclusion	• Could you recommend this concert or performer to others? Why or why not?

AL Booster

- Did you have any expectations or preconceptions about the concert before you went?
- What made the concert memorable for you? Was it the music itself, the performance, the atmosphere, or something else?
- Did this concert inspire you in any way, or leave you with any lasting impressions?

Useful Expressions

have an opportunity to-v ~할 기회가 있다   immediately 즉시   take place 열리다, 개최되다   venue (콘서트, 스포츠 경기 등) 장소
intimate 친밀한   carefully chosen 신중하게 고른   enhance 높이다   be filled with ~으로 가득 차 있다   enthusiastic 열정적인
enjoyable 즐거운   feel a mix of emotions 만감이 교차하다   a sense of connection with ~와의 유대감   standout 두드러지는
magical 마법의   incredibly 믿을 수 없을 정도로   crowd 군중

Pattern Drills 패턴 학습

Practice using the given sentence patterns to help you deliver your response clearly.
주어진 문장 패턴을 익혀 답변이 명확하게 전달될 수 있도록 연습해 보세요.

①
> The concert took place at _____.

- a massive auditorium with state-of-the-art acoustics
- a large stadium with seating capacity for thousands of fans
- a sprawling open-air arena on the outskirts of town

②
> I went to the concert with _____, which made the experience _____.

- my best friends / more enjoyable
- my sister / even more special
- my mother / more memorable
- my classmates / more exciting

③
> One of the standout moments was when _____.

- the singer hit the high note perfectly
- the singer performed an incredible guitar solo
- the band played a special version of one of my favorite songs

④
> I would highly recommend _____ if you have the chance.

- trying out that new restaurant
- watching that movie
- visiting the park

Mini Actual Test 연습 문제 🎧 6_1.mp3

Respond to the following question while keeping in mind what you have learned.
앞서 배운 내용을 떠올리면서 다음 질문에 답변해 보세요.

> Can you tell me about the most recent concert you went to? When was it? Who was the performer? What made it so memorable? Please tell me about it in detail.

Model Answer 모범 답안

 6_2.mp3

Enhance your response by referring to the model answer.
다음 모범 답안을 참고하여 여러분의 답변을 발전시켜 보세요.

> I recently had the opportunity to attend a concert by an indie band that I am a big fan of. This was not my first concert, but it was definitely a unique experience. I learned about the concert from the band's website, and I immediately knew that I had to attend. The concert took place at a small music venue downtown, and the atmosphere was very cozy and intimate. The sound quality was excellent, and it was clear that the venue was carefully chosen to enhance the musical experience. The band played a mix of old and new songs, and the audience was filled with enthusiastic fans. I went to the concert with some friends, which made the experience even more enjoyable. I felt a mix of emotions during the concert — excitement, joy, and a sense of connection with the music and the other fans. One of the standout moments was when the band played a special version of one of my favorite songs. It was a magical experience that I will never forget. Overall, the concert was incredibly memorable for me. It was not only the music but also the intimate atmosphere and the enthusiastic crowd that made it so special. I would highly recommend attending one of their concerts if you have the chance.

Level Up to AL   AL 공략하기

Read the examples below and see how IH-level sentences can be rephrased at the AL level.
다음 예시를 읽고 IH 수준의 문장을 어떻게 AL 수준으로 바꾸어 말할 수 있는지 살펴보세요.

IH	→	AL
❶ This was not my first concert, but it was definitely a unique experience.	→	While I had attended previous concerts, this particular one stood out as an exceptional and distinct experience.
❷ It was a magical experience that I will never forget.	→	The experience was enchanting and memorable, and it will stay with me forever.
❸ Overall, the concert was incredibly memorable for me.	→	Overall, the concert had a significant impact on me and will always remain vivid in my mind.

출제 가능성 ★★★★☆

Q2 I'll give you a situation and ask you to act it out. You want to watch a performance with your friends. Call the ticket office and ask 3~4 questions in order to buy tickets.

Question Analysis 질문 분석

Answer the following questions and identify the key matter and the information to be included in your response.
다음 질문에 답하며 답변의 주제와 반드시 포함되어야 할 내용이 무엇인지 파악해 보세요.

1. What is going to be the key matter of your response?
2. What information should your response include?

Warm Your Brain Up 브레인스토밍

Answer the following questions for ideas.
다음 질문에 답하며 답변 소재를 발굴해 보세요.

Intro
- To whom are you planning to make a call?
- How will you greet the person when they answer the phone?
- What is the primary reason for your call?

Body
- Which performance are you interested in attending?
- On which date would you like to attend?
- What additional information would you like to know?

Conclusion
- How would you verify the ticket price and seat reservation?
- How would you conclude the conversation before ending the call?

AL Booster

- What are some common concerns or issues that may arise when buying tickets for a performance?
- How can you ensure that you get the best tickets possible for your group?

Useful Expressions
purchase 구매하다 upcoming 다가오는 performance 공연 provide A with B A에게 B를 제공하다 musical 뮤지컬
dates 날짜 times 시간대 available 이용할 수 있는 process 과정 reserve 예약하다 seat 좌석 assistance 도움
confirm 확인하다 total price 총 가격 selected seat 선택된 좌석 proceed with ~을 진행하다 ticket office 매표소

Pattern Drills 패턴 학습

Practice using the given sentence patterns to help you deliver your response clearly.
주어진 문장 패턴을 익혀 답변이 명확하게 전달될 수 있도록 연습해 보세요.

❶ Can you tell me what dates and times are available for _____?
- the movie *Goodbye*
- the concert next weekend
- the theater performance in May

❷ Could you please explain the process for _____?
- purchasing the tickets online
- exchanging tickets
- getting a refund
- upgrading seats

❸ Is it possible to reserve _____?
- seats in the front row
- a table for two at the restaurant
- a room with a balcony

❹ Could you also confirm _____?
- the seat numbers
- the location of the seats
- the availability of group discounts
- the age restriction for the performance

Mini Actual Test 연습 문제

🎧 6_3.mp3

Respond to the following question while keeping in mind what you have learned.
앞서 배운 내용을 떠올리면서 다음 질문에 답변해 보세요.

> Let's suppose you and your friends want to see a performance. Call the ticket office and ask 3-4 questions to purchase tickets.

Model Answer 모범 답안

 6_4.mp3

Enhance your response by referring to the model answer.
다음 모범 답안을 참고하여 여러분의 답변을 발전시켜 보세요.

> Good afternoon, I would like to purchase tickets for the upcoming performance. Could you please provide me with some information? I appreciate your help. I'm interested in watching the musical *Dear My Friends* with some friends. Can you tell me what dates and times are available next week? Okay. What is the price for the tickets? Oh, okay. Is it possible to reserve seats together for three people? Thank you for your assistance thus far. Could you also confirm the total price for three tickets in the selected seats? Alright, that sounds great. I will proceed with purchasing the tickets by visiting the ticket office. Thank you!

Level Up to AL AL 공략하기

Read the examples below and see how IH-level sentences can be rephrased at the AL level.
다음 예시를 읽고 IH 수준의 문장을 어떻게 AL 수준으로 바꾸어 말할 수 있는지 살펴보세요.

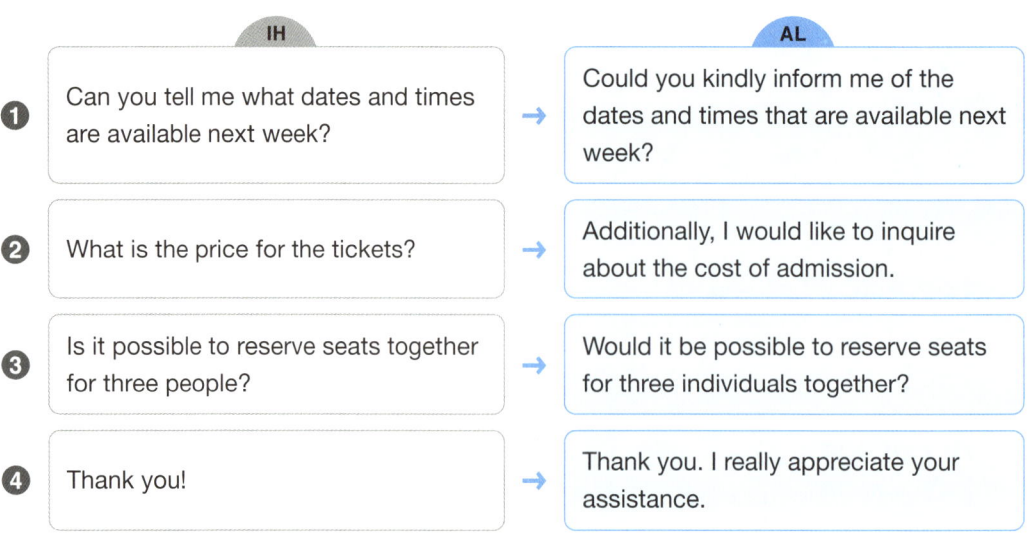

출제 가능성 ★★★☆☆

Q3 Have you ever had tickets for a performance or other event but you couldn't go? What was the problem? How did this affect your plan?

Question Analysis 질문 분석

Answer the following questions and identify the key matter and the information to be included in your response.
다음 질문에 답하며 답변의 주제와 반드시 포함되어야 할 내용이 무엇인지 파악해 보세요.

1. What is going to be the key matter of your response?
2. What information should your response include?

Warm Your Brain Up 브레인스토밍

Answer the following questions for ideas.
다음 질문에 답하며 답변 소재를 발굴해 보세요.

Intro	• What was the performance that you had tickets for and couldn't attend? • What were the reasons that prevented you from attending?
Body	• How did you feel? Why? • How did it affect your original plans? • How did you ultimately resolve the issue and what was the outcome?
Conclusion	• What did you learn from this experience? • What advice would you give to someone who is facing a similar situation?

AL Booster

- Did you seek help from anyone in order to solve the problem?
- Did you try to reschedule the event or sell the tickets?
- What steps would you take in the future to avoid such a situation?

Useful Expressions

encounter 맞닥뜨리다   family emergency 급한 집안 사정   come up 생기다, 발생하다   at the last minute 막판에   disappointed 실망한   look forward to -ing ~할 것을 고대하다   for weeks 몇 주 동안   cancellation 취소   make arrangements with ~와 약속을 정하다   plan the outing 외출 계획을 세우다   ticket seller 매표소   offer a refund 환불해 주다   grateful 감사하는   have a backup plan 비상시 대책이 있다   in case of ~의 경우에   unexpected event 뜻밖의 사건   regrettable 유감스러운   learning opportunity 배움의 기회   apply to ~에 적용하다   future situation 미래 상황

Pattern Drills 패턴 학습

Practice using the given sentence patterns to help you deliver your response clearly.
주어진 문장 패턴을 익혀 답변이 명확하게 전달될 수 있도록 연습해 보세요.

> The problem was that _____ at the last minute.

❶
- the flight got canceled
- the weather took a turn for the worse
- the hotel overbooked their rooms
- the shipment was delayed

> I was disappointed as _____.

❷
- my favorite restaurant was closed when I got there
- the concert was canceled due to the unforeseen circumstances
- the movie was not available on any streaming platform

> Despite the situation, I contacted _____.

❸
- customer support to report the issue
- the airline to reschedule my flight
- my professor to explain why I missed the deadline for the assignment

> This experience taught me _____.

❹
- the importance of saving money for emergencies
- the value of patience and perseverance
- to appreciate the small things in life
- to prioritize my time and focus on what really matters

Mini Actual Test 연습 문제   🎧 6_5.mp3

Respond to the following question while keeping in mind what you have learned.
앞서 배운 내용을 떠올리면서 다음 질문에 답변해 보세요.

> Have you ever encountered a situation where you had tickets for a performance or event but were unable to attend? What issue did you face and how did you solve the problem?

Model Answer 모범 답안

 6_6.mp3

Enhance your response by referring to the model answer.
다음 모범 답안을 참고하여 여러분의 답변을 발전시켜 보세요.

> Yes, I have encountered a situation where I had tickets to a concert but was unable to attend. The problem was that a family emergency came up at the last minute, and I had to leave town. I was disappointed as I had been looking forward to the concert for weeks. I had even made arrangements to do something with my friends right after the concert, but all those plans got disrupted. We had been planning the outing for a long time, and it was unfortunate that I had to miss it. However, I contacted the ticket seller and explained my situation. They were able to offer me a refund, although it was not the same as being able to attend the concert. In spite of missing the concert, I was grateful for the option of a refund. This experience taught me the importance of having a backup plan in case of unexpected events. Overall, it was a regrettable experience, but it was a learning opportunity that I can apply to future situations.

Level Up to AL AL 공략하기

Read the examples below and see how IH-level sentences can be rephrased at the AL level.
다음 예시를 읽고 IH 수준의 문장을 어떻게 AL 수준으로 바꾸어 말할 수 있는지 살펴보세요.

IH		AL
❶ I was disappointed as I had been looking forward to the concert for weeks.	→	I felt let down since I had been eagerly anticipating the concert for weeks.
❷ They were able to offer me a refund, although it was not the same as being able to attend the concert.	→	While I was grateful for the possibility of a refund provided by the ticket seller, it was clear that it could not replace the experience of being present at the concert.
❸ Overall, it was a regrettable experience, but it was a learning opportunity that I can apply to future situations.	→	Overall, although the experience was disheartening, it also presented an opportunity for growth that can be applied to comparable scenarios in the future.

Chapter 4

Listening to Music 음악 감상

✓ Strategy Check 주제 관련 전략

Check the following strategies related to the topic of this chapter.
이 챕터의 주제와 관련된 시험 대비 전략을 확인해 보세요.

IH Essential

- The Background Survey question 5 asks about your hobbies or interests. It is a multiple-choice question where you must select at least one option. As mentioned in the previous chapter, the topics you choose in the Background Survey could be used to create test questions. Therefore, you must consider whether you can sufficiently explain the chosen topic in English before making your selection.
백그라운드 서베이 5번은 취미나 관심사를 묻는 질문입니다. 선택지 중 최소 1개 이상을 선택해야 하는 질문으로, 이전 챕터에서 언급했듯이 백그라운드 서베이에서 선택한 항목과 관련하여 시험 문제가 출제될 수 있으므로, 선택지를 고르기 전 본인이 충분히 영어로 설명할 수 있는 소재인지 반드시 생각해 보아야 합니다.

- Among the choices, "Listening to music" is particularly easy to answer. Not only that, but it also allows you to prepare your response in connection with the topic of "Performances" and "Concerts" discussed in the previous chapter, making it possible to efficiently prepare for the exam.
선택지 중 '음악 감상하기'는 특히 답변하기 쉬운 소재입니다. 뿐만 아니라 이전 챕터에서 다룬 '공연, 콘서트' 소재와도 연계하여 답변을 준비할 수 있어 효율적인 시험 대비가 가능해집니다.

- If you choose "Listening to music," you may receive questions about the devices you use to listen to music. Also, regardless of the exam difficulty level you selected during the orientation, there is a frequent occurrence of questions asking you to perform a role play. Therefore, refer to this textbook and prepare thoroughly for various types of questions.
'음악 감상하기'를 선택할 경우, 음악을 들을 때 사용하는 기기에 관해 질문을 받을 수 있습니다. 또한 오리엔테이션에서 본인이 선택한 시험 난이도와 관계 없이 역할극을 해 보라는 문제가 자주 출제되는 편이니 본 교재를 참고하여 다양한 유형의 문제에 철저하게 대비해 보세요.

AL Booster

- If you choose only "Listening to music" in Background Survey question 5, the probability of this topic being included in the exam doubles.
백그라운드 서베이 5번에서 '음악 감상하기'만 선택하는 경우, 본 주제가 시험에 출제될 확률은 2배가 됩니다.

- If you choose a difficulty level of 5 or higher during the orientation, you may encounter questions that require you to compare two musicians or music genres, or questions related to the development of music equipment and technology. Therefore, if your goal is to achieve an AL level, you must be prepared for more challenging music-related questions as well.
오리엔테이션에서 시험 난이도를 5 이상으로 선택하는 경우, 두 음악가 또는 음악 장르를 비교하거나 음악 장비 및 기술의 발전에 관해 묻는 질문이 출제될 수 있습니다. 따라서 AL 획득을 목표로 하고 있다면, 다소 까다로운 음악 관련 질문까지 대비해야 합니다.

❓ Frequently Asked Questions 빈출 질문 유형

Here are the most frequently asked question types related to the topic. Try to identify the key matter of the question and the information that should be included in your response.
이 챕터의 주제와 관련해 자주 출제되는 질문 유형들을 확인해 보세요. 그리고 각 질문의 중심 소재와 답변에 어떤 정보를 포함시켜야 하는지 파악해 보세요.

Favorite Genre & Musician	• You indicated in the survey that you like music. What kind of music do you like? • Choose two types of music you usually listen to and describe the differences between them. What are the characteristics of each type of music? Give me as many details as possible. • Tell me about your favorite musician or singer. What kind of songs does he / she sing? Why do you like him or her? • Choose two musicians or singers you like and describe differences between them. Which do you like better? Why? Tell me as many details as you can.
Place & Time & Device	• You indicated in the survey that you like listening to music. When do you usually listen to music? Where do you usually listen to music? • What do you use to listen to music? Give me as many details as you can about your music-playing device.
Experience	• Tell me about an experience when you listened to live music. What kind of live music do you like? Where did you go and whom did you go with? Give me as many details about that experience as possible. • I'd like to know how you became interested in music or what made you like to listen to music. Tell me about that experience in detail.
Role-play	• I also enjoy listening to music. Ask me three or four questions about the kinds of music that I like to listen to. • I'd like to give you a situation and ask you to act it out. You want to buy an MP3 player. Before you make a purchase, call a friend who has one and ask 3 or 4 questions about his or her MP3 player. • I'm sorry but there's a problem which I want you to resolve. You have borrowed an MP3 player from your friend but broke it accidentally. Call your friend and explain the situation. Give some suggestions to deal with this problem.

Chapter 4 — Listening to Music 음악 감상

Unit 07　Combo Set (1)

MP3 바로가기

출제 가능성 ★★★★★

Q1 You indicated in the survey that you like music. What kind of music do you like?

Question Analysis 질문 분석

Answer the following questions and identify the key matter and the information to be included in your response.
다음 질문에 답하며 답변의 주제와 반드시 포함되어야 할 내용이 무엇인지 파악해 보세요.

1. What is going to be the key matter of your response?
2. What information should your response include?

Warm Your Brain Up 브레인스토밍

Answer the following questions for ideas.
다음 질문에 답하며 답변 소재를 발굴해 보세요.

Intro	• What is your general opinion about music? • What is your favorite music genre?
Body	• Why do you like the music genre? • What are the characteristics of the music that you appreciate? • How does the music make you feel?
Conclusion	• How has your appreciation for music influenced other aspects of your life? • Is there anything else you would like to add about your love of music and why you enjoy it so much?

AL Booster

- How have music genres evolved over time?
- Do you think your music preferences will continue to evolve? Why or why not?
- What do you think your music preferences say about you as a person?

Useful Expressions

a variety of 다양한　depending on ~에 따라　mood 기분　occasion 상황, 경우　upbeat 쾌활한　catchy 기억하기 쉬운　feel down 기분이 울적하다　energize 활기를 불어넣다　feature 특징을 이루다　relatable 공감이 가는, 연결되어 있다고 느끼는　lyric 가사　everyday people 평범한 사람들　on a personal level 개인적으로, 개인 차원에서　struggle 몸부림, 싸움　appreciate 감상하다　evolution 진화　cultural 문화적인　societal factor 사회적 요인　discover 발견하다　artist 예술가　latest trend 최신 동향　stay up-to-date with 최신 동향을 파악하다

Pattern Drills 패턴 학습

Practice using the given sentence patterns to help you deliver your response clearly.
주어진 문장 패턴을 익혀 답변이 명확하게 전달될 수 있도록 연습해 보세요.

① If I had to choose one favorite, it would be _____.
- classical music
- action movies
- mystery novels

② One reason I like _____ is because of its _____.
- electronic music / unique and futuristic sound
- jazz music / musical expression
- country music / storytelling aspect and relatable lyrics

③ This makes it easy for me to _____.
- connect with the song's emotions
- understand the song's message
- appreciate the depth and meaning behind the song's lyrics
- feel a connection with the artist

④ Another aspect of the music genre that I appreciate is _____.
- its cultural significance
- its ability to evoke powerful emotions
- the creativity and talent of the musicians who produce it

Mini Actual Test 연습 문제   🎧 7_1.mp3

Respond to the following question while keeping in mind what you have learned.
앞서 배운 내용을 떠올리면서 다음 질문에 답변해 보세요.

> **What kind of music do you like? Why?**

Model Answer 모범 답안

🎧 7_2.mp3

Enhance your response by referring to the model answer.
다음 모범 답안을 참고하여 여러분의 답변을 발전시켜 보세요.

> I enjoy listening to a variety of music genres depending on my mood and the occasion. However, if I had to choose one favorite, it would be pop music. One reason I like pop music is because of its upbeat and catchy melodies. Whenever I'm feeling down, listening to a pop song instantly lifts my spirits and energizes me. Additionally, pop music often features relatable lyrics that express the emotions and experiences of everyday people. This makes it easy for me to connect with the songs on a personal level and feel like I'm not alone in my struggles or joys. Another aspect of pop music that I appreciate is its evolution over time. It's interesting to see how the genre has changed and been influenced by different cultural and societal factors. I enjoy discovering new artists and following the latest trends in pop music. In summary, pop music is my favorite genre because of its catchy melodies, relatable lyrics, and evolving nature. Listening to pop music is not only a source of entertainment for me but also a way to connect with others and stay up-to-date with the latest trends.

Level Up to AL AL 공략하기

Read the examples below and see how IH-level sentences can be rephrased at the AL level.
다음 예시를 읽고 IH 수준의 문장을 어떻게 AL 수준으로 바꾸어 말할 수 있는지 살펴보세요.

IH		AL
❶ Whenever I'm feeling down, listening to a pop song instantly lifts my spirits and energizes me.	→	When I am feeling sad or depressed, playing a pop song immediately boosts my mood and revitalizes me.
❷ ··· and feel like I'm not alone in my struggles or joys.	→	··· and sense a connection to others who may be experiencing similar challenges or pleasures as me.

출제 가능성 ★★★★★

Q2 What do you use to listen to music? Give me as many details about your music-playing device as you can.

Question Analysis 질문 분석

Answer the following questions and identify the key matter and the information to be included in your response.
다음 질문에 답하며 답변의 주제와 반드시 포함되어야 할 내용이 무엇인지 파악해 보세요.

1. What is going to be the key matter of your response?
2. What information should your response include?

Warm Your Brain Up 브레인스토밍

Answer the following questions for ideas.
다음 질문에 답하며 답변 소재를 발굴해 보세요.

Intro	• What kind of music-playing device do you use (smartphone, tablet, computer, dedicated music player, etc.)? • What are the reasons you prefer this device?
Body	• What are the main features of the device? • How do those features enhance your enjoyment of music? • Do you have any accessories to enhance your music-listening experience?
Conclusion	• What do you like about your music-playing device? • Are there any areas where you feel your device could be improved?

AL Booster

- What kind of headphones or speakers do you use with your device? Why?
- How much storage space does your device have for music?
- What are the platforms you use to listen to music?

Useful Expressions

most of the time 대부분의 시간   handy 편리한   access 접근하다   music collection 음악 컬렉션   anytime 언제든지
anywhere 어디서든지   decent 괜찮은   focus on the music 음악에 집중하다   wireless earbuds 무선 이어폰   comfortable 편안한
for long periods 오랜 기간 동안   storage capacity 저장 용량   store music 음악을 저장하다   stream music 음악을 스트리밍하다
popular platform 인기 있는 플랫폼   organize a playlist 재생 목록을 정리하다   create a playlist 재생 목록을 만들다
perfect music companion 완벽한 음악 동반자   convenience 편의성   enhance 향상시키다

Chapter 4 Listening to Music 음악 감상

Pattern Drills 패턴 학습

Practice using the given sentence patterns to help you deliver your response clearly.
주어진 문장 패턴을 익혀 답변이 명확하게 전달될 수 있도록 연습해 보세요.

I use _____ to listen to music most of the time.

①
- my laptop
- my portable speaker
- my smartwatch
- my car stereo

They're comfortable to wear _____.

②
- during my daily commute to work
- while exercising at the gym
- on long flights or road trips
- while doing household chores

My phone has _____, allowing me to _____.

③
- a large storage capacity / store a vast collection of music
- a fast internet connection / stream high-quality music
- Bluetooth connectivity / pair it with my car's audio system while driving

To _____, I use different applications.

④
- discover new music
- synchronize my music across all my devices
- manage my music library

Mini Actual Test 연습 문제   7_3.mp3

Respond to the following question while keeping in mind what you have learned.
앞서 배운 내용을 떠올리면서 다음 질문에 답변해 보세요.

> How do you listen to music? What kind of music-playing device do you usually use?

Model Answer 모범 답안

🎧 7_4.mp3

Enhance your response by referring to the model answer.
다음 모범 답안을 참고하여 여러분의 답변을 발전시켜 보세요.

> I use my smartphone to listen to music most of the time. It's handy because I can access my music collection anytime and anywhere since my phone is always with me. The phone also has a decent speaker, which I use to listen to music without headphones when I'm alone. However, when I want to focus on the music and have a better listening experience, I prefer using my wireless earbuds. They provide great sound quality, and they're comfortable to wear for long periods. My phone has a large storage capacity, allowing me to store a lot of music, and I can also stream music from popular platforms like YouTube. To organize my music collection, I use different applications and create playlists. Overall, my smartphone is the perfect music companion for me because it offers convenience, good sound quality, and useful features that enhance my listening experience.

Level Up to AL AL 공략하기

Read the examples below and see how IH-level sentences can be rephrased at the AL level.
다음 예시를 읽고 IH 수준의 문장을 어떻게 AL 수준으로 바꾸어 말할 수 있는지 살펴보세요.

IH	AL
❶ I use my smartphone to listen to music most of the time.	→ I use my smartphone as my primary music-playing device.
❷ The phone also has a decent speaker, which I use to listen to music without headphones when I'm alone.	→ The phone also has a good-quality speaker that allows me to enjoy my favorite tracks without headphones when I'm alone.
❸ They provide great sound quality, and they're comfortable to wear for long periods.	→ They offer exceptional sound quality and are comfortable to wear for extended periods.

출제 가능성 ★★★★☆

Q3 I'd like to know how you became interested in music or what made you like to listen to music. Tell me about that experience in detail.

Question Analysis 질문 분석

Answer the following questions and identify the key matter and the information to be included in your response.
다음 질문에 답하며 답변의 주제와 반드시 포함되어야 할 내용이 무엇인지 파악해 보세요.

1. What is going to be the key matter of your response?
2. What information should your response include?

Warm Your Brain Up 브레인스토밍

Answer the following questions for ideas.
다음 질문에 답하며 답변 소재를 발굴해 보세요.

Intro	• What is your first memory of music? • Who introduced you to music and how did they influence your taste? • What are some of your favorite music memories?
Body	• What genre of music did you first enjoy listening to? • When did you first discover your love for music? • What sparked your interest in music?
Conclusion	• How has your love for music grown and evolved over the years? • What role does music play in your life today?

AL Booster

- How has music affected your life?
- What are some future goals you have related to music?

Useful Expressions

be interested in ~에 관심이 있다   as long as I can remember 내가 기억하는 한   remember -ing ~했던 것을 기억하다
sing along (노래를) 따라 부르다   explore 탐험하다   speak to A emotionally A에게 감정적으로 호소하다(다가가다)   ballad 발라드
lyric 가사   melody 멜로디, 곡조   touch one's soul 마음을 움직이다   move 감동시키다   from then on 그 이후로
be hooked on 중독되다, 빠지다   express one's emotion 감정을 표현하다   feel the same way 같은 감정을 느끼다   essential 필수적인
seek out ~을 찾아내다   diverse 다양한, 다채로운   enrich 풍부하게 하다

Pattern Drills 패턴 학습

Practice using the given sentence patterns to help you deliver your response clearly.
주어진 문장 패턴을 익혀 답변이 명확하게 전달될 수 있도록 연습해 보세요.

① I've been interested in _____ for as long as I can remember.
- sports
- cooking
- technology

② I remember _____ even before I could speak.
- dancing to my favorite song
- humming along to nursery rhymes
- my parents playing classical music around the house

③ From then on, I was hooked on _____.
- jazz music and started my album collection
- musical theater
- reading mystery novels

④ Today, _____ is / are an essential part of my life, and I can't imagine living without it / them.
- exercise and meditation
- reading and writing
- spending time with my family

Mini Actual Test 연습 문제　🎧 7_5.mp3

Respond to the following question while keeping in mind what you have learned.
앞서 배운 내용을 떠올리면서 다음 질문에 답변해 보세요.

> Can you describe what led to your interest in music and what specifically drew you to it? Please provide a detailed account of this experience.

Model Answer 모범 답안

 7_6.mp3

Enhance your response by referring to the model answer.
다음 모범 답안을 참고하여 여러분의 답변을 발전시켜 보세요.

> I've been interested in music for as long as I can remember. When I was a child, my parents were always playing music around the house, and I remember dancing and singing along even before I could speak. As I got older, I started to appreciate music more and began to explore different genres. I remember the first time I heard a song that really spoke to me emotionally. It was a ballad with beautiful lyrics and a melody that touched my soul. The song moved me in a way that no other form of art ever had before. From then on, I was hooked on music and started to listen to it all the time. I found that music was a way for me to express my emotions and connect with others who felt the same way. As I learned more about music, I also began to appreciate the artistry and skill that goes into creating it. Today, music is an essential part of my life, and I can't imagine living without it. I continue to seek out new and diverse sounds to enrich my experiences.

Level Up to AL AL 공략하기

Read the examples below and see how IH-level sentences can be rephrased at the AL level.
다음 예시를 읽고 IH 수준의 문장을 어떻게 AL 수준으로 바꾸어 말할 수 있는지 살펴보세요.

	IH	→	AL
❶	I've been interested in music for as long as I can remember.	→	Since my earliest memories, music has been a constant presence in my life.
❷	As I got older, I started to appreciate music more and began to explore different genres.	→	As I grew older, my interest in music deepened, and I began to explore different genres and artists.
❸	I was hooked on music and started to listen to it all the time.	→	I was completely hooked on music, and it became a fundamental part of my life.
❹	Today, music is an essential part of my life, and I can't imagine living without it.	→	Today, I cannot imagine my life without music. It remains a central part of my daily routine.

Chapter 4 Listening to Music 음악 감상

Unit 08 Combo Set (2)

출제 가능성 ★★★★★

Q1 I'd like to give you a situation and ask you to act it out. You want to buy an MP3 player. Before you make a purchase, call a friend who has one and ask 3 or 4 questions about his or her MP3 player.

Question Analysis 질문 분석

Answer the following questions and identify the key matter and the information to be included in your response.
다음 질문에 답하며 답변의 주제와 반드시 포함되어야 할 내용이 무엇인지 파악해 보세요.

1. What is going to be the key matter of your response?
2. What information should your response include?

Warm Your Brain Up 브레인스토밍

Answer the following questions for ideas.
다음 질문에 답하며 답변 소재를 발굴해 보세요.

Intro	• How would you greet your friend? • What is the purpose of the phone call?
Body	• What questions should you ask a friend who owns an MP3 player? • What features would you look for in a MP3 Player? • How would you respond to your friend's answers?
Conclusion	• What is an appropriate way to thank a friend who has helped you? • How would you end the conversation before hanging up?

AL Booster

- How might the answers to these questions influence your purchasing decision?
- What are some polite ways to ask for information when you have a question?

Useful Expressions

recently 최근에   wonder if ~인지 궁금하다   advice 조언, 충고   storage space 저장 공간   impressive 인상적인
battery life 배터리 수명   last 지속되다   navigate the menu 메뉴를 이용하여 이동하다   exactly 정확히, 딱 맞게
sound quality 음질   compared to ~와 비교해서   on the market 시장에서   for myself 나 자신을 위해서

Pattern Drills 패턴 학습

Practice using the given sentence patterns to help you deliver your response clearly.
주어진 문장 패턴을 익혀 답변이 명확하게 전달될 수 있도록 연습해 보세요.

I heard that you recently bought _____.

①
- a new MP3 player
- a fancy new phone
- a subscription to a music streaming service

I'm thinking about _____, and I was wondering if you could give me some advice.

②
- buying a new laptop
- taking up hiking
- traveling to Japan

How about _____?

③
- the brand reputation
- the storage capacity
- the camera quality
- the screen size

How does _____ compare to other MP3 players on the market?

④
- the durability
- the display quality
- the noise cancellation feature

Mini Actual Test 연습 문제   8_1.mp3

Respond to the following question while keeping in mind what you have learned.
앞서 배운 내용을 떠올리면서 다음 질문에 답변해 보세요.

> I'm going to give you a situation to act out. Your friend recently bought an MP3 player. You have also wanted to buy one for a long time. Ask your friend three or four questions about his or her new MP3 player.

Model Answer 모범 답안

Enhance your response by referring to the model answer.
다음 모범 답안을 참고하여 여러분의 답변을 발전시켜 보세요.

> Hi, it's me! How are you doing? I heard that you recently bought an MP3 player. I'm also thinking about buying one and I was wondering if you could give me some advice. Well, first of all, how much storage space does your MP3 player have? Wow, that's pretty impressive! How about the battery life? How long does it last? That sounds perfect! How easy is it to navigate the menu and find the songs you want to listen to? That's exactly what I'm looking for. One last question—how does the sound quality compare to other MP3 players on the market? Awesome, thank you so much for all of the information. I think I might just have to get one of these MP3 players for myself! Thanks again. Talk to you later!

Level Up to AL AL 공략하기

Read the examples below and see how IH-level sentences can be rephrased at the AL level.
다음 예시를 읽고 IH 수준의 문장을 어떻게 AL 수준으로 바꾸어 말할 수 있는지 살펴보세요.

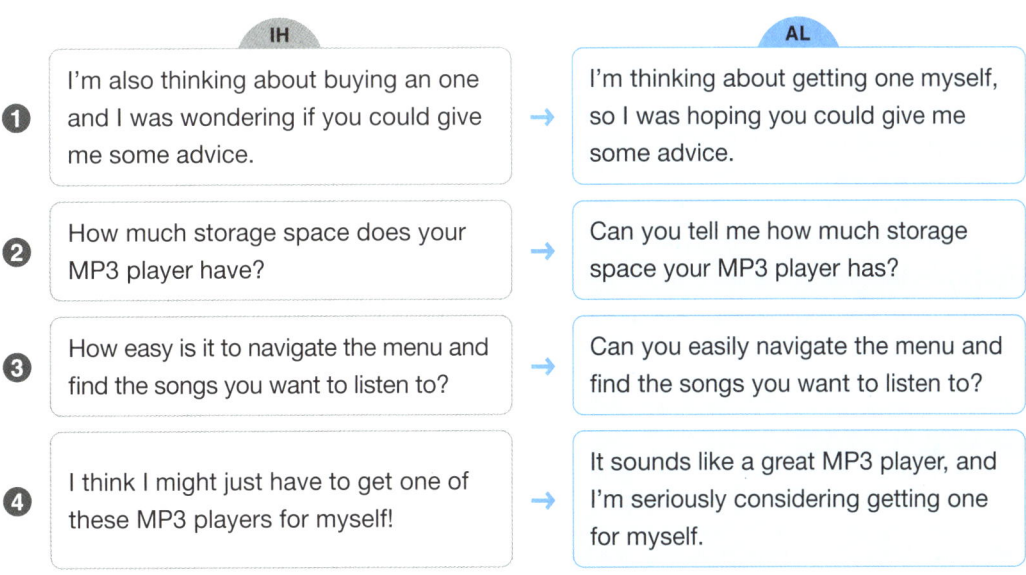

출제 가능성 ★★★★★

Q2 I'm sorry, but there's a problem which I want you to resolve. You have borrowed an MP3 player from your friend but broke it accidentally. Call your friend and explain the situation. Give some suggestions to deal with this problem.

> **Question Analysis** 질문 분석

Answer the following questions and identify the key matter and the information to be included in your response.
다음 질문에 답하며 답변의 주제와 반드시 포함되어야 할 내용이 무엇인지 파악해 보세요.

1. What is going to be the key matter of your response?
2. What information should your response include?

> **Warm Your Brain Up** 브레인스토밍

Answer the following questions for ideas.
다음 질문에 답하며 답변 소재를 발굴해 보세요.

Intro	• How would you start the conversation? • What is the purpose of the phone call?
Body	• What happened to the MP3 player? • What are your suggestions for resolving the problem? • How will you communicate these suggestions to your friend?
Conclusion	• What is an appropriate way to apologize to a friend? • How would you end the conversation before hanging up?

AL Booster

• How would you feel if you found out that the MP3 player you had borrowed from your friend was broken?
• How will you make sure your friend is satisfied with the solution?

Useful Expressions

lend 빌려주다   accidentally 우연히, 사고로   at the gym 체육관에서   must have p.p. 분명히 ~했을 것이다
fall out of one's pocket ~의 주머니에서 빠지다   get damaged 손상되다   feel terrible 기분이 매우 안 좋다
make it right 바로잡다, 보상하다   pay for ~을 지불하다   repairs 수리   replace A with B A를 B로 대체하다   option 선택
whatever 무엇이든   as soon as possible 가능한 빨리   understanding 이해해 주는   bye for now 잠시 안녕

Pattern Drills 패턴 학습

Practice using the given sentence patterns to help you deliver your response clearly.
주어진 문장 패턴을 익혀 답변이 명확하게 전달될 수 있도록 연습해 보세요.

I need to talk to you about _____.

①
- something urgent
- something important
- the travel arrangements for our upcoming business trip

I was thinking that I could either _____ or _____.

②
- get it repaired / buy you a new one
- go to the gym / go for a hike
- take the bus / ride my bike

Or if you'd prefer, I could just _____.

③
- lend you my own MP3 player for the time being
- give you some money towards buying a new MP3 player

Again, I'm really sorry about _____.

④
- losing it
- my mistake
- what happened to your device

Mini Actual Test 연습 문제 🎧 8_3.mp3

Respond to the following question while keeping in mind what you have learned.
앞서 배운 내용을 떠올리면서 다음 질문에 답변해 보세요.

> I'm afraid that there is a problem that you need to solve. You borrowed an MP3 player from one of your friends. Unfortunately, you broke it by mistake. Call your friend and explain the situation, giving two or three alternatives.

Model Answer 모범 답안

 8_4.mp3

Enhance your response by referring to the model answer.
다음 모범 답안을 참고하여 여러분의 답변을 발전시켜 보세요.

> Hi, it's me. I need to talk to you about something important. Well, you remember the MP3 player you lent me last week? I accidentally broke it. I'm really sorry. I was at the gym and it must have fallen out of my pocket and gotten damaged. I feel terrible about it and I want to make it right. I was thinking that I could either pay for the cost of repairs or replace it with a new one. Which option do you prefer? Well, I am not sure about how much it would cost to repair, but I can check. Or if you'd prefer, I could just buy you a new one. I'll do whatever you think is best. Sure, I'll check and let you know as soon as possible. Again, I'm really sorry about this. Will do. Thanks for your understanding. Bye for now.

Level Up to AL AL 공략하기

Read the examples below and see how IH-level sentences can be rephrased at the AL level.
다음 예시를 읽고 IH 수준의 문장을 어떻게 AL 수준으로 바꾸어 말할 수 있는지 살펴보세요.

IH		AL
❶ I need to talk to you about something important.	→	I have an important matter to discuss with you.
❷ Well, you remember the MP3 player you lent me last week?	→	Well, do you happen to recall the MP3 player you graciously lent me last week?
❸ I feel terrible about it and I want to make it right.	→	I sincerely apologize for my carelessness and I want to make amends.

출제 가능성 ★★★★★

Q3 Tell me about an experience where any device you had broke down. Provide the background surrounding this situation and describe what happened. Also, how did you solve the problem?

Question Analysis 질문 분석

Answer the following questions and identify the key matter and the information to be included in your response.
다음 질문에 답하며 답변의 주제와 반드시 포함되어야 할 내용이 무엇인지 파악해 보세요.

1. What is going to be the key matter of your response?
2. What information should your response include?

Warm Your Brain Up 브레인스토밍

Answer the following questions for ideas.
다음 질문에 답하며 답변 소재를 발굴해 보세요.

Intro	• What device did you have that broke down? • When and where did it break down?
Body	• What happened to it? • How did you feel when you found out that it didn't work properly? • Did you try to troubleshoot the problem yourself or seek help from someone else?
Conclusion	• How did you ultimately solve the problem? • What did you learn from this experience?

AL Booster

- What was the context surrounding the situation?
- What advice would you give to someone who is dealing with a broken musical device or piece of equipment?

Useful Expressions

once (과거) 언젠가   break down 고장 나다   cheap 저렴한   one day 어느 날   work out 운동하다
drop A on the floor A를 바닥에 떨어뜨리다   turn on 켜다   refuse to ~을 거부하다   start up 시작이 되다, 시동이 걸리다
frustrated 좌절한   a bunch of 다수의   electronics store 전자 제품 가게   be repaired 수리되다   higher-quality 고급의
everyday use 일상적인 사용   inconvenience 불편함   invest in ~에 투자하다   better-quality 더 좋은(높은) 품질의   device 장치

Chapter 4 Listening to Music 음악 감상

Pattern Drills 패턴 학습

Practice using the given sentence patterns to help you deliver your response clearly.
주어진 문장 패턴을 익혀 답변이 명확하게 전달될 수 있도록 연습해 보세요.

1
I once had an experience with _____ that broke down.
- a guitar amplifier
- headphones
- earbuds

2
I accidentally dropped _____ on the floor.
- the phone
- the remote control
- the case

3
I was frustrated because I had just _____.
- purchased new batteries for it
- downloaded a new album onto it
- finished recording a song with it

4
I decided to purchase _____ that I could use for both _____ and _____.
- headphones / listening to music / taking calls
- a portable sound system / indoor parties / outdoor events
- a high-quality guitar / recording / live performances

Mini Actual Test 연습 문제 🎧 8_5.mp3

Respond to the following question while keeping in mind what you have learned.
앞서 배운 내용을 떠올리면서 다음 질문에 답변해 보세요.

> Can you share with me a situation in which a musical instrument or piece of equipment that you owned stopped working? Please give context to the event and explain what happened. Also, explain what steps you took to address and resolve the issue.

Model Answer 모범 답안

 8_6.mp3

Enhance your response by referring to the model answer.
다음 모범 답안을 참고하여 여러분의 답변을 발전시켜 보세요.

> I once had an experience with an MP3 player that broke down. It was a cheap player that I had purchased for working out at the gym. One day, while I was working out, I accidentally dropped the MP3 player on the floor. When I tried to turn it on, it refused to start up. I was frustrated because I had just downloaded a bunch of new songs. I took the player to an electronics store to see if it could be repaired, but they told me it would be cheaper to just buy a new one. I decided to purchase a new, high-quality player that I could have for both working out and everyday use. While it was an inconvenience to have to replace the player, I was able to learn from the experience and invest in a better-quality device.

Level Up to AL AL 공략하기

Read the examples below and see how IH-level sentences can be rephrased at the AL level.
다음 예시를 읽고 IH 수준의 문장을 어떻게 AL 수준으로 바꾸어 말할 수 있는지 살펴보세요.

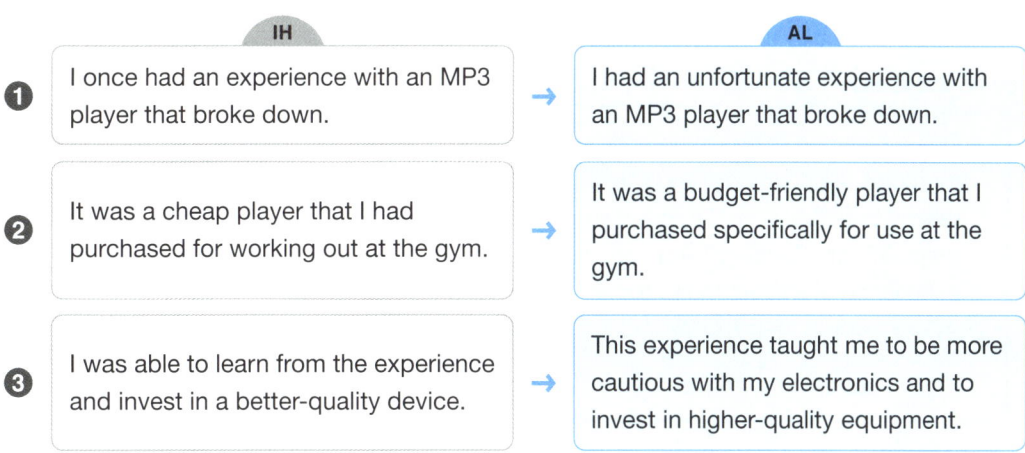

Chapter 5

Reading · Cooking 독서·요리

✓ Strategy Check 주제 관련 전략

Check the following strategies related to the topic of this chapter.
이 챕터의 주제와 관련된 시험 대비 전략을 확인해 보세요.

IH Essential

- Try selecting "Reading books" and "Cooking" among the options in Background Survey question 5. Both topics are commonly encountered in daily life, making it easy to prepare answers. Moreover, they can be related to questions frequently asked about "Residence" and "Vacations," which will enhance your efficiency in preparing for the exam.
  백그라운드 서베이 5번 선택지 중, '독서'와 '요리하기'를 선택해 보세요. 두 주제 모두 일상 생활에서 흔히 접할 수 있으므로 답변을 준비하기 용이할 뿐만 아니라, '거주지'와 '휴가' 관련하여 자주 출제되는 문제와도 연계할 수 있어 시험 대비 효율을 높여줄 것입니다.

- If you choose "Reading books" in Background Survey question 5, it is important to have your thoughts organized regarding your favorite books or authors as well as how you purchase books. Additionally, be prepared to answer questions that may vary, such as recent or memorable books you've read, your reading habits, etc. This will help you avoid being flustered when you are asked some challenging questions related to reading.
  백그라운드 서베이 5번에서 '독서'를 선택할 경우, 좋아하는 책 또는 작가, 책을 구매하는 방법에 관하여 본인의 생각을 정리해 두는 것이 중요합니다. 뿐만 아니라 최근에 읽었거나 기억에 남는 책, 본인만의 독서 습관 등 변형 문제가 출제되어도 당황하지 않도록 독서와 관련하여 다방면으로 답변을 준비할 필요가 있습니다.

- If you choose "Cooking," you can easily prepare for questions related to other topics such as "daily activities at home," "spending vacations at home," "activities during holidays," and more. Utilize what you've learned and prepared from this chapter to practice answering questions of other topics as well.
  '요리하기'를 선택하면 '평소 집에서 하는 일,' '집에서 보내는 휴가,' '명절에 하는 일' 등 다른 주제와 관련하여 출제되는 문제에도 쉽게 대비할 수 있습니다. 이번 챕터에서의 학습 내용을 활용하여 다른 질문에 답변하는 연습도 해 보세요.

AL Booster

- One advantage of preparing answers related to "Cooking" is that you can also utilize them for topics such as "food" and "holidays." For instance, one frequently presented question related to holidays is, "Describe your most memorable holiday." Using the materials you prepared for "Cooking," you can elaborate on "the dishes you enjoy cooking and the experience of sharing those dishes with your family" as a response to this question.
  '요리하기'와 관련하여 준비한 답변은 돌발 주제인 '음식,' '명절' 등에도 활용할 수 있다는 장점이 있습니다. 예를 들어, 명절과 관련하여 자주 출제되는 돌발 문제 중 하나가 '가장 기억에 남는 명절에 관해 설명해 보라'는 것입니다. 이 질문에 대한 답변으로, '요리하기'에서 준비한 소재를 활용하여 '평소 자주 하는 요리와 해당 요리를 가족과 나눠 먹은 경험'에 대해 서술할 수 있습니다.

❓ Frequently Asked Questions 빈출 질문 유형

Here are the most frequently asked question types related to the topic. Try to identify **the key matter** of the question and **the information** that should be included in your response.

이 챕터의 주제와 관련해 자주 출제되는 질문 유형들을 확인해 보세요. 그리고 각 질문의 중심 소재와 답변에 어떤 정보를 포함시켜야 하는지 파악해 보세요.

Reading Books

- What kind of books do you read? How often do you read? Tell me about your reading habits in as much detail as possible.
- Who is your favorite author? What kinds of books did he or she write? Why do you like the author?
- Why did you become interested in reading? Did anyone influence you? Tell me why you are interested in reading.
- Have any books had a positive effect on you? I'd like to know about one of those books.

Buying Books

- How do you purchase books? Do you prefer going to a physical bookstore or using an online bookstore?
- Some people learn about books by reading book reviews. Do you read reviews before deciding to purchase a book? Why or why not?

Cooking

- What types of things do you enjoy cooking? Please choose one and explain why you enjoy cooking it. Provide several details about the dish, including how to prepare it.
- How did you first become interested in cooking? How did you learn to cook different foods?
- Think about a time something unexpected happened while you were cooking. What kind of food were you trying to cook? What was the problem?
- Has there been any change in the way you cook between this year and last year? What kind of change? What caused it?

Chapter 5 Reading·Cooking 독서·요리

Unit 09 Combo Set (1)

MP3 바로가기

출제 가능성 ★★★★☆

Q1 How do you purchase books? Do you prefer going to a physical bookstore or using an online bookstore?

▶ Question Analysis 질문 분석

Answer the following questions and identify the key matter and the information to be included in your response.
다음 질문에 답하며 답변의 주제와 반드시 포함되어야 할 내용이 무엇인지 파악해 보세요.

1. What is going to be the key matter of your response?
2. What information should your response include?

▶ Warm Your Brain Up 브레인스토밍

Answer the following questions for ideas.
다음 질문에 답하며 답변 소재를 발굴해 보세요.

Intro	• What are the different ways to purchase a book? • In your case, which is the better option for purchasing a book, a physical bookstore or an online bookstore?
Body	• What are the advantages or disadvantages of using an online bookstore? • What are the benefits or drawbacks of going to a physical bookstore?
Conclusion	• Overall, what factors influence your decision to purchase a book from a physical store or an online store?

AL Booster

- How can comparing prices between different sellers on online bookstores benefit a book buyer?
- How does the selection of books differ between physical and online bookstores?
- How can reading online reviews benefit a book buyer?

Useful Expressions

when it comes to ~에 관해서라면   physical bookstore 오프라인 서점   as for me 내 경우에는   prefer to ~하는 것을 선호하다
offer convenience 편의를 제공하다   browse 둘러보다   a wide selection 다양한   specific title 특정 제목   niche topic 특정 분야
budget 예산   limited selection 한정된 종류   compare prices 가격을 비교하다   seller 판매자   feature 특징
get the most value for one's money ~가 지불한 값어치만큼 좋은 것을 얻다(사다)   review 후기   recommendation 추천
convenient 편리한   cost-effective 비용 효율이 높은, 가성비가 좋은

Pattern Drills 패턴 학습

Practice using the given sentence patterns to help you deliver your response clearly.
주어진 문장 패턴을 익혀 답변이 명확하게 전달될 수 있도록 연습해 보세요.

❶
When it comes to _____, there are two main options: _____ and _____.

- exercising / cardio / strength training
- cooking / following a recipe / improvising
- managing stress / practicing meditation / doing exercise

❷
Another advantage of using online bookstores is the ability to _____.

- download e-books instantly
- easily compare prices
- read reviews from other customers
- pre-order books before their official release date

❸
This is helpful for me when trying to _____.

- organize my thoughts and ideas
- plan out my daily schedule
- pursue personal and professional growth

❹
I find it to be a/an _____ option for buying books.

- time-saving
- affordable
- convenient

Mini Actual Test 연습 문제   🎧 9_1.mp3

Respond to the following question while keeping in mind what you have learned.
앞서 배운 내용을 떠올리면서 다음 질문에 답변해 보세요.

> When buying a book, do you prefer visiting a traditional bookstore or shopping at an online bookstore?

Model Answer 모범 답안

Enhance your response by referring to the model answer.
다음 모범 답안을 참고하여 여러분의 답변을 발전시켜 보세요.

> When it comes to purchasing books, there are two main options: physical bookstores and online bookstores. As for me, I prefer to use online bookstores. There are several reasons for this. Firstly, online bookstores offer a lot of convenience. I can browse through a wider selection of books and find specific titles or niche topics that may not be available in physical bookstores. Secondly, online bookstores usually offer better prices, which is great for my budget. Although I do miss the experience of browsing through physical bookstores, they often have limited selections. This makes it difficult for me to find a specific book quickly. Another advantage of using online bookstores is the ability to compare prices between different sellers. This feature helps me find the best deal and get the most value for my money. Additionally, many online bookstores offer helpful reviews and recommendations from other customers. This is important for me when trying to decide which book to purchase. Overall, while I do miss the experience of browsing physical bookstores, I find online bookstores to be a more convenient and cost-effective option for buying books.

Level Up to AL AL 공략하기

Read the examples below and see how IH-level sentences can be rephrased at the AL level.
다음 예시를 읽고 IH 수준의 문장을 어떻게 AL 수준으로 바꾸어 말할 수 있는지 살펴보세요.

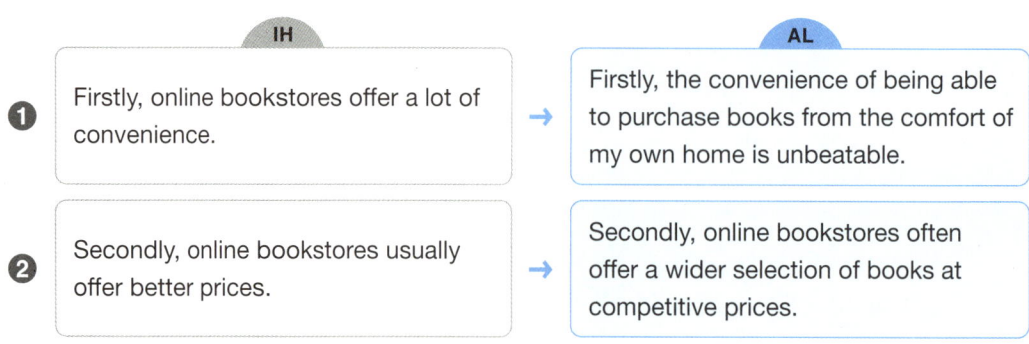

출제 가능성 ★★★☆☆

Q2 Why did you become interested in reading? Did anyone influence you? Tell me why you are interested in reading.

Question Analysis 질문 분석

Answer the following questions and identify the key matter and the information to be included in your response.
다음 질문에 답하며 답변의 주제와 반드시 포함되어야 할 내용이 무엇인지 파악해 보세요.

1. What is going to be the key matter of your response?
2. What information should your response include?

Warm Your Brain Up 브레인스토밍

Answer the following questions for ideas.
다음 질문에 답하며 답변 소재를 발굴해 보세요.

Intro	• What is your earliest memory of reading? How did it make you feel? • Did you grow up in a household where reading was encouraged?
Body	• How has your love for reading evolved over time? • What do you enjoy most about reading? • What kind of books do you prefer and why? • What role does reading play in your life now?
Conclusion	• What impact has reading had on your life? • Would you recommend reading to others? Why?

AL Booster

- Has anyone in your life encouraged or influenced your love for reading? How?
- How did you develop a love for reading?
- Who helped you discover new authors and genres?

Useful Expressions

passion 열정   used to ~하곤 했다   early exposure to 어린 시절 ~에 대한 노출   develop a love for ~을 사랑하게 되다
grow on 점점 좋아지다   literature 문학   escape 탈출하다   stories 이야기, 소설   discover 발견하다   genre 장르
play an important role 중요한 역할을 하다   critical thinking 비판적 사고   empathy 감정 이입, 공감

Pattern Drills 패턴 학습

Practice using the given sentence patterns to help you deliver your response clearly.
주어진 문장 패턴을 익혀 답변이 명확하게 전달될 수 있도록 연습해 보세요.

1
_____ has been a passion of mine since I was young.
- Reading books
- Riding bikes
- Playing sports

2
Reading became a way for me to _____.
- relax and unwind after a long day
- improve my vocabulary and language skills
- cope with difficult emotions or experiences

3
_____ has played an important role in my life.
- Reading
- Nature
- Family

4
I highly recommend reading to anyone who wants to _____.
- broaden their horizons
- learn new things
- escape into a different world for a while

Mini Actual Test 연습 문제

🎧 9_3.mp3

Respond to the following question while keeping in mind what you have learned.
앞서 배운 내용을 떠올리면서 다음 질문에 답변해 보세요.

> How did you first become interested in reading? When was it? Did anyone influence you?

Model Answer 모범 답안

Enhance your response by referring to the model answer.
다음 모범 답안을 참고하여 여러분의 답변을 발전시켜 보세요.

> I love reading, and it has been a passion of mine since I was young. My parents used to read to me every night before bed, and I always looked forward to this special time. This early exposure to books and reading helped me develop a love for literature that has continued to this day. As I grew older, reading became a way for me to escape and explore new worlds and ideas. I enjoy reading all kinds of books, but if I had to pick just one kind, it would be novels because they allow me to become part of the characters and their world. My parents introduced me to reading, and my English teacher in high school helped me discover new authors but the genre that I loved. Reading has played an important role in my life. It has not only helped me develop important skills like critical thinking and empathy, but it has also given me a better understanding of the world around me. I highly recommend reading to anyone who wants to escape, learn, and grow.

Level Up to AL AL 공략하기

Read the examples below and see how IH-level sentences can be rephrased at the AL level.
다음 예시를 읽고 IH 수준의 문장을 어떻게 AL 수준으로 바꾸어 말할 수 있는지 살펴보세요.

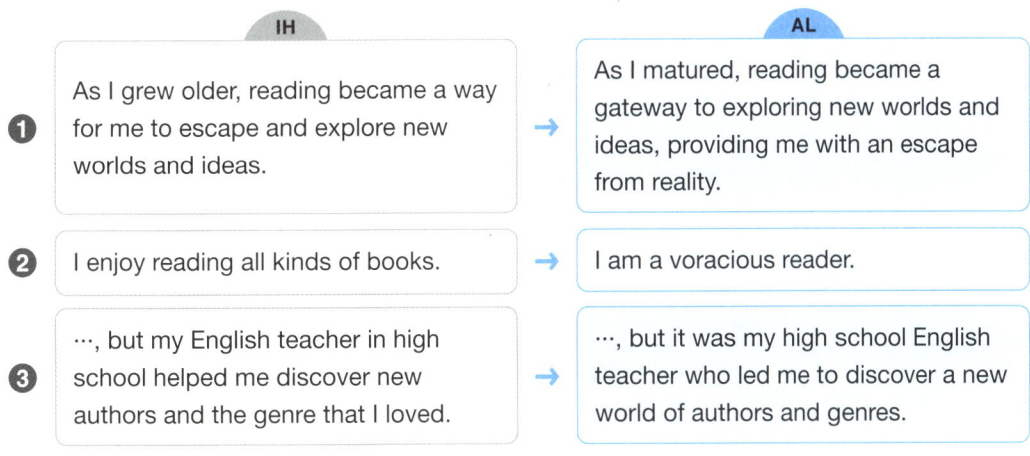

출제 가능성 ★★★☆☆

Q3 Have any books had a positive effect on you? I'd like to know about one of those books.

Question Analysis 질문 분석

Answer the following questions and identify the key matter and the information to be included in your response.
다음 질문에 답하며 답변의 주제와 반드시 포함되어야 할 내용이 무엇인지 파악해 보세요.

1. What is going to be the key matter of your response?
2. What information should your response include?

Warm Your Brain Up 브레인스토밍

Answer the following questions for ideas.
다음 질문에 답하며 답변 소재를 발굴해 보세요.

Intro	• What is the title of the book that had a positive effect on you? • Who or what influenced you to read the book?
Body	• What were the main themes in the book? • How did the book influence your thoughts, feelings, or actions? • Which character in the book inspired you and how?
Conclusion	• What lessons did you learn from the book? • Would you recommend this book to others? Why or why not?

AL Booster

- Did the book change the way you view the world or certain issues?
- How did it help you develop your thinking skills and empathy?

Useful Expressions

positive 긍정적인   have an impact 영향을 미치다   connect with ~에 공감하다   get lost 빠져들다   racism 인종차별   injustice 불평등   empathy 공감 능력   treat others 다른 사람을 대하다   kindness 친절   stand up for ~을 지지하다   critical thinking skill 비판적 사고 능력   perspective 관점   particularly 특별히   be inspired by ~에 의해 영감을 받다   role model 닮고 싶은(모범이 되는) 사람   justice 정의   have a lasting impact on ~에 대한 영향이 오래 지속되다   through literature 문학을 통해

Pattern Drills 패턴 학습

Practice using the given sentence patterns to help you deliver your response clearly.
주어진 문장 패턴을 익혀 답변이 명확하게 전달될 수 있도록 연습해 보세요.

I really connected with _____.

1
- the main character in the book
- the message of the book
- the author's writing style
- the emotions portrayed in the novel

The book made me think deeply about _____.

2
- the concept of human nature
- the importance of family values
- the political landscape of our country

The book showed me the importance of _____.

3
- forgiveness and how it can lead to healing
- self-reflection and how it can lead to personal growth
- being true to oneself, even when it's difficult

I was particularly inspired by _____.

4
- the main character's determination
- the author's use of vivid imagery
- the way the author tackled complex social issues

Mini Actual Test 연습 문제

🎧 9_5.mp3

Respond to the following question while keeping in mind what you have learned.
앞서 배운 내용을 떠올리면서 다음 질문에 답변해 보세요.

> Can you tell me about a book that has been particularly memorable for you? What is the book about? In what ways has reading this book influenced you?

Model Answer 모범 답안

Enhance your response by referring to the model answer.
다음 모범 답안을 참고하여 여러분의 답변을 발전시켜 보세요.

> I have always loved reading books, and there is one book that has had a very positive impact on me. It is *To Blind Runner* by Harris Kim. I really connected with the story and the characters, and I got lost in the world that Kim created. The book made me think deeply about important themes like racism, injustice, and empathy. It showed me the importance of treating others with kindness and standing up for what is right. Reading this book helped me develop my critical thinking skills and my ability to understand others' perspectives. I was particularly inspired by the character of George Frank, who taught me about the importance of being a good role model and standing up for justice. I believe that *To Blind Runner* is a very special book, and it has had a lasting impact on me. I highly recommend it to anyone who wants to learn and grow through literature.

Level Up to AL AL 공략하기

Read the examples below and see how IH-level sentences can be rephrased at the AL level.
다음 예시를 읽고 IH 수준의 문장을 어떻게 AL 수준으로 바꾸어 말할 수 있는지 살펴보세요.

IH → **AL**

❶ I got lost in the world that Kim created. → I found myself absorbed in the world that Kim created.

❷ The book made me think deeply about important themes like racism, injustice, and empathy. It showed me the importance of treating others with kindness and standing up for what is right. → The book's themes of racism, injustice, and empathy opened my eyes to the importance of standing up for what is right and treating others with respect and kindness.

Chapter 5 Reading · Cooking 독서·요리

Unit 10 Combo Set (2)

출제 가능성 ★★★☆☆

Q1 What What kinds of food do you enjoy cooking? Please choose one and explain why you enjoy cooking it. Provide several details about the dish, including how to prepare it.

Question Analysis 질문 분석

Answer the following questions and identify the key matter and the information to be included in your response.
다음 질문에 답하며 답변의 주제와 반드시 포함되어야 할 내용이 무엇인지 파악해 보세요.

1. What is going to be the key matter of your response?
2. What information should your response include?

Warm Your Brain Up 브레인스토밍

Answer the following questions for ideas.
다음 질문에 답하며 답변 소재를 발굴해 보세요.

Intro	What type of dish do you enjoy cooking? Why is this dish your favorite to prepare?
Body	• What are the ingredients for this dish? • What kitchen tools do you need to cook it? • How do you cook the dish?
Conclusion	• Why do you like making the dish? • What is your favorite part of making this dish?

AL Booster

- What are some cooking techniques that are essential for making this dish?
- How does the dish reflect your personal preferences?

Useful Expressions

carbonara 카르보나라 (이탈리아 파스타 요리)   change up 변화를 주다, 바꾸다   by -ing ~하면서, ~함으로써   ingredient 재료
consist of ~을 포함하다, ~으로 구성되다   key 중요한   have a great taste 맛이 좋다   texture 질감   frying pan 프라이팬
crispy 바삭한   black pepper 후추   bowl 그릇   mix everything together 모두 섞다   coat 코팅하다   noodle 면
turn out 결과적으로 ~이 되다   vegetable 채소   one's go-to dish ~가 자주 먹는 요리   tasty 맛있는   flavor 맛

Pattern Drills 패턴 학습

Practice using the given sentence patterns to help you deliver your response clearly.
주어진 문장 패턴을 익혀 답변이 명확하게 전달될 수 있도록 연습해 보세요.

❶
> The dish consists of just a few key ingredients like _____.

- chicken, rice, and spices
- bread, cheese, and tomato sauce
- fish, vegetables, and herbs

❷
> To prepare this dish, I start by _____.

- boiling a pot of water
- chopping up some vegetables
- preheating the oven

❸
> I really like making this dish because _____.

- it's a quick and easy meal
- it allows me to be creative
- it reminds me of my childhood

❹
> Overall, _____ is my go-to dish for a _____ dinner.

- Stir-fried rice / quick
- Small-sized pizza / tasty
- Fish en papillote / fancy

Mini Actual Test 연습 문제 🎧 10_1.mp3

Respond to the following question while keeping in mind what you have learned.
앞서 배운 내용을 떠올리면서 다음 질문에 답변해 보세요.

> What's your favorite dish to prepare? Why do you like making it? How do you make it?

⊙ Model Answer 모범 답안

 10_2.mp3

Enhance your response by referring to the model answer.
다음 모범 답안을 참고하여 여러분의 답변을 발전시켜 보세요.

> I really enjoy cooking different foods, but one of my favorite dishes is spaghetti carbonara. I like this dish because it is easy to make and you can change it up by adding different ingredients. The dish consists of just a few key ingredients like spaghetti, eggs, cheese, and bacon, and it has a great taste. To prepare this dish, I start by cooking the spaghetti until it is just the right texture. Then I cook some bacon in a frying pan until it is crispy. After that, I mix some eggs, cheese, and black pepper in a bowl to make a sauce. I add the cooked spaghetti to the frying pan and stir it well to mix with the bacon. Finally, I turn the heat down and pour the prepared sauce into the pan. Then I mix everything together until the sauce coats the noodles. I really like making this dish because it is fast and easy, and it always turns out to be really yummy. I also like that I can add other things like vegetables or different types of meat to make it even more interesting. Overall, spaghetti carbonara is my go-to dish for a quick and tasty dinner.

⊙ Level Up to AL AL 공략하기

Read the examples below and see how IH-level sentences can be rephrased at the AL level.
다음 예시를 읽고 IH 수준의 문장을 어떻게 AL 수준으로 바꾸어 말할 수 있는지 살펴보세요.

IH		AL
❶ I like this dish because it is easy to make and you can change it up by adding different ingredients.	→	What draws me to this dish is that it is easy to make, and I can use various ingredients to cook it differently.
❷ I really like making this dish because it is fast and easy, and it always turns out to be really yummy.	→	I love the process of making this dish because it is quick and easy, yet the end result is a delicious and satisfying meal.

출제 가능성 ★★★★☆

Q2 Think about a time something unexpected happened while you were cooking. What kind of food were you trying to cook? What was the problem?

Question Analysis 질문 분석

Answer the following questions and identify the key matter and the information to be included in your response.
다음 질문에 답하며 답변의 주제와 반드시 포함되어야 할 내용이 무엇인지 파악해 보세요.

1. What is going to be the key matter of your response?
2. What information should your response include?

Warm Your Brain Up 브레인스토밍

Answer the following questions for ideas.
다음 질문에 답하며 답변 소재를 발굴해 보세요.

Intro	• What was the dish you were trying to cook? • What was the occasion?
Body	• What unexpected event occurred during your cooking process? • How did you react to the unexpected event? • How did the dish turn out in the end?
Conclusion	• What did you learn from this experience? • Did you have to make any adjustments to the dish or the cooking process because of the unexpected event?

AL Booster

• Why is it important to embrace unexpected events in the kitchen and learn from them?

Useful Expressions

as planned 계획대로   boil 끓이다   strain 걸러내다   accidentally 우연히   drop 떨어뜨리다   drain 배수구   disappointed 실망한
a new batch of 새로운 한 묶음의   think fast 빠르게 생각하다   leftover 남은 음식   in the fridge 냉장고 안에
cook up 요리해서 만들어 내다   mix A with B A와 B를 섞다   be a substitute for ~을 대신하다   be impressed with ~에 감명받다
lead to ~로 이어지다   discovery 발견   adaptable 적응할 수 있는   creative 창의적인

Pattern Drills 패턴 학습

Practice using the given sentence patterns to help you deliver your response clearly.
주어진 문장 패턴을 익혀 답변이 명확하게 전달될 수 있도록 연습해 보세요.

① One time I was making _____, and things didn't go as planned.
- pancakes
- cookies
- beef stew

② I was disappointed because I didn't have enough ingredients to _____.
- prepare a fancy dinner for my guests
- cook my favorite pasta dish
- make a cake for my friend's birthday

③ It turned out to be a great substitute for _____.
- the missing ingredient in the dish
- the expensive ingredient in the recipe
- sugar in the dessert

④ This experience taught me that _____.
- being creative in the kitchen can result in delicious meals
- cooking is not always predictable
- experimenting with ingredients can result in surprising and delightful dishes

Mini Actual Test 연습 문제

🎧 10_3.mp3

Respond to the following question while keeping in mind what you have learned.
앞서 배운 내용을 떠올리면서 다음 질문에 답변해 보세요.

> While you were cooking, did something funny or unexpected occur? What was it? Tell me the whole story.

Model Answer 모범 답안  10_4.mp3

Enhance your response by referring to the model answer.
다음 모범 답안을 참고하여 여러분의 답변을 발전시켜 보세요.

> Spaghetti is one of my favorite meals to cook for dinner because it's simple and delicious. However, one time I was making spaghetti for my family, and things didn't go as planned. After boiling the pasta, I went to strain it, but I accidentally dropped it all down the drain. I was disappointed because I didn't have enough ingredients to make a new batch of pasta. I had to think fast and get creative. I remembered that I had some leftover rice in the fridge and quickly cooked up some vegetables to add to the sauce. I mixed the rice with the sauce, and it turned out to be a great substitute for spaghetti. My family was surprised but impressed with the new dish. This experience taught me that sometimes mistakes can lead to new discoveries. It also taught me to be adaptable and creative in the kitchen.

Level Up to AL AL 공략하기

Read the examples below and see how IH-level sentences can be rephrased at the AL level.
다음 예시를 읽고 IH 수준의 문장을 어떻게 AL 수준으로 바꾸어 말할 수 있는지 살펴보세요.

IH → **AL**

❶ After boiling the pasta, I went to strain it, but I accidentally dropped it all down the drain.
→ I had already boiled the pasta and was getting ready to strain it, but as I went to pour it into the colander, the pasta slipped out of the pot and went straight down the drain.

❷ It also taught me to be adaptable and creative in the kitchen.
→ It also encouraged me to be more adaptable in the kitchen and to experiment with different ingredients.

출제 가능성 ★★★☆☆

Q3 Has there been any change in the way you cook between this year and last year? What kind of change? What caused it?

Question Analysis 질문 분석

Answer the following questions and identify the key matter and the information to be included in your response.
다음 질문에 답하며 답변의 주제와 반드시 포함되어야 할 내용이 무엇인지 파악해 보세요.

1. What is going to be the key matter of your response?
2. What information should your response include?

Warm Your Brain Up 브레인스토밍

Answer the following questions for ideas.
다음 질문에 답하며 답변 소재를 발굴해 보세요.

Intro	• Has your cooking changed over the past year? • What was your cooking routine like last year?
Body	• What changes have you made to your cooking this year and why? • What has caused your cooking habits to change?
Conclusion	• What have you learned from the changes in your cooking habits?

AL Booster

- What types of meals have you started cooking more often this year?
- What are the new things that you have started cooking?

Useful Expressions

notice 알아차리다 cooking habit 요리 습관 work from home 재택근무하다 elaborate 정교한, 복잡한
try new recipes 새로운 요리법을 시도하다 experiment 시도하다, 실험하다 in pursuit of ~을 추구하며 as a result 그 결과로
simple and quick 간단하고 빠른 stir-fry 볶음 요리 pre-made 미리 만들어진 seasoning 양념 save time 시간을 절약하다
miss the joy of -ing ~하는 즐거움을 그리워하다 complicated 복잡한 efficient 효율적인

Pattern Drills 패턴 학습

Practice using the given sentence patterns to help you deliver your response clearly.
주어진 문장 패턴을 익혀 답변이 명확하게 전달될 수 있도록 연습해 보세요.

Last year, I was working from home and had more time to _____.

❶
- enjoy the process of cooking
- try out different ingredients and techniques
- perfect my culinary skills

I would spend hours in the kitchen _____.

❷
- trying out new recipes from my favorite cooking blog
- preparing a special dinner for my friends and family
- baking various desserts such as cookies and pies

I've started cooking _____ meals.

❸
- quick and easy
- healthy and nutritious
- budget-friendly

This change has also taught me to _____.

❹
- appreciate the simplicity of certain dishes
- prioritize my time and find more efficient ways to cook
- be more adaptable in the kitchen

Mini Actual Test 연습 문제   🎧 10_5.mp3

Respond to the following question while keeping in mind what you have learned.
앞서 배운 내용을 떠올리면서 다음 질문에 답변해 보세요.

Have you made any changes to the way you cook compared to last year? What particular changes did you make and why?

Model Answer 모범 답안

 10_6.mp3

Enhance your response by referring to the model answer.
다음 모범 답안을 참고하여 여러분의 답변을 발전시켜 보세요.

> I've noticed that my cooking habits have changed a lot between this year and last year. Last year, I was working from home and had more time to cook elaborate meals. I would spend hours in the kitchen trying new recipes and experimenting with different recipes and ingredients. I often spent hours in the kitchen in pursuit of the perfect meal. However, my schedule has become busier this year, and I don't have as much free time as before. As a result, I've started cooking more simple and quick meals, such as stir-fries, salads, and sandwiches. I've also started using more pre-made sauces and seasonings to save time. While I miss the joy of spending hours in the kitchen, I've learned that cooking doesn't always have to be complicated to be delicious. This change has also taught me to be more efficient and creative with my cooking.

Level Up to AL AL 공략하기

Read the examples below and see how IH-level sentences can be rephrased at the AL level.
다음 예시를 읽고 IH 수준의 문장을 어떻게 AL 수준으로 바꾸어 말할 수 있는지 살펴보세요.

IH → **AL**

① I've noticed that my cooking habits have changed a lot between this year and last year. → Over the past year, I have observed a significant shift in my cooking habits.

② As a result, I've started cooking more simple and quick meals. → In response to this, I have changed my approach to cooking and have begun preparing simple, easy-to-make meals.

③ I've learned that cooking doesn't always have to be complicated to be delicious. → I have come to realize that delicious food can be made without being overly complicated.

Chapter 6

Exercise 운동

✓ Strategy Check 주제 관련 전략

Check the following strategies related to the topic of this chapter.
이 챕터의 주제와 관련된 시험 대비 전략을 확인해 보세요.

IH Essential

- Background Survey question 6 is about your favorite "Exercise," and you must select at least one option from the choices provided. It is appropriate to choose 2 to 3 different types of exercises, and if you wish to select more, it is recommended to group together related exercises to prepare your answers.
  백그라운드 서베이 6번은 본인이 즐겨 하는 '운동'에 관한 질문으로 최소 1가지 이상의 선택지를 선택해야 합니다. 2~3가지 종목을 선택하는 것이 적절하며, 그 이상을 선택하고 싶을 경우 연계하여 답변을 준비할 수 있는 종목들을 묶어서 선택하길 추천합니다.

- It is recommended to choose some or all of "Jogging," "Walking," and "Hiking/Trekking." Since those types of exercises are similar, you will be able to respond smoothly to any of the topics related to jogging, walking, hiking, and trekking by preparing several answer frameworks.
  답변 연계가 가능한 '조깅,' '걷기,' '하이킹, 트레킹' 중 일부 또는 전부를 선택하길 추천합니다. 운동을 하는 장소, 준비물, 기억에 남는 경험 등에 관해 몇 가지 답변 프레임을 준비해 놓으면 '조깅,' '걷기,' '하이킹, 트레킹' 중 어떤 주제가 출제되어도 무난하게 답변할 수 있습니다.

- If you choose "Do not exercise at all," the probability of exercise-related questions being presented in the exam will be significantly reduced or even eliminated.
  '운동을 전혀 하지 않음'을 선택하면 운동 관련 질문이 아예 출제되지 않을 확률이 높아집니다.

AL Booster

- If you choose sports like "Soccer" or "Basketball" among the options in Background Survey question 6, there is a possibility that a question may be asked about explaining the rules of the game. As it can be a challenging question to answer, it is recommended to avoid selecting ball-game sports if possible. However, if you still wish to choose those, it's advisable to familiarize yourself with the specific terminology and expressions related to each sport and practice their accurate pronunciation.
  백그라운드 서베이 6번 선택지 중 '축구,' '농구' 등 구기 종목을 선택할 경우 경기 규칙에 관해 설명하라는 문제가 출제될 수 있습니다. 답변이 까다로운 질문이기 때문에 가급적 구기 종목은 선택하지 않는 것을 추천합니다. 그럼에도 구기 종목을 선택하고자 할 때에는, 각 종목의 전문 용어와 특정 표현을 익혀 두고 정확한 발음을 연습해 두는 것이 좋습니다.

❓ Frequently Asked Questions 빈출 질문 유형

Here are the most frequently asked question types related to the topic. Try to identify the key matter of the question and the information that should be included in your response.
이 챕터의 주제와 관련해 자주 출제되는 질문 유형들을 확인해 보세요. 그리고 각 질문의 중심 소재와 답변에 어떤 정보를 포함시켜야 하는지 파악해 보세요.

Jogging & Walking & Hiking

- How far and how long do you usually jog / walk / hike? Do you jog / walk / hike every day or once a week? Tell me about your jogging / walking / hiking routine.
- What do you need to go jogging / walking / hiking? What are the things you prepare or do in order to avoid injuries while jogging / walking / hiking?
- Tell me about the most interesting place you've ever gone for a jog / walk / hike. Where was it? Why was this place so interesting? Who did you go with? What was your time there like?
- People say that jogging / walking / hiking is a good activity for your health. Tell me about the social, physical, and mental benefits of jogging / walking / hiking. What do you think are the advantages of it compared to other activities or sports? Tell me about it in detail.
- Do people in your country jog / walk / hike more or less frequently compared to the past? Why do you think people have decided to walk more or less often than they did before? Tell me in detail.

Role-play

- I'd like to give you a situation and ask you to act it out. A friend has asked you to go for a jog / walk / hike. Ask your friend three to four questions about these plans.
- I'm going to give you a situation to act out. Unfortunately, you just found out that you will be unable to join your friend for a hike as planned. Contact your friend and explain why you will not be able to join him / her. Finally, offer two or three options to solve this issue.
- Here is a situation. You want to walk / jog / hike with your friend at a park in your neighborhood. Call your friend and ask some questions to organize a walk / jog / hike together.

Chapter 6 Exercise 운동

Unit 11 Combo Set (1)

MP3 바로가기

출제 가능성 ★★★☆☆

Q1 How far and how long do you usually jog? Do you jog every day or once a week? Tell me about your jogging routine.

Question Analysis 질문 분석

Answer the following questions and identify the key matter and the information to be included in your response.
다음 질문에 답하며 답변의 주제와 반드시 포함되어야 할 내용이 무엇인지 파악해 보세요.

1. What is going to be the key matter of your response?
2. What information should your response include?

Warm Your Brain Up 브레인스토밍

Answer the following questions for ideas.
다음 질문에 답하며 답변 소재를 발굴해 보세요.

Intro	• How long have you been jogging? • How far and how long do you usually jog?
Body	• How often do you jog? • Do you prefer jogging alone or with a partner / group? • Where do you usually jog?
Conclusion	• How has it impacted your overall health and wellbeing? • Do you have any advice for someone who wants to start a jogging routine?

AL Booster

- How do you measure your distance and time when jogging?
- How do you stay motivated to keep up your jogging routine?

Useful Expressions

cover a distance 거리를 이동하다　keep track of ~을 기록하다　progress 진척　fitness tracker 피트니스 추적기
motivate 동기를 부여하다　alone 혼자서　so that ~하기 위하여　clear one's mind ~의 마음을 비우다　vary 변화하다, 달라지다
nearby trail 인근 산책로　make sure 확실히 하다　routine 규칙적으로 하는 일, (판에 박힌) 일상　good quality 고품질
running shoes 운동화　do stretching 스트레칭 하다　do strength training exercises 근력 운동을 하다
improve one's fitness ~의 체력을 향상시키다　challenging 도전적인　stay motivated 의욕을 잃지 않다
adjust one's routine ~의 일과를 조정하다　active 활동적인　focused 집중하는

122 Compact OPIc 컴팩트 오픽

Pattern Drills 패턴 학습

Practice using the given sentence patterns to help you deliver your response clearly.
주어진 문장 패턴을 익혀 답변이 명확하게 전달될 수 있도록 연습해 보세요.

❶ I usually jog for _____ and cover a distance of _____.
- 45 minutes / 5 kilometers on weekends
- 20 minutes / 2 kilometers before work
- 30 minutes / 3.5 kilometers every day

❷ To keep track of my progress, I use _____.
- a workout journal
- a project management tool
- a fitness application

❸ I make sure to wear _____.
- comfortable clothes
- clothes suitable for the weather
- a hat and sunglasses

❹ It can be challenging to _____.
- push myself to jog faster or farther
- jog alone in the dark
- jog when feeling under the weather

Mini Actual Test 연습 문제   🎧 11_1.mp3

Respond to the following question while keeping in mind what you have learned.
앞서 배운 내용을 떠올리면서 다음 질문에 답변해 보세요.

> Can you describe your jogging routine? How far and how long do you typically jog? How often do you do it?

Model Answer 모범 답안

Enhance your response by referring to the model answer.
다음 모범 답안을 참고하여 여러분의 답변을 발전시켜 보세요.

> I've been jogging every day for the past two years. I usually jog for about 30 minutes and cover a distance of around 3 kilometers. To keep track of my progress, I use a fitness tracker, which also helps motivate me to keep going. I usually prefer to jog alone so that I can think and clear my mind. My jogging route varies and includes places like the park near my house and some nearby trails. During my jogging routine, I make sure to wear comfortable clothes and good quality running shoes. I do some stretching before and after jogging because it is the best way to warm your body up and also cool it down. It can be challenging to stay motivated, but I try to change up my routes and listen to music to keep things interesting. If I get hurt or feel tired, I rest and adjust my routine. Jogging has helped me become more healthy, active, and more focused overall.

Level Up to AL AL 공략하기

Read the examples below and see how IH-level sentences can be rephrased at the AL level.
다음 예시를 읽고 IH 수준의 문장을 어떻게 AL 수준으로 바꾸어 말할 수 있는지 살펴보세요.

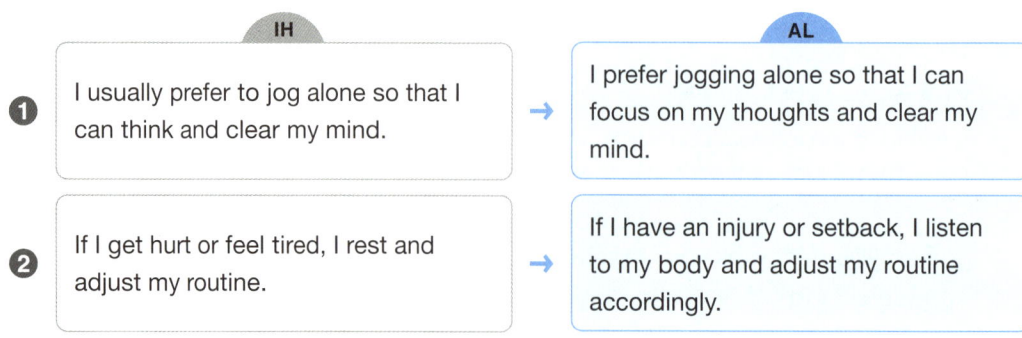

Q2 What do you need to go jogging? What are the things you prepare or do in order to avoid injuries while jogging?

출제 가능성 ★★★★☆

Question Analysis 질문 분석

Answer the following questions and identify the key matter and the information to be included in your response.
다음 질문에 답하며 답변의 주제와 반드시 포함되어야 할 내용이 무엇인지 파악해 보세요.

1. What is going to be the key matter of your response?
2. What information should your response include?

Warm Your Brain Up 브레인스토밍

Answer the following questions for ideas.
다음 질문에 답하며 답변 소재를 발굴해 보세요.

Intro	• What are the essential items needed to go jogging? • What do you wear for jogging?
Body	• What should be done to avoid injuries while jogging? • What type of gear can help prevent injuries?
Conclusion	• What is your overall opinion of jogging as an exercise? • How can jogging be a safe and enjoyable exercise?

AL Booster

- What are some accessories that may be helpful when you jog?
- What should be done if you experience an injury while jogging?

Useful Expressions

in order to ~하기 위해서   essential 필수적인   clothing 의류   breathable 통기성이 있는   a good pair of 한 켤레의 좋은 ~   perhaps 아마도   water bottle 물병   materials 소재   wick away 빨아들이다   sweat 땀   breathe 숨 쉬다   supportive 지지력이 있는   terrain 지형   avoid injuries 부상을 피하다   warming up 준비 운동   wear gear 장비를 착용하다   sweatband 땀 흡수 밴드   compression sleeve 압박 보호대   seek medical attention 의료진의 치료를 받다   as needed 필요에 따라   stay fit 건강을 유지하다   appropriate gear 적절한 장비   adequate preparation 충분한 준비

Pattern Drills 패턴 학습

Practice using the given sentence patterns to help you deliver your response clearly.
주어진 문장 패턴을 익혀 답변이 명확하게 전달될 수 있도록 연습해 보세요.

1
In order to go jogging, there are a few items that _____.
- I always pack in my gym bag
- I check before leaving the house
- I need to purchase first

2
When I choose clothing for jogging, I make sure to _____.
- select colors that are visible to drivers
- check the weather forecast ahead of time
- wear layers

3
To avoid injuries while jogging, I always _____.
- warm up and stretch my muscles
- wear appropriate shoes
- pay attention to the terrain

4
I believe that jogging is a(n) _____.
- fun way to explore new areas
- great way to relieve stress
- effective way to improve my physical fitness

Mini Actual Test 연습 문제 🎧 11_3.mp3

Respond to the following question while keeping in mind what you have learned.
앞서 배운 내용을 떠올리면서 다음 질문에 답변해 보세요.

> Is there anything you have to prepare before you go for a jog? What clothing do you wear when you go jogging? Please describe it in detail.

Model Answer 모범 답안

 11_4.mp3

Enhance your response by referring to the model answer.
다음 모범 답안을 참고하여 여러분의 답변을 발전시켜 보세요.

> In order to go jogging, there are a few items that I consider essential. These include clothing that is both comfortable and breathable, a good pair of running shoes, and perhaps additional items such as a fitness tracker or a water bottle. When I choose clothing for jogging, I make sure to wear materials that will wick away sweat and allow my skin to breathe. My shoes should be comfortable, supportive, and appropriate for the type of terrain I'll be jogging on. To avoid injuries while jogging, I always prepare my body by stretching and warming up before I start my jog. I also make sure to wear gear like a sweatband or compression sleeve, which can help prevent injuries. If I do experience an injury, I make sure to rest and seek medical attention as needed. Overall, with appropriate gear and adequate preparation, I believe that jogging is a safe and fun way for me to stay fit and healthy.

Level Up to AL AL 공략하기

Read the examples below and see how IH-level sentences can be rephrased at the AL level.
다음 예시를 읽고 IH 수준의 문장을 어떻게 AL 수준으로 바꾸어 말할 수 있는지 살펴보세요.

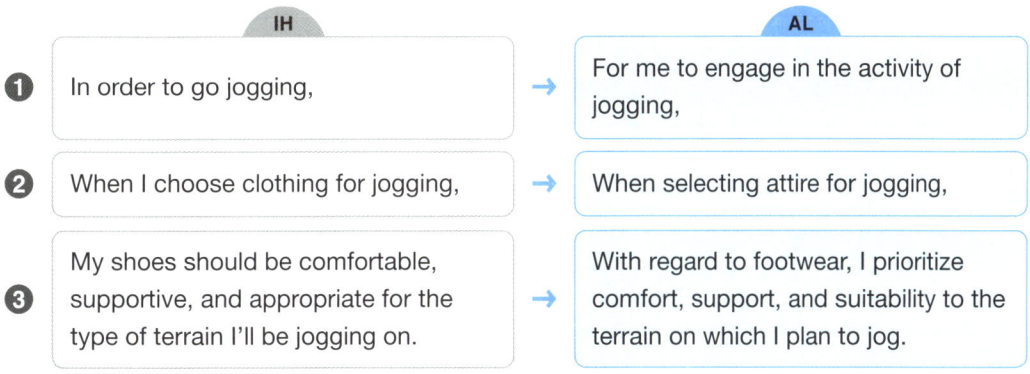

출제 가능성 ★★★★☆

Q3 Tell me about the most interesting place you've ever gone for a jog. Where was it? Why was this place so interesting? Who did you go with? What was your time there like?

> **Question Analysis** 질문 분석

Answer the following questions and identify the key matter and the information to be included in your response.
다음 질문에 답하며 답변의 주제와 반드시 포함되어야 할 내용이 무엇인지 파악해 보세요.

1. What is going to be the key matter of your response?
2. What information should your response include?

> **Warm Your Brain Up** 브레인스토밍

Answer the following questions for ideas.
다음 질문에 답하며 답변 소재를 발굴해 보세요.

Intro	• Where did you go for a jog? • What are the distinctive features of the place?
Body	• Whom did you go jogging with and why? • Do you think the place you had chosen was nice for a jog? • What were the pros and cons of the place for joggers?
Conclusion	• What's your overall experience of the place?

AL Booster

- What did you see at the place?
- What was the atmosphere of the place?

Useful Expressions

national park 국립 공원 hometown 고향 be full of ~으로 가득 차다 wildlife 야생 동물 peaceful 평화로운 alone 혼자서 가다 clear one's head ~의 머릿속을 정리하다 get some exercise 운동을 하다 be close to ~에 가깝다 feel like ~같은 느낌이 들다 be surrounded by ~으로 둘러싸여 있다 cool breeze 시원한 바람 distance 거리 scenery 경치 fresh air 신선한 공기 escape from ~에서 탈출하다 noise 소음 hustle 바쁘게 사는 (하는) 것 everyday life 일상적인 삶 definitely 확실히, 분명히

128 Compact OPIc 컴팩트 오픽

Pattern Drills 패턴 학습

Practice using the given sentence patterns to help you deliver your response clearly.
주어진 문장 패턴을 익혀 답변이 명확하게 전달될 수 있도록 연습해 보세요.

❶
One of the most interesting places I've gone for a jog was _____.
- a hilly countryside with breathtaking views
- a peaceful forest trail with chirping birds
- a historical town with charming architecture

❷
The park was full of _____.
- beautiful trees and wildlife
- tourists and colorful umbrellas
- lush greenery and tall trees

❸
What made _____ so interesting to me was _____.
- jogging / I became more alive while doing it
- the museum / it had a lot of interactive exhibits
- the restaurant / it served food from a variety of different cultures

❹
It was a great way to _____.
- enjoy the outdoors and get some fresh air
- improve my physical health and fitness
- explore new places

Mini Actual Test 연습 문제   🎧 11_5.mp3

Respond to the following question while keeping in mind what you have learned.
앞서 배운 내용을 떠올리면서 다음 질문에 답변해 보세요.

> Think of a memorable place you've gone for a jog. What was your experience like? Describe the place and your experience there in detail.

Model Answer 모범 답안

 11_6.mp3

Enhance your response by referring to the model answer.
다음 모범 답안을 참고하여 여러분의 답변을 발전시켜 보세요.

> One of the most interesting places I've gone for a jog was a national park near my hometown. The park was full of beautiful trees and wildlife, and it was very peaceful to jog there. I went alone because I wanted to clear my head and get some exercise, but I saw many families and couples enjoying the park as well. What made this place so interesting to me was the fact that it was so close to the city, but it felt like I was in a different world. I loved being surrounded by nature and feeling the cool breeze on my face. I didn't worry about my time or distance; I just enjoyed the scenery and fresh air. It was a great way to escape the hustle and bustle of everyday life. Overall, it was a wonderful experience, and I would definitely go back for another jog in the park.

Level Up to AL AL 공략하기

Read the examples below and see how IH-level sentences can be rephrased at the AL level.
다음 예시를 읽고 IH 수준의 문장을 어떻게 AL 수준으로 바꾸어 말할 수 있는지 살펴보세요.

	IH	→	AL
❶	What made this place so interesting to me was the fact that it was so close to the city, but it felt like I was in a different world.	→	What struck me about this place was its proximity to the city. It was like entering a whole new world just a short distance away.
❷	I didn't worry about my time or distance; I just enjoyed the scenery and fresh air.	→	Instead of fixating on my pace or the number of kilometers I ran, I simply appreciated the beauty of my surroundings and the feeling of the crisp air on my skin.

Chapter 6 Exercise 운동

Unit 12 Combo Set (2)

MP3 바로가기

출제 가능성 ★★★★☆

Q1 I'd like to give you a situation and ask you to act it out. A friend has asked you to go for a hike. Ask your friend three to four questions about the plan.

Question Analysis 질문 분석

Answer the following questions and identify the key matter and the information to be included in your response.
다음 질문에 답하며 답변의 주제와 반드시 포함되어야 할 내용이 무엇인지 파악해 보세요.

1. What is going to be the key matter of your response?
2. What information should your response include?

Warm Your Brain Up 브레인스토밍

Answer the following questions for ideas.
다음 질문에 답하며 답변 소재를 발굴해 보세요.

Intro	How would you feel about being asked to go for a hike? What are some important factors to consider before going on a hike?
Body	• What questions should you ask a friend who has invited you? • What do you expect the start time and the duration of the hike to be? • What are the things you think to bring for a hike?
Conclusion	• How would you end the conversation?

AL Booster

• How would you react to your friend's response?

Useful Expressions

invite A to B A를 B에 초대하다   particular 특정한   trail 등산로   have A in mind A를 생각하고 있다   up for ~을 기꺼이 하고 싶은   explore 탐험하다   waterfall 폭포   difficulty level 난이도   tend to ~하는 경향이 있다   work well 잘 맞다   definitely 확실히   backpack 배낭   get out in nature 자연 속으로 나가다   enjoy some fresh air 신선한 공기를 즐기다

Pattern Drills 패턴 학습

Practice using the given sentence patterns to help you deliver your response clearly.
주어진 문장 패턴을 익혀 답변이 명확하게 전달될 수 있도록 연습해 보세요.

❶
> Do you have any _____ in mind?

- particular destination
- specific trail

❷
> I love hiking and I'm always up for _____.

- challenging myself on difficult trails
- admiring stunning views along the way
- meeting fellow hikers on the trail

❸
> _____ works well for me.

- An early start time
- Meeting at the coffee shop near the trailhead
- Splitting the hike into two days

❹
> It's always great to _____.

- get away from the city
- visit new places and experience new cultures
- have some quiet time to reflect and recharge

Mini Actual Test 연습 문제 🎧 12_1.mp3

Respond to the following question while keeping in mind what you have learned.
앞서 배운 내용을 떠올리면서 다음 질문에 답변해 보세요.

> Here is a situation to act out. Your friend has invited you to go for a hike. Ask your friend three or four questions regarding the plan.

Model Answer 모범 답안

🎧 12_2.mp3

Enhance your response by referring to the model answer.
다음 모범 답안을 참고하여 여러분의 답변을 발전시켜 보세요.

> Hey, thanks for inviting me to go hiking! I'm really excited about it. Do you have any particular trail in mind? I love hiking and I'm always up for exploring new trails. Oh, so you are thinking of going up to the waterfall. That sounds great! How long is the hike and what's the difficulty level? Excellent, the plan sounds perfect. What time are you thinking of starting the hike? I tend to wake up early, so an early start time works well for me. Great, that works for me too. I'll definitely bring a backpack with some water and snacks. Is there anything else you think we should bring? Sounds like a plan. I'm looking forward to it! It's always fun to get out in nature and enjoy some fresh air and exercise.

Level Up to AL AL 공략하기

Read the examples below and see how IH-level sentences can be rephrased at the AL level.
다음 예시를 읽고 IH 수준의 문장을 어떻게 AL 수준으로 바꾸어 말할 수 있는지 살펴보세요.

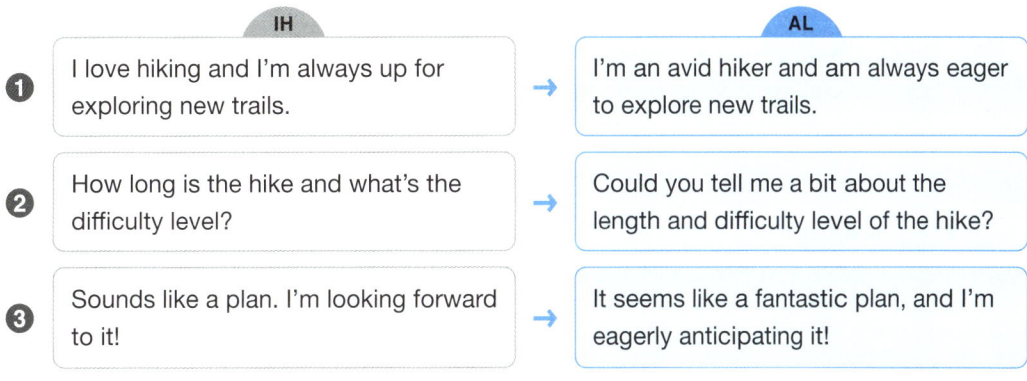

IH → **AL**

1. I love hiking and I'm always up for exploring new trails. → I'm an avid hiker and am always eager to explore new trails.

2. How long is the hike and what's the difficulty level? → Could you tell me a bit about the length and difficulty level of the hike?

3. Sounds like a plan. I'm looking forward to it! → It seems like a fantastic plan, and I'm eagerly anticipating it!

출제 가능성 ★★★★★

I'm going to give you a situation to act out. Unfortunately, you just found out that you will be unable to join your friend for a hike as planned. Contact your friend and explain why you will not be able to join him / her. Finally, offer two or three options to solve this issue.

Question Analysis 질문 분석

Answer the following questions and identify the key matter and the information to be included in your response.
다음 질문에 답하며 답변의 주제와 반드시 포함되어야 할 내용이 무엇인지 파악해 보세요.

1. What is going to be the key matter of your response?
2. What information should your response include?

Warm Your Brain Up 브레인스토밍

Answer the following questions for ideas.
다음 질문에 답하며 답변 소재를 발굴해 보세요.

Intro	• What is the purpose of the contact? • What is the situation you need to address?
Body	• What reasons can you give to explain why you cannot join your friend? • How can you communicate this to your friend in a nice way? • What options can you offer to solve the issue?
Conclusion	• How will you end the conversation before hanging up?

AL Booster
• How will you make sure your friend is satisfied with the solution?

Useful Expressions
join 합류하다　look forward to ~을 고대하다　unfortunately 불행히도　Something came up. 일이 생겼다.
deal with ~을 처리하다, 다루다　make the most of the weekend 주말을 최대한으로 즐기다　reschedule 일정을 변경하다
explore 탐험하다　local sights 지역의 볼거리　check out 살펴보다　open up 개장하다　If all else fails, 다른 방법이 없으면,
game night (특히 친구들과) 게임을 즐기는 밤　figure out 해결하다　going forward 앞으로 진행될

Pattern Drills 패턴 학습

Practice using the given sentence patterns to help you deliver your response clearly.
주어진 문장 패턴을 익혀 답변이 명확하게 전달될 수 있도록 연습해 보세요.

❶ Unfortunately, something came up _____.
- at the last minute
- at work that I need to deal with
- with my family that requires my attention

❷ I've got a few ideas on _____.
- some fun and creative activities to do
- how to plan a memorable vacation

❸ How about we reschedule _____.
- our plan for a hike this week
- our dinner plans for next week
- our outdoor picnic for tomorrow morning

❹ And if all else fails, how about _____?
- we order some pizza and have a movie night instead
- we cook a meal at home
- we take public transportation

Mini Actual Test 연습 문제   🎧 12_3.mp3

Respond to the following question while keeping in mind what you have learned.
앞서 배운 내용을 떠올리면서 다음 질문에 답변해 보세요.

> You were supposed to go on a hike with your friend, but something has come up and you won't be able to make it. Contact your friend and let him/her know why you won't be able to join him/her. Suggest two or three options to resolve this issue.

Model Answer 모범 답안

Enhance your response by referring to the model answer.
다음 모범 답안을 참고하여 여러분의 답변을 발전시켜 보세요.

> Hey, what's up? Listen, I've got some bad news. I won't be able to join you for our hike this weekend. I know, I know, I was really looking forward to it too. Unfortunately, something came up with my family and I have to deal with that. But don't worry, I've got a few ideas for how we can still hang out. How about we reschedule the hike for next weekend when I'm free? Or we could explore some local sights together instead— maybe check out the new park that just opened up? And if all else fails, how about we have a fun game night at my place? No matter what we decide, I'm sure we'll still have a great time. Let me know what you think, and we can figure out the best plan going forward. Thanks for understanding.

Level Up to AL AL 공략하기

Read the examples below and see how IH-level sentences can be rephrased at the AL level.
다음 예시를 읽고 IH 수준의 문장을 어떻게 AL 수준으로 바꾸어 말할 수 있는지 살펴보세요.

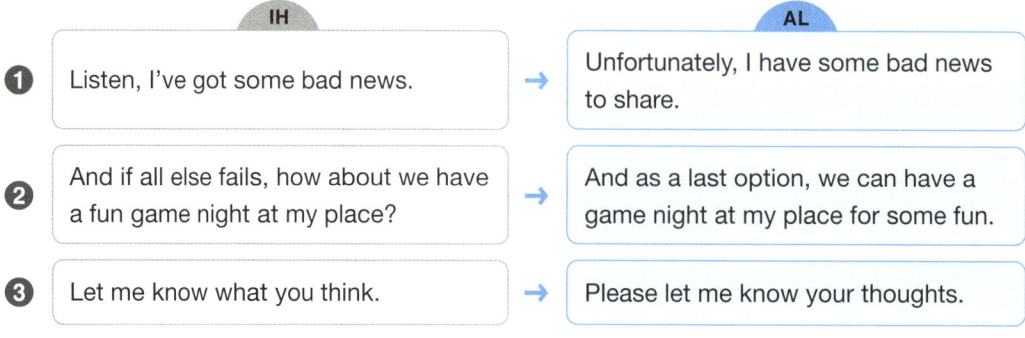

출제 가능성 ★★★☆☆

Q3 Are people in your country hiking more or less frequently compared to the past? Why do you think people have decided to walk more or less often than they did before? Tell me in detail.

Question Analysis 질문 분석

Answer the following questions and identify the key matter and the information to be included in your response.
다음 질문에 답하며 답변의 주제와 반드시 포함되어야 할 내용이 무엇인지 파악해 보세요.

1. What is going to be the key matter of your response?
2. What information should your response include?

Warm Your Brain Up 브레인스토밍

Answer the following questions for ideas.
다음 질문에 답하며 답변 소재를 발굴해 보세요.

Intro	• What is the current state of hiking in your country? • How has the popularity of hiking changed over the years?
Body	• Do you often go for a hike? If not, why do you think you don't get to go for a hike often? • Why do you think more/less people are hiking nowadays?
Conclusion	• Do you think hiking will get more popular or the opposite?

AL Booster

- Are there any cultural or societal factors that have influenced this trend?
- Have changes in technology or transportation affected the popularity of hiking?

Useful Expressions

frequently 자주   walk long distance 긴 거리를 걷다   realize 깨닫다   see A as a way to A를 ~하는 방법으로 보다
maintain one's physical well-being ~의 신체 건강을 유지하다   spend time outside 야외에서 시간을 보내다   as much 그만큼
pervasive 널리 퍼져 있는, 만연하는   feel overwhelmed 압도되는 느낌을 받다   fast-paced 빠른 속도의   urban 도시의
turn to ~으로 전환하다   appreciate 감상하다   hiking trails and routes 하이킹 코스 및 경로   factor 요인   contribute to ~에 기여하다
growing popularity 상승하는 인기   continue to 계속해서 ~하다   in the years to come 앞으로 몇 년 간

Pattern Drills 패턴 학습

Practice using the given sentence patterns to help you deliver your response clearly.
주어진 문장 패턴을 익혀 답변이 명확하게 전달될 수 있도록 연습해 보세요.

There are a few reasons why _____.

❶
- people prefer to hike more than they used to
- people love staying at home rather than going for a hike
- people enjoy walking in nature

Many people in my country want to spend time _____.

❷
- exploring the outdoors
- with their families and friends
- pursuing their passions and hobbies

More and more people are turning to _____ as a way to _____.

❸
- working out in nature / maintain their physical and mental health
- meditation / improve their mental health
- going to a gym / exercise regularly

There is more information available about _____.

❹
- healthy eating habits
- advances in technology and innovation
- the benefits of exercise and physical activity

Mini Actual Test 연습 문제 🎧 12_5.mp3

Respond to the following question while keeping in mind what you have learned.
앞서 배운 내용을 떠올리면서 다음 질문에 답변해 보세요.

> Can you tell me if people in your country are hiking more or less often than they used to? Please explain in detail the reasons why you think this is the case.

Model Answer 모범 답안

 12_6.mp3

Enhance your response by referring to the model answer.
다음 모범 답안을 참고하여 여러분의 답변을 발전시켜 보세요.

> In the past few years, people in my country, Korea, are hiking more frequently than before. This means they are walking long distances in nature. There are a few reasons why this has happened. Firstly, many Koreans are realizing the importance of exercise for their health. They want to be healthy and active, and they see hiking as a way to maintain their physical well-being. Secondly, many people in my country want to spend time outside in nature and not use technology as much. As technology has become more pervasive in our daily lives, many Koreans have started to feel overwhelmed by the fast-paced, urban lifestyle. As a result, more and more people are turning to nature as a way to escape the stress and noise of the city. Hiking is a great way to do this because it allows people to explore nature and appreciate its beauty. Lastly, there is more information available about hiking trails and routes. This helps people plan their hike and enjoy it more. All these factors have contributed to the growing popularity of hiking in my country, and I believe it will continue to be a popular activity in the years to come.

Level Up to AL AL 공략하기

Read the examples below and see how IH-level sentences can be rephrased at the AL level.
다음 예시를 읽고 IH 수준의 문장을 어떻게 AL 수준으로 바꾸어 말할 수 있는지 살펴보세요.

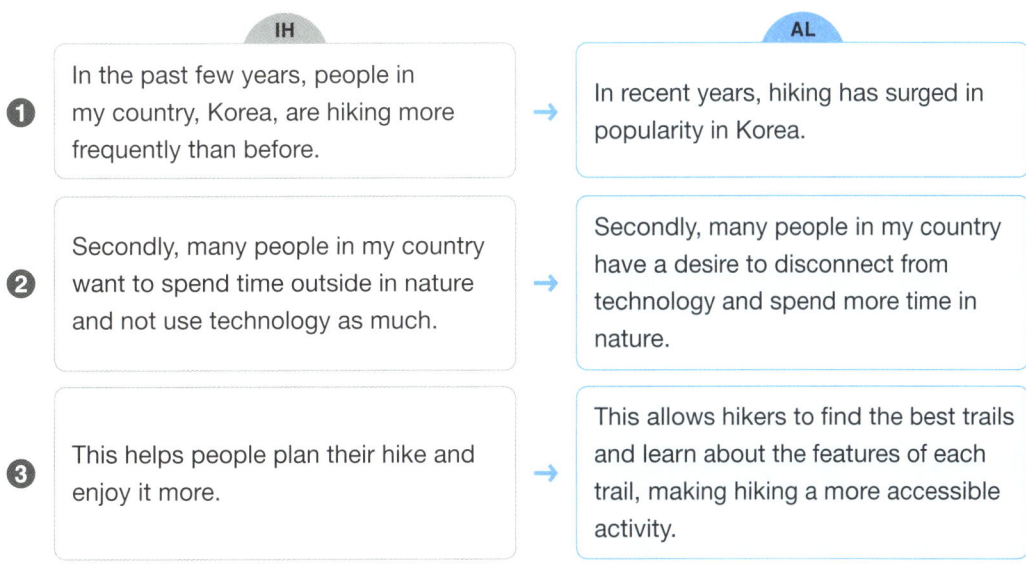

IH		AL
❶ In the past few years, people in my country, Korea, are hiking more frequently than before.	→	In recent years, hiking has surged in popularity in Korea.
❷ Secondly, many people in my country want to spend time outside in nature and not use technology as much.	→	Secondly, many people in my country have a desire to disconnect from technology and spend more time in nature.
❸ This helps people plan their hike and enjoy it more.	→	This allows hikers to find the best trails and learn about the features of each trail, making hiking a more accessible activity.

Chapter 7

Travel·Business Trip 여행·출장

✓ Strategy Check 주제 관련 전략

Check the following strategies related to the topic of this chapter.
이 챕터의 주제와 관련된 시험 대비 전략을 확인해 보세요.

IH Essential

- In Background Survey question 7, the last question, you will be asked to select at least one option from the 5 choices related to your vacation or business trip experiences. In this case, it is recommended to choose only one option, specifically "Spending vacations at home."
  백그라운드 서베이 마지막 질문인 7번에서는 본인의 휴가나 출장 경험과 관련해 5개 선택지 중 최소 1개 이상을 선택하게 됩니다. 이때 '집에서 보내는 휴가' 하나만 선택할 것을 추천합니다.

- Choosing the minimum number of options in question 7 makes it easier to prepare your responses. Selecting "Spending vacations at home" restricts the activities and places during the vacation, making it relatively easy to prepare your response. Additionally, since you will be describing activities inside your home, you can utilize everyday and easy words, which is an advantage.
  7번에서는 최소한의 선택지를 골라야 답변을 준비하기 쉬워집니다. '집에서 보내는 휴가'를 선택하면 활동 및 활동 반경을 제한할 수 있으므로 답변을 준비하기가 비교적 수월해집니다. 뿐만 아니라 집안에서 하는 일을 묘사하게 되므로 일상적이고 쉬운 단어들을 활용할 수 있다는 이점이 있습니다.

- Furthermore, selecting "Spending vacations at home" allows you to prepare responses that can be related to questions presented in other topics. For instance, questions about "residence" that ask about "household chores" or "how you spend time at home" are frequently asked. In such cases, you can utilize the answers you prepared regarding "Spending vacations at home" to respond to these questions.
  뿐만 아니라, '집에서 보내는 휴가'를 선택할 경우 다른 주제에서 출제되는 질문들과도 연계하여 답변을 준비할 수 있습니다. 예를 들어, '거주지'와 관련하여 '집안일' 또는 '집에서 시간을 보내는 법'을 묻는 질문이 자주 출제되는데, 이때 '집에서 보내는 휴가'와 관련하여 준비했던 답변들을 활용해 볼 수 있습니다.

AL Booster

- Even if you choose "Spending vacations at home" in the Background Survey, you are not obligated to provide answers only related to indoor activities. For example, if a question is asked about "what you did during your last vacation at home," you can respond by saying "I originally planned to spend my vacation at home, but due to a fan breaking down, I ended up going outside." You can seamlessly continue your response by applying the materials you learned in previous chapters about topics like "Watching movies" or "Walking" and adapt them to the question.
  백그라운드 서베이에 '집에서 보내는 휴가'를 선택하여 관련 문제가 출제되었다 하더라도, 반드시 실내에서 일어난 일에 관해 답변할 필요는 없습니다. 예를 들어, '지난 휴가 때 집에서 한 일'을 묻는 문제가 출제된다면 '원래 집에서 휴가를 보내려 했으나, 선풍기가 고장나는 바람에 밖으로 나가게 되었다'고 답변할 수 있고, 이전 챕터에서 학습한 '영화 보기,' '걷기' 등과 관련된 소재를 응용하여 자연스럽게 답변을 이어갈 수 있습니다.

❓ Frequently Asked Questions 빈출 질문 유형

Here are the most frequently asked question types related to the topic. Try to identify the key matter of the question and the information that should be included in your response.
이 챕터의 주제와 관련해 자주 출제되는 질문 유형들을 확인해 보세요. 그리고 각 질문의 중심 소재와 답변에 어떤 정보를 포함시켜야 하는지 파악해 보세요.

Vacation at Home	• You indicated in the survey that you stay at home during your vacation. Tell me about the things you do during the vacation • Who are the people you would like to see and spend time with on your vacation? • Describe some of the things you would like to do with people you visit or see during your vacation. • You indicated that you take vacations at home. What do people in your country normally do on their vacations? How has the way they spend vacations changed over the years? Give me specific examples. • What are some advantages of spending vacations at home? Please tell me in detail.
Experience	• Tell me about what you did during your last vacation. How did your vacation start and how did it end? What did you do each day? • Tell me about the most memorable vacation you have spent at home. Who were you with? What did you do? What made the vacation more special?

Chapter 7 Travel · Business Trip 여행·출장

Unit 13　Combo Set (1)

출제 가능성 ★★★★☆

Q1 You indicated in the survey that you stay at home during your vacation. Tell me about the things you do during the vacation.

Question Analysis 질문 분석

Answer the following questions and identify the key matter and the information to be included in your response.
다음 질문에 답하며 답변의 주제와 반드시 포함되어야 할 내용이 무엇인지 파악해 보세요.

1. What is going to be the key matter of your response?
2. What information should your response include?

Warm Your Brain Up 브레인스토밍

Answer the following questions for ideas.
다음 질문에 답하며 답변 소재를 발굴해 보세요.

Intro	• Why do you prefer to stay at home during your vacation? • What are some advantages of a staycation?
Body	• What are some activities you enjoy doing during your staycation? • How do you usually plan your staycation activities? • Who do you like to spend time with during your vacation?
Conclusion	• Would you recommend taking a staycation to others? Why or why not? • Do you think you will continue to take staycations in the future? Why or why not?

AL Booster

- Do you have any staycation routines or traditions?
- How is it different when you spend your holidays at home compared to when you spend your holidays hanging out with people and doing outdoor activities?

Useful Expressions

staycation 집에서의 휴가　relaxing 편안한, 여유로운　nearby 근처의; 인근에　try new recipes 새로운 요리를 시도하다
local park 지역 공원　museum 박물관　beforehand 미리, 사전에　have a good mix of ~을 적절히 조합하다, 조화롭게 섞다
self-care 자기 관리　transportation 교통수단　explore 탐방하다　local area 지역, 현지　continue -ing 계속 ~하다
encourage 격려하다, 권장하다　give it a try 시도해 보다

Pattern Drills 패턴 학습

Practice using the given sentence patterns to help you deliver your response clearly.
주어진 문장 패턴을 익혀 답변이 명확하게 전달될 수 있도록 연습해 보세요.

① I like to stay home for my vacation instead of traveling because _____.

- it allows me to spend quality time with my family
- it gives me the opportunity to explore my local area
- it gives me the chance to catch up on my reading

② During my staycation, I spend time with _____.

- my loved ones
- my pets and take them for long walks
- myself and focus on personal growth

③ One thing my family likes to do is _____.

- have a picnic in the park
- go to a nearby art exhibit
- go on a day trip to a nearby town

④ I think it's a good idea to try a staycation if _____.

- you want to save money on travel expenses such as lodging
- you want to support local businesses and restaurants in your area
- you want to have a flexible schedule

Mini Actual Test 연습 문제 🎧 13_1.mp3

Respond to the following question while keeping in mind what you have learned.
앞서 배운 내용을 떠올리면서 다음 질문에 답변해 보세요.

> While staying home during vacations, what activities do you usually enjoy doing? Please describe the activities you like to do in detail.

Model Answer 모범 답안

 13_2.mp3

Enhance your response by referring to the model answer.
다음 모범 답안을 참고하여 여러분의 답변을 발전시켜 보세요.

> I like to stay home for my vacation instead of traveling because it's cheaper and more relaxing. During my staycation, I spend time with my family and do fun things nearby. I like to watch movies, read books, try new recipes, and go to local parks and museums. I plan what I want to do beforehand so I can have a good mix of rest and fun. One thing my family likes to do is have a game night and cook a special meal together. I also enjoy taking some time for self-care, doing things such as going for a walk or taking a bath. Staying home for vacation has a lot of benefits, like being able to relax without the stress of travel. It also saves money on transportation and hotels, so you can use it for other things. I think it's a good idea to try a staycation if you need a break but can't travel. You can relax and have fun with your family while exploring your local area. I plan to continue taking staycations in the future and encourage others to give it a try.

Level Up to AL AL 공략하기

Read the examples below and see how IH-level sentences can be rephrased at the AL level.
다음 예시를 읽고 IH 수준의 문장을 어떻게 AL 수준으로 바꾸어 말할 수 있는지 살펴보세요.

IH → **AL**

① I like to stay home for my vacation instead of traveling because it's cheaper and more relaxing. → I prefer staycations rather than traveling because they are more relaxing and cost-effective.

② I spend time with my family and do fun things nearby. → I enjoy spending quality time with my family and exploring local attractions.

③ I think it's a good idea to try a staycation if you need a break but can't travel. → I highly recommend taking a staycation, especially for those who need a break but cannot afford to travel.

출제 가능성 ★★★★★

Q2 Tell me about what you did during your last vacation. How did your vacation start and how did it end? What did you do each day?

Question Analysis 질문 분석

Answer the following questions and identify the key matter and the information to be included in your response.
다음 질문에 답하며 답변의 주제와 반드시 포함되어야 할 내용이 무엇인지 파악해 보세요.

1. What is going to be the key matter of your response?
2. What information should your response include?

Warm Your Brain Up 브레인스토밍

Answer the following questions for ideas.
다음 질문에 답하며 답변 소재를 발굴해 보세요.

Intro	• What type of vacation did you take? • Where did you go for your vacation? • When did you take this vacation?
Body	• How did your vacation start? • What did you do on the next day of your vacation? • How did your vacation end?
Conclusion	• What did you enjoy the most during your vacation? • Would you like to take this vacation again in the future?

AL Booster

• What are the benefits of a staycation?

Useful Expressions

relax 휴식하다   recharge 재충전하다   leisure time 여가 시간   backyard 뒷마당   organize the closet 옷장을 정리하다
feel energized 활기를 느끼다   go for a morning walk 아침 산책을 하다   a variety of 여러 가지의   old classics 옛 고전 작품
catch up on 따라잡다   house chores 집안일   laundry 세탁물   vacuum 청소기를 돌리다   end with ~로 마무리되다   takeout 외식
refresh 활기를 되찾다   highly recommend 강력히 추천하다   need a break 휴식이 필요하다   cannot afford to ~할 여유가 없다
take time off work 휴가를 내다   comforts of home 집에서 느끼는 편안함

Pattern Drills 패턴 학습

Practice using the given sentence patterns to help you deliver your response clearly.
주어진 문장 패턴을 익혀 답변이 명확하게 전달될 수 있도록 연습해 보세요.

❶
I started my staycation with _____.
- a lazy morning in bed
- a delicious breakfast in bed
- a trip to the local farmer's market

❷
The next day, I felt energized after _____ and spent the rest of the day _____.
- a good night's sleep / exploring the city
- a morning jog / listening to music
- a refreshing shower / catching up on some reading

❸
The day ended with _____.
- a delicious meal and a cozy movie night
- a relaxing bubble bath and a good book
- a family game night and some homemade snacks

❹
Overall, a staycation is a great way to _____.
- spend quality time with your family
- explore your local area
- be productive and work on home improvement

Mini Actual Test 연습 문제  13_3.mp3

Respond to the following question while keeping in mind what you have learned.
앞서 배운 내용을 떠올리면서 다음 질문에 답변해 보세요.

> Tell me about the last time you spent your vacation at home. How did your vacation start and end? What did you do? Did you meet someone? Describe everything you did.

Model Answer 모범 답안

 13_4.mp3

Enhance your response by referring to the model answer.
다음 모범 답안을 참고하여 여러분의 답변을 발전시켜 보세요.

> During my last vacation, I decided to stay at home and enjoy a staycation. It was a great chance to relax, recharge, and enjoy some leisure time. I started my staycation with a relaxing morning at home. On the first day, I had a late breakfast and spent some time reading a book in my backyard. In the afternoon, I cleaned the kitchen and organized my closet before enjoying a nice dinner and watching a movie. The next day, I felt energized after going for a morning walk in the park and spent the rest of the day watching a variety of movies, including old classics. On the third day, I caught up on some TV shows and did some house chores, like doing the laundry, cleaning the bathroom, and vacuuming the living room. The day ended with takeout from my favorite restaurant and another movie. Overall, a staycation is a great way to recharge and refresh without the stress of travel. I highly recommend it to anyone who needs a break but cannot afford to travel. You can enjoy all the comforts of home and recharge without the stress of travel.

Level Up to AL AL 공략하기

Read the examples below and see how IH-level sentences can be rephrased at the AL level.
다음 예시를 읽고 IH 수준의 문장을 어떻게 AL 수준으로 바꾸어 말할 수 있는지 살펴보세요.

IH → **AL**

① It was a great chance to relax, recharge, and enjoy some leisure time. → It was a wonderful opportunity to unwind, recharge, and indulge in some leisure activities.

② … and spent the rest of the day watching a variety of movies, including old classics. → … and watched a variety of movies, ranging from comedies to dramas and even some old classics that I had not seen in a while for the rest of the day.

출제 가능성 ★★★★☆

Q3 You indicated that you take vacations at home. What do people in your country normally do on their vacations? How has the way they spend vacations changed over the years? Give me specific examples.

Question Analysis 질문 분석

Answer the following questions and identify the key matter and the information to be included in your response.
다음 질문에 답하며 답변의 주제와 반드시 포함되어야 할 내용이 무엇인지 파악해 보세요.

1. What is going to be the key matter of your response?
2. What information should your response include?

Warm Your Brain Up 브레인스토밍

Answer the following questions for ideas.
다음 질문에 답하며 답변 소재를 발굴해 보세요.

Intro	• What are some common ways that people in your country typically spend their vacations? • How did people normally spend their vacations in the past?
Body	• How have vacation activities changed over time? • What factors have contributed to these changes?
Conclusion	• Overall, what can we learn from these changes?

AL Booster

• Can you provide a specific example that illustrates the changes in vacation activities over time?

Useful Expressions

home country 고국   be not the case 실제로는 그렇지 않다   over time 시간이 지남에 따라   opt for ~을 선택하다
enjoy the comforts of ~의 편안함을 즐기다   environment (주변) 환경   due in part to 부분적으로는 ~때문에
economic reason 경제적 이유   become more aware of ~에 대해 더 많이 인식하게 되다   stay close 가까이에 머물다
the goal of ~의 목표   relaxation 휴식, 안정   remain the same 변함없이 유지되다

148 Compact OPIc 컴팩트 오픽

Pattern Drills 패턴 학습

Practice using the given sentence patterns to help you deliver your response clearly.
주어진 문장 패턴을 익혀 답변이 명확하게 전달될 수 있도록 연습해 보세요.

① In my home country, many people _____.
- value family and spend a lot of time with them
- celebrate the New Year with a big feast
- enjoy spicy food and various cultural festivals

② Now, more and more people are opting for _____.
- remote work opportunities
- minimalist lifestyles
- eco-friendly products

③ They choose to enjoy the comforts of _____.
- their own homes
- family and close friends
- a home-cooked meal instead of eating out

④ People are becoming more aware of _____.
- the benefits of mindfulness for overall well-being
- the need to reduce carbon emissions
- the importance of recycling

Mini Actual Test 연습 문제 🎧 13_5.mp3

Respond to the following question while keeping in mind what you have learned.
앞서 배운 내용을 떠올리면서 다음 질문에 답변해 보세요.

> You mentioned that you prefer to spend your vacations at home. Can you share with me the typical activities or traditions that people in your country engage in during their vacations? How have they evolved over time?

Model Answer 모범 답안

 13_6.mp3

Enhance your response by referring to the model answer.
다음 모범 답안을 참고하여 여러분의 답변을 발전시켜 보세요.

> In my home country, many people take vacations at home, just like I did during my last break. However, this was not always the case. In the past, people often traveled to other cities or even other countries for their vacations. But over time, the way people spend their vacations has changed. Now, more and more people are opting for staycations. They choose to relax at home, spend time with their families, and enjoy the comforts of their own environment. This change is due in part to economic reasons, as travel can be expensive, but also because people are becoming more aware of the importance of self-care and rest. For example, during my staycation, I was able to read books, watch movies, and take walks while staying close to home. While the way people spend their vacations may have changed, the goal of rest and relaxation remains the same.

Level Up to AL AL 공략하기

Read the examples below and see how IH-level sentences can be rephrased at the AL level.
다음 예시를 읽고 IH 수준의 문장을 어떻게 AL 수준으로 바꾸어 말할 수 있는지 살펴보세요.

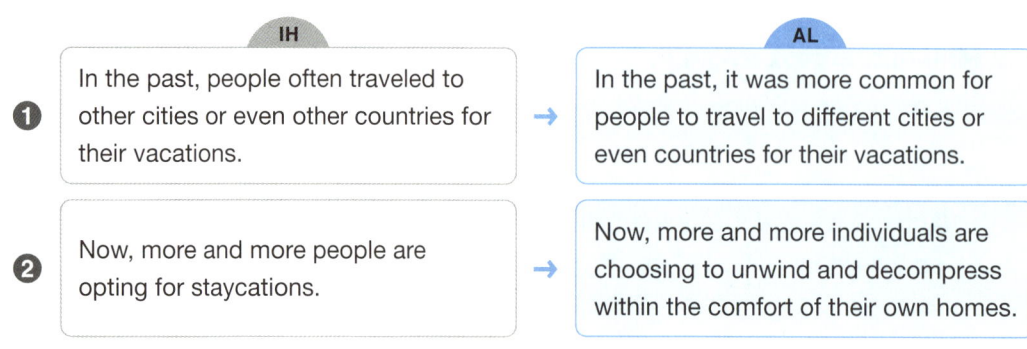

Chapter 7 Travel·Business Trip 여행·출장

Unit 14 Combo Set (2)

MP3 바로가기

출제 가능성 ★★★★☆

Q1 Who are the people you would like to see and spend time with on your vacation?

Question Analysis 질문 분석

Answer the following questions and identify the key matter and the information to be included in your response.
다음 질문에 답하며 답변의 주제와 반드시 포함되어야 할 내용이 무엇인지 파악해 보세요.

1. What is going to be the key matter of your response?
2. What information should your response include?

Warm Your Brain Up 브레인스토밍

Answer the following questions for ideas.
다음 질문에 답하며 답변 소재를 발굴해 보세요.

Intro	• Who are the people that you want to spend your vacation with? • What are the reasons that you chose these people?
Body	• What things would you like to do with these people? • Can you give an example of a vacation experience that highlights the importance of spending time with those people?
Conclusion	• What impact can the people we spend our time with during vacation have on our experience?

AL Booster

• What are some benefits of spending quality time with your loved ones during vacation?

Useful Expressions

bond with ~와 유대감(친밀한 관계)를 형성하다   loved one 사랑하는 사람   make memories 추억을 만들다
feel comfortable -ing ~하는 데 편안함을 느끼다   catch up with ~와 그간 못한 근황 얘기를 나누다   share stories 이야기를 공유하다
take a vacation trip 휴가에 여행을 가다   filled with ~으로 가득 찬   laughter 웃음   cherish 소중히 여기다   closest to ~에 가장 가까운
greatly 크게   impact 영향을 미치다   essential 필수적인   choose wisely 현명하게 선택하다   enjoy the time with ~와 있는 시간을 즐기다
care about ~을 신경 쓰다, 중요하게 생각하다

Pattern Drills 패턴 학습

Practice using the given sentence patterns to help you deliver your response clearly.
주어진 문장 패턴을 익혀 답변이 명확하게 전달될 수 있도록 연습해 보세요.

① The people I would like to spend my vacation with are _____.
- my childhood friends
- my parents
- my college roomates

② They are the ones who _____.
- know me the best
- make me feel at ease
- share my interests and hobbies

③ It was such a wonderful time filled with _____.
- excitement and energy
- joy and relaxation
- meaningful conversations and deep connections

④ The people we spend our time with during vacation can _____.
- greatly influence our mood and level of happiness
- make or break our experience
- help us create unforgettable memories

Mini Actual Test 연습 문제   🎧 14_1.mp3

Respond to the following question while keeping in mind what you have learned.
앞서 배운 내용을 떠올리면서 다음 질문에 답변해 보세요.

> Who would you like to spend time with during your vacation?

Model Answer 모범 답안

 14_2.mp3

Enhance your response by referring to the model answer.
다음 모범 답안을 참고하여 여러분의 답변을 발전시켜 보세요.

> Vacations are a wonderful time to bond with loved ones and make memories. The people I would like to spend my vacation with are my family and close friends. They are the ones who understand me the most and with whom I feel most comfortable being myself. I would love to catch up with them, share stories, and create new memories together. For example, I took a vacation trip with my family last summer. It was such a wonderful time filled with laughter and love, and it made me realize how much I cherish the time spent with those closest to me. Truly, the people we spend our time with during vacation can greatly impact our experience. Thus, I believe it's essential to choose wisely and enjoy the time with those we care most about.

Level Up to AL AL 공략하기

Read the examples below and see how IH-level sentences can be rephrased at the AL level.
다음 예시를 읽고 IH 수준의 문장을 어떻게 AL 수준으로 바꾸어 말할 수 있는지 살펴보세요.

IH → **AL**

❶ They are the ones who understand me the most and with whom I feel most comfortable being myself. → They are the ones who possess a profound understanding of my personality and accept me unconditionally.

❷ Thus, I believe it's essential to choose wisely and enjoy the time with those we care most about. → Therefore, I strongly believe that it is crucial to carefully select our vacation companions and cherish the time spent with those who are dear to us.

출제 가능성 ★★★★☆

Q2 Describe some of the things you would like to do with people you visit or see during your vacation.

Question Analysis 질문 분석

Answer the following questions and identify the key matter and the information to be included in your response.
다음 질문에 답하며 답변의 주제와 반드시 포함되어야 할 내용이 무엇인지 파악해 보세요.

1. What is going to be the key matter of your response?
2. What information should your response include?

Warm Your Brain Up 브레인스토밍

Answer the following questions for ideas.
다음 질문에 답하며 답변 소재를 발굴해 보세요.

Intro	• What does vacation time mean to you? • What do you usually do during your vacation?
Body	• What are some specific activities that you would like to do during vacation time? • Why do you want to do those activities? • Who are the people you would like to do those activities with?
Conclusion	• How would you conclude your thoughts on vacation time based on your answer?

AL Booster

• What is a potential activity that can be enjoyed with friends and family during vacation time?

Useful Expressions

a perfect opportunity to ~할 수 있는 완벽한 기회   recharge 재충전하다   especially 특히   even if 비록 ~이더라도
in the local area 지역 내에서   plan 계획하다   invite over 집으로 초대하다   bond with ~와 유대감을 형성하다   fresh air 신선한 공기
sunshine 햇살   arrange a movie night 영화 보는 밤을 계획하다   create a cozy atmosphere 아늑한 분위기를 만들다
play board games 보드게임을 하다   friendly 친근한, 우호적인   competitive 경쟁적인   dull 따분한

154 Compact OPIc 컴팩트 오픽

Pattern Drills 패턴 학습

Practice using the given sentence patterns to help you deliver your response clearly.
주어진 문장 패턴을 익혀 답변이 명확하게 전달될 수 있도록 연습해 보세요.

❶ Vacation time is a perfect opportunity to _____.
- try new activities and hobbies
- disconnect from technology
- relax both physically and mentally

❷ Even if I am at home during vacation, I still like to _____.
- read books and get lost in a good story
- exercise and stay active by going for walks
- organize my space and belongings

❸ This would be a great way to bond with my loved ones while _____.
- enjoying some delicious food
- taking a break from our busy lives
- having meaningful conversations

❹ This activity is perfect for _____.
- relieving stress
- cooling down on a hot summer day
- enjoying nature and getting some fresh air

Mini Actual Test 연습 문제

🎧 14_3.mp3

Respond to the following question while keeping in mind what you have learned.
앞서 배운 내용을 떠올리면서 다음 질문에 답변해 보세요.

> Can you describe some of the activities you would enjoy doing with the people you spend time with on vacation?

Model Answer 모범 답안

Enhance your response by referring to the model answer.
다음 모범 답안을 참고하여 여러분의 답변을 발전시켜 보세요.

> Vacation time is a perfect opportunity to relax and recharge, especially when staying at home. Even if I am at home during vacation, I still like to find things to do in the local area. I love to plan fun activities with the people I like. Firstly, I would love to have a barbecue in the backyard and invite friends and family over for a delicious meal. This would be a great way to bond with my loved ones while enjoying some fresh air and sunshine. Secondly, I would like to arrange a movie night and enjoy some popcorn and snacks while watching my favorite films with my family or friends. This activity is perfect for relaxing and creating a cozy atmosphere at home. Lastly, I would love to play board games or card games together because these can be a lot of fun and create a friendly, competitive environment. In conclusion, staying at home during vacation time does not have to be dull or boring, and there are many ways to have fun while spending time with those closest to me.

Level Up to AL AL 공략하기

Read the examples below and see how IH-level sentences can be rephrased at the AL level.
다음 예시를 읽고 IH 수준의 문장을 어떻게 AL 수준으로 바꾸어 말할 수 있는지 살펴보세요.

IH → **AL**

❶ Even if I am at home during vacation, I still like to find things to do in the local area. I love to plan fun activities with the people I like.
→ Even when I'm staying at home, I enjoy engaging in local activities and planning enjoyable things to do with the people around me.

❷ This activity is perfect for relaxing and creating a cozy atmosphere at home.
→ This activity is perfect for unwinding and creating a relaxing atmosphere in the comfort of my own home.

출제 가능성 ★★★★★

Q3 Tell me about the most memorable vacation you have spent at home. Who were you with? What did you do? What made the vacation more special?

Question Analysis 질문 분석

Answer the following questions and identify the key matter and the information to be included in your response.
다음 질문에 답하며 답변의 주제와 반드시 포함되어야 할 내용이 무엇인지 파악해 보세요.

1. What is going to be the key matter of your response?
2. What information should your response include?

Warm Your Brain Up 브레인스토밍

Answer the following questions for ideas.
다음 질문에 답하며 답변 소재를 발굴해 보세요.

Intro	• Where was your most memorable vacation spent? • Who were you with during the vacation?
Body	• What did you do with those people during the vacation? • What was one of the best parts of the vacation?
Conclusion	• Why was the vacation more special compared to others? • Why is this vacation so unforgettable for you?

AL Booster

• How did the vacation bring you and the people you spent time with closer?

Useful Expressions

memorable 기억에 남는   actually 사실은   travel far away 멀리 여행하다   amazing 놀라운, 멋진   explore 탐방하다
art museum 미술관   historical 역사상의, 역사와 관련된   historic 역사적으로 중요한, 역사에 남을 만한   landmark 주요 지형지물
take a cooking class 요리 수업을 듣다   homemade 집에서 만든   plenty of 충분한   feel rushed 서두르는 느낌이 들다
sleep in 늦잠 자다   usual 보통의   in short 간단히 말해서   spend quality time (특히 친밀한 사람들과) 소중한 시간을 보내다

Chapter 7 Travel·Business Trip 여행·출장   **157**

> **Pattern Drills** 패턴 학습

Practice using the given sentence patterns to help you deliver your response clearly.
주어진 문장 패턴을 익혀 답변이 명확하게 전달될 수 있도록 연습해 보세요.

❶
One of the best parts was when _____.
- we saw the stunning sunset
- we reached the summit of the mountain
- we discovered a new favorite dish at a local restaurant

❷
We had a lot of fun and also _____.
- got to know each other better
- learned some valuable cooking skills
- got some exercise while hiking up the mountain trail

❸
In short, my most memorable vacation was spent at(in) _____ with _____.
- home / my family
- the mountains / a group of friends
- a nearby park / my friends

❹
We had a great time _____.
- relaxing, having a good conversation, and enjoying time together
- catching up with old friends from college
- exploring the national park and seeing all the wildlife

> **Mini Actual Test** 연습 문제   🎧 14_5.mp3

Respond to the following question while keeping in mind what you have learned.
앞서 배운 내용을 떠올리면서 다음 질문에 답변해 보세요.

Can you describe a vacation you had at home that you remember the most? Who did you spend it with? What activities did you do? What made it a special experience?

Model Answer 모범 답안

 14_6.mp3

Enhance your response by referring to the model answer.
다음 모범 답안을 참고하여 여러분의 답변을 발전시켜 보세요.

> One of my most memorable vacations was actually spent at home with my family. We didn't travel far away, but we still had an amazing time together. During this vacation, I was with my parents and my younger sister. We decided to stay at home and do things we hadn't done before. I suggested a game called "Halli Galli" that a group of people can enjoy. Every member of my family has a strong desire for winning, so the game was very intense. However, we had a lot of fun and also became closer as a family. This vacation was more special than others because we had plenty of time to spend together without feeling rushed. We also slept in, had casual dinner together, played other board games, and watched movies. It was a nice break from our usual busy schedules and we enjoyed each other's company. In short, my most memorable vacation was spent at home with my family. We had a great time playing games and spending quality time together. It's a vacation that I'll never forget.

Level Up to AL AL 공략하기

Read the examples below and see how IH-level sentences can be rephrased at the AL level.
다음 예시를 읽고 IH 수준의 문장을 어떻게 AL 수준으로 바꾸어 말할 수 있는지 살펴보세요.

	IH		AL
❶	We didn't travel far away, but we still had an amazing time together.	→	We didn't venture far from home, but we still had an extraordinary time together.
❷	However, we had a lot of fun and also became closer as a family.	→	However, we had an absolute blast and our family bond was strengthened.
❸	It's a vacation that I'll never forget.	→	It's a vacation that I will always cherish.

Chapter 7 Travel·Business Trip 여행·출장 **159**

Section 02

Random Question Topics

돌발 주제

- Chapter 8 　날씨·계절 Weather·Season
- Chapter 9 　재활용 Recycling
- Chapter 10　패션·산업 Fashion·Industry
- Chapter 11　지형·환경 이슈 Environmental Issues
- Chapter 12　교통·건강 Transportation·Health
- Chapter 13　은행 Bank
- Chapter 14　기술·인터넷 Technology·Internet
- Chapter 15　명절·모임 Holiday·Gathering

Chapter 8

Weather · Season 날씨·계절

✓ Strategy Check 주제 관련 전략

Check the following strategies related to the topic of this chapter.
이 챕터의 주제와 관련된 시험 대비 전략을 확인해 보세요.

IH Essential

- In the OPIc test, there are also randomly chosen topics that are not related to the Background Survey responses. The topics covered in this chapter, such as "Weather" and "Seasons," are also included among the topics that may unexpectedly appear during the exam.
  오픽 시험에는 백그라운드 서베이 응답과 관계 없이 임의로 출제되는 주제들도 있습니다. 이번 챕터의 주제인 '날씨'와 '계절' 관련 주제들도 돌발 주제에 포함됩니다.

- When topics like "Weather" and "Seasons" are presented, there might be instances where three questions are consecutively given in a combo format or only two questions are asked. Referring to the materials in this textbook, recall and organize your experiences and thoughts on "Weather" and "Seasons" to prepare your answers.
  '날씨'와 '계절' 주제가 출제되는 경우 3개 문제가 콤보 형태로 연달아 출제되거나, 2개 문제만이 출제되는 경우도 있습니다. 본 교재의 문제들을 참고하여 '날씨'나 '계절'에 관련된 다양한 경험과 생각을 떠올려 보고 이를 답변으로 정리해 놓을 필요가 있습니다.

- Expand upon your ideas using the theme of the four seasons in Korea. Even just summarizing the characteristics of each season and the weather features for each season will enable you to derive various answers based on them.
  한국의 사계절을 키워드로 아이디어를 확장시켜 보세요. 사계절의 특징과 계절별 날씨의 특징만 정리해 두어도, 그를 기반으로 다양한 답변을 도출할 수 있습니다.

AL Booster

- "Weather" and "Seasons" are occasionally presented as the first question topic in the actual exam. As these are frequently asked topics, it is strongly recommended to prepare your answers regarding "Weather" and "Seasons" thoroughly.
  '날씨'와 '계절'은 간혹 본시험의 첫 번째 질문 주제로 출제되기도 합니다. 이처럼 출제 빈도가 잦은 주제이기 때문에 '날씨'와 '계절'에 관해서는 반드시 답변을 준비해 보길 권장합니다.

❓ Frequently Asked Questions 빈출 질문 유형

Here are the most frequently asked question types related to the topic. Try to identify the key matter of the question and the information that should be included in your response.
이 챕터의 주제와 관련해 자주 출제되는 질문 유형들을 확인해 보세요. 그리고 각 질문의 중심 소재와 답변에 어떤 정보를 포함시켜야 하는지 파악해 보세요.

Weather	• Tell me about the weather where you are today. What is happening right now? • Tell me about your favorite type of weather. How does the weather affect your mood? Provide as many details as possible. • How has the weather in your country changed over the years? What was the weather like when you were a child? How different is it now? • Have you ever experienced something memorable because of the weather? Please explain what happened and why it was memorable. Give me as many details as possible.
Season	• How does the weather in your country change along the seasons? Are there distinct changes in the seasons? Provide a detailed description of each season. • Identify your favorite season and describe some of the activities that you do during this time of year.

Chapter 8 Weather · Season 날씨 · 계절

Unit 15 Combo Set (1)

출제 가능성 ★★★★☆

Q1 What is the weather like in your country? Are there distinct changes in the seasons? Provide a detailed description of each season.

Question Analysis 질문 분석

Answer the following questions and identify the key matter and the information to be included in your response.
다음 질문에 답하며 답변의 주제와 반드시 포함되어야 할 내용이 무엇인지 파악해 보세요.

1. What is going to be the key matter of your response?
2. What information should your response include?

Warm Your Brain Up 브레인스토밍

Answer the following questions for ideas.
다음 질문에 답하며 답변 소재를 발굴해 보세요.

Intro	• What is the weather like in Korea?
Body	• What is the weather like during spring in Korea? • When does summer start in Korea, and what is the weather like during this season? • What is the weather like during the fall season in Korea, and what outdoor activities are popular during this season? • What is the weather like during the winter season in Korea?
Conclusion	• What is the main point that you would like to recap?

AL Booster

• What unique features does each season in Korea have?

Useful Expressions

be famous for ~으로 유명하다   lovely 사랑스러운, 멋진   cherry blossom 벚꽃   Celsius 섭씨   occasional 가끔의, 때때로인
rain shower 소나기   humid 습한   heavy rainfall 호우, 장대비   thunderstorm 천둥 번개   outdoor activity 야외 활동
comfortable season 쾌적한 계절   plenty of sunshine 맑은 날씨, 많은 일조량   with temperatures below zero 영하의 기온과 함께
provide 제공하다   snow-covered 눈으로 덮인   frozen 얼어 붙은   in short 간단히 말해서   diverse 다양한   unique 독특한
throughout the year 연중 내내

Pattern Drills 패턴 학습

Practice using the given sentence patterns to help you deliver your response clearly.
주어진 문장 패턴을 익혀 답변이 명확하게 전달될 수 있도록 연습해 보세요.

①

Spring is a lovely season when _____.

- the trees become green again
- the temperature starts to warm up
- people enjoy outdoor activities like picnics

②

The weather is usually between _____ degrees Celsius, with _____.

- 25 to 35 / high humidity and frequent thunderstorms
- -5 to 5 / snow and strong winds
- 10 to 20 / mild temperatures and plenty of sunshine

③

This season is a favorite time for _____.

- outdoor concerts in the park
- road trips
- outdoor enthusiasts to go hiking in the mountains

④

Despite the cold, it provides _____.

- beautiful scenery and landscapes
- perfect conditions for winter sports
- stunning views of snow-covered trees

Mini Actual Test 연습 문제 🎧 15_1.mp3

Respond to the following question while keeping in mind what you have learned.
앞서 배운 내용을 떠올리면서 다음 질문에 답변해 보세요.

> Can you describe the weather patterns in your country? Are there any noticeable variations between the different seasons? Describe in detail.

Model Answer 모범 답안  15_2.mp3

Enhance your response by referring to the model answer.
다음 모범 답안을 참고하여 여러분의 답변을 발전시켜 보세요.

> Korea is famous for its four distinct seasons, each with its own weather patterns. Spring is a lovely season when the cherry blossoms bloom. The weather is usually between 10 to 20 degrees Celsius, with clear skies and occasional rain showers. Summer starts in June, and it is the hottest and most humid season. The temperatures often go over 30 degrees Celsius with heavy rainfall and thunderstorms, making outdoor activities hard. Fall begins in September, and it is the most comfortable season, with cool, fresh air, clear skies, and plenty of sunshine. This season is a favorite time for outdoor activities like hiking and camping. Winter starts in December, and it is the coldest season, with temperatures below zero and lots of snow. Despite the cold, it provides beautiful views of snow-covered mountains and frozen lakes. In short, Korea's diverse weather patterns offer both unique experiences and beauty throughout the year.

Level Up to AL AL 공략하기

Read the examples below and see how IH-level sentences can be rephrased at the AL level.
다음 예시를 읽고 IH 수준의 문장을 어떻게 AL 수준으로 바꾸어 말할 수 있는지 살펴보세요.

출제 가능성 ★★★★☆

Q2
Identify your favorite season and describe some of the activities that you do during this time of year.

Question Analysis 질문 분석

Answer the following questions and identify the key matter and the information to be included in your response.
다음 질문에 답하며 답변의 주제와 반드시 포함되어야 할 내용이 무엇인지 파악해 보세요.

1. What is going to be the key matter of your response?
2. What information should your response include?

Warm Your Brain Up 브레인스토밍

Answer the following questions for ideas.
다음 질문에 답하며 답변 소재를 발굴해 보세요.

Intro	• What is your favorite season? • What is the weather usually like in this season?
Body	• What do you love to do during this season? • Do you have one specific experience that is particularly memorable from this season? • What are fun activities that people enjoy during this season?
Conclusion	• What is the main point that you would like to recap?

AL Booster

• What are the benefits that you can get from the activities during the season?

Useful Expressions

not too hot 너무 ~하지 않은   be perfect for ~에 완벽하다   outdoor activities 야외 활동   in the woods 숲속에서
change color 색이 바뀌다   amazing 놀라운   nearby 인근의   cool breeze 시원한 바람   good for one's brain ~의 두뇌에 좋은
cozy 아늑한   provide 제공하다   appreciate 감상하다   nature's beauty 자연의 아름다움   various 다양한
enrich one's life ~의 삶을 풍요롭게 하다

Chapter 8 Weather·Season 날씨·계절

Pattern Drills 패턴 학습

Practice using the given sentence patterns to help you deliver your response clearly.
주어진 문장 패턴을 익혀 답변이 명확하게 전달될 수 있도록 연습해 보세요.

❶
Fall is my favorite season because _____.
- it's a great time to read
- it's a perfect time to be cozy indoors
- it provides a chance to enjoy nature's beauty

❷
I love hiking in the woods during the fall because _____.
- the leaves make the scenery spectacular
- the fresh air makes me feel alive
- the cooler temperature makes it easier to explore new trails and paths

❸
Fall is also a great time for other activities that are _____.
- good for your physical health, such as running or hiking
- intellectually stimulating, such as reading books or attending lectures
- creative and artistic, such as painting or drawing

❹
Overall, fall provides an opportunity to _____.
- slow down and appreciate the beauty of nature
- learn and grow
- engage in self-care and focus on my mental and physical health

Mini Actual Test 연습 문제   🎧 15_3.mp3

Respond to the following question while keeping in mind what you have learned.
앞서 배운 내용을 떠올리면서 다음 질문에 답변해 보세요.

> What is your favorite season and what are some of the activities you typically engage in during that time of the year?

Model Answer 모범 답안

 15_4.mp3

Enhance your response by referring to the model answer.
다음 모범 답안을 참고하여 여러분의 답변을 발전시켜 보세요.

> Fall is my favorite season because it's beautiful and there are lots of things to do. The weather is usually nice, not too hot and not too cold, which is perfect for outdoor activities. I love hiking in the woods during the fall because the leaves on the trees change color, and it looks amazing. One time last fall, I went hiking with some friends in a nearby park and it was great. The cool breeze, the sound of the leaves moving, and the singing birds made it a really special time that I won't forget. Fall is also a great time for other activities that are fun and good for your brain. For example, I love to read during the fall because it's nice to spend time inside and get cozy with a good book. Overall, fall provides an opportunity to appreciate nature's beauty and enjoy various activities that can enrich our lives.

Level Up to AL AL 공략하기

Read the examples below and see how IH-level sentences can be rephrased at the AL level.
다음 예시를 읽고 IH 수준의 문장을 어떻게 AL 수준으로 바꾸어 말할 수 있는지 살펴보세요.

IH → **AL**

❶ The weather is usually nice, not too hot and not too cold, which is perfect for outdoor activities. → The mild and comfortable weather is perfect for outdoor activities, such as hiking in the woods.

❷ For example, I love to read during the fall because it's nice to spend time inside and get cozy with a good book. → With the cooler weather, I find it enjoyable to curl up in a cozy spot with a good book.

출제 가능성 ★★★★★

Q3 Have you ever experienced something memorable because of the severe weather condition? Please explain what happened and why it was memorable. Give me as many details as possible.

> ### Question Analysis 질문 분석
> Answer the following questions and identify the key matter and the information to be included in your response.
> 다음 질문에 답하며 답변의 주제와 반드시 포함되어야 할 내용이 무엇인지 파악해 보세요.
>
> 1. What is going to be the key matter of your response?
> 2. What information should your response include?

> ### Warm Your Brain Up 브레인스토밍
> Answer the following questions for ideas.
> 다음 질문에 답하며 답변 소재를 발굴해 보세요.

Intro	• What was the experience you had related to severe weather conditions?
Body	• What happened and what was the problem? • How did you deal with the situation? • Did you experience any difficulty dealing with the problem?
Conclusion	• What did the experience teach you?

AL Booster
• Who else was affected by the weather? How did you cope with that?

Useful Expressions
severe 심각한   unpredictable 예측할 수 없는   damage 손상, 피해   heavy rain 호우, 장대비   flooding 침수, 홍수
be flooded 침수되다, 홍수에 잠기다   belongings 소지품   move around 이동하다   water supply 수도 공급   be affected 영향을 받다
deal with ~을 처리하다, 다루다   stay calm 차분하게 있다   follow instructions 지시를 따르다   local authority 지역 당국
in a safe place 안전한 장소에   unless ~하지 않는 한   offer A B A에게 B를 제공하다   shelter 대피소   be prepared 대비하다, 각오하다
challenging time 어려운 시기

Pattern Drills 패턴 학습

Practice using the given sentence patterns to help you deliver your response clearly.
주어진 문장 패턴을 익혀 답변이 명확하게 전달될 수 있도록 연습해 보세요.

❶

One experience I had related to severe weather conditions was _____.

- during a snowstorm last winter
- when a tornado hit my hometown
- during a heatwave that caused power outages in my city

❷

The situation was concerning because _____.

- the heavy winds had knocked down power lines
- the smoke from the forest fires was making it difficult to breathe
- the hailstorm had damaged the roofs of many houses in the neighborhood

❸

We dealt with the situation by _____.

- following the emergency evacuation procedures
- gathering food and water supplies to last us through the storm
- contacting our insurance company to file a claim for the damages

❹

Overall, the experience taught me the importance of _____.

- having a plan in place for unexpected events
- following instructions from local authorities during a crisis
- staying calm during challenging situations

Mini Actual Test 연습 문제   🎧 15_5.mp3

Respond to the following question while keeping in mind what you have learned.
앞서 배운 내용을 떠올리면서 다음 질문에 답변해 보세요.

> Severe weather conditions can do a lot of damage. Tell me about an experience you had related to severe weather conditions. What was the problem? How did you deal with that situation?

Model Answer 모범 답안

Enhance your response by referring to the model answer.
다음 모범 답안을 참고하여 여러분의 답변을 발전시켜 보세요.

> Severe weather conditions can be unpredictable and cause a lot of damage. One experience I had related to severe weather conditions was when we had heavy rains in my city. The problem was that the heavy rains caused flooding in several areas, including my neighborhood. The streets were flooded, and water entered some houses, damaging furniture and other belongings. The situation was concerning because it was difficult to move around, and the water supply was also affected. However, my family and I dealt with the situation by staying calm and following the instructions provided by local authorities. We made sure to keep our valuable belongings and important documents in a safe place. We didn't go out unless we had to. We also helped our neighbors by offering them food and shelter. Overall, the experience taught me the importance of being prepared and helping others during challenging times.

Level Up to AL AL 공략하기

Read the examples below and see how IH-level sentences can be rephrased at the AL level.
다음 예시를 읽고 IH 수준의 문장을 어떻게 AL 수준으로 바꾸어 말할 수 있는지 살펴보세요.

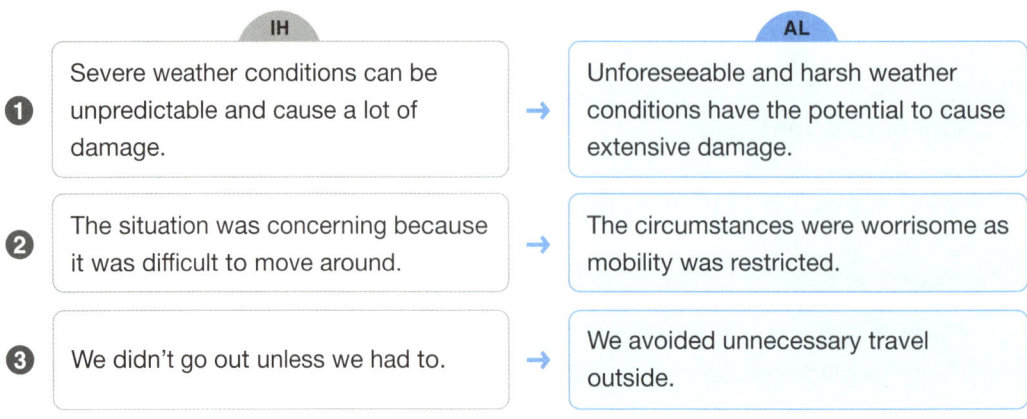

Chapter 8 Weather·Season 날씨·계절

Unit 16 Combo Set (2)

출제 가능성 ★★★★☆

Q1 Tell me about the weather where you are these days. What is happening right now?

 Question Analysis 질문 분석

Answer the following questions and identify the key matter and the information to be included in your response.
다음 질문에 답하며 답변의 주제와 반드시 포함되어야 할 내용이 무엇인지 파악해 보세요.

1. What is going to be the key matter of your response?
2. What information should your response include?

Warm Your Brain Up 브레인스토밍

Answer the following questions for ideas.
다음 질문에 답하며 답변 소재를 발굴해 보세요.

Intro	What is the current season in Korea? How is the temperature during the current period?
Body	• How is the weather condition during this time of the season? • How would you describe the environment or nature during this time? • What occasional weather phenomenon affects your country during this period?
Conclusion	• What is the overall description of the weather?

AL Booster
• What are some recommended activities to do during this season?

Useful Expressions

depending on ~에 따라 current period 현재 시기 in the middle of ~의 도중에, 중간에 moderately 적당히 average 평균
occasional 가끔의 rain shower 소나기 season ~의 철, 한창인 시기 bloom 개화하다 lilac 라일락 acacia 아카시아
air quality 대기질 yellow dust storm 황사 폭풍 blow from ~에서 불어오다 respiratory problem 호흡기 문제
despite ~에도 불구하고 at the moment 현재는 pleasant 쾌적한, 즐거운 inviting 매력적인

Pattern Drills 패턴 학습

Practice using the given sentence patterns to help you deliver your response clearly.
주어진 문장 패턴을 익혀 답변이 명확하게 전달될 수 있도록 연습해 보세요.

❶
_____ varies depending on the time of year.
- The number of tourists who visit our city
- The availability of certain fruits
- The frequency and severity of storms in my country

❷
During the current period, which is the middle of spring, the temperature is _____.
- hovering around 20 degrees Celsius
- moderate and comfortable
- ideal for going on hikes

❸
Despite this, it's still a great time to _____.
- enjoy outdoor sports and activities
- relax and spend time with friends and family
- enjoy the fresh air and soak up the sunshine

❹
Overall, the weather in Korea at the moment is _____.
- refreshing, with clear blue skies
- favorable for a range of activities
- mild and comfortable

Mini Actual Test 연습 문제   🎧 16_1.mp3

Respond to the following question while keeping in mind what you have learned.
앞서 배운 내용을 떠올리면서 다음 질문에 답변해 보세요.

> Can you describe the current weather conditions where you are located and what's happening at the moment?

Model Answer 모범 답안

 16_2.mp3

Enhance your response by referring to the model answer.
다음 모범 답안을 참고하여 여러분의 답변을 발전시켜 보세요.

> The weather in Korea varies depending on the time of year. During the current period, which is the middle of spring, the temperature is moderately comfortable, averaging about 20 degrees Celsius with occasional rain showers. The cherry blossom season has just ended, and now the trees are blooming with other flowers, such as lilac and acacia. The air quality is good, with blue skies and fresh air. However, the occasional yellow dust storm caused by sand blowing from China's deserts can cause respiratory problems for some people. Despite this, it's still a great time to go outside and enjoy the beauty of nature. Overall, the weather in Korea at the moment is pleasant and inviting, and it's perfect for outdoor activities like hiking or enjoying a picnic in the park.

Level Up to AL AL 공략하기

Read the examples below and see how IH-level sentences can be rephrased at the AL level.
다음 예시를 읽고 IH 수준의 문장을 어떻게 AL 수준으로 바꾸어 말할 수 있는지 살펴보세요.

IH → **AL**

❶ The air quality is good, with blue skies and fresh air. → The air quality is satisfactory, with clear blue skies and a refreshing breeze.

❷ Despite this, it's still a great time to go outside and enjoy the beauty of nature. → Despite this, it's an ideal time to relish the natural beauty by indulging in outdoor activities such as hiking or picnicking in the park.

출제 가능성 ★★★★☆

Q2 Tell me about your favorite type of weather. How does the weather affect your mood? Provide as many details as possible.

Question Analysis 질문 분석

Answer the following questions and identify the key matter and the information to be included in your response.
다음 질문에 답하며 답변의 주제와 반드시 포함되어야 할 내용이 무엇인지 파악해 보세요.

1. What is going to be the key matter of your response?
2. What information should your response include?

Warm Your Brain Up 브레인스토밍

Answer the following questions for ideas.
다음 질문에 답하며 답변 소재를 발굴해 보세요.

Intro	• What kind of weather do you enjoy the most? • How does this weather make you feel?
Body	• What activities do you like to do during this type of weather? • How does this weather impact your mood?
Conclusion	• What is the overall effect of your favorite weather on your well-being?

AL Booster

• What is your least favorite type of weather? How do you feel when the weather is not your favorite?

Useful Expressions

light breeze 가벼운 바람   energized 활기찬   motivated 동기를 부여 받은   a sense of ~의 느낌   warmth 따뜻함   positivity 긍정
gentle breeze 부드러운 바람   cool down 시원하게 하다   keep A comfortable A를 편안하게 하다   combination 조합
elevate one's mood ~의 기분을 고조하다   boost one's productivity ~의 생산성을 높이다   sluggish 기력이 떨어지는
unmotivated 의욕이 없는   look forward to ~을 기대하다, 고대하다   have a huge impact on ~에 큰 영향을 미치다   well-being 건강 상태

Pattern Drills 패턴 학습

Practice using the given sentence patterns to help you deliver your response clearly.
주어진 문장 패턴을 익혀 답변이 명확하게 전달될 수 있도록 연습해 보세요.

❶
I really enjoy _____.
- a spring day with a gentle rain
- a crisp, cold morning with fresh snow on the ground
- a warm summer evening with clear skies

❷
This type of weather makes me _____.
- happy and energized
- inspired and creative

❸
The combination of _____ is perfect for _____.
- cool weather and colorful leaves / a scenic autumn hike
- snowfall and a fireplace / a cozy winter evening
- a gentle rain and cozy indoors / a relaxing day of reading

❹
On days when the weather is _____, I tend to feel _____.
- rainy / a bit gloomy
- extremely hot / exhausted
- extremely cold / numb

Mini Actual Test 연습 문제   🎧 16_3.mp3

Respond to the following question while keeping in mind what you have learned.
앞서 배운 내용을 떠올리면서 다음 질문에 답변해 보세요.

> Can you tell me your favorite weather condition and how it impacts your mood? Please explain it with as many details as you can.

Model Answer 모범 답안

 16_4.mp3

Enhance your response by referring to the model answer.
다음 모범 답안을 참고하여 여러분의 답변을 발전시켜 보세요.

> My favorite type of weather is a warm, sunny day with a light breeze. This type of weather makes me feel happy, energized, and motivated. The sunshine brings a sense of warmth and positivity, while the gentle breeze cools me down just enough to keep me comfortable. I love to spend time outside during this kind of weather, whether it's going for a walk, having a picnic, or simply sitting in a park. The combination of sunshine and a light breeze is perfect for outdoor activities, and it helps to elevate my mood and boost my productivity. On days when the weather is cloudy or rainy, I tend to feel a bit sluggish and unmotivated, so I always look forward to sunny days. Overall, warm, sunny weather with a light breeze is my favorite type of weather, and it has a huge impact on my mood and overall well-being.

Level Up to AL AL 공략하기

Read the examples below and see how IH-level sentences can be rephrased at the AL level.
다음 예시를 읽고 IH 수준의 문장을 어떻게 AL 수준으로 바꾸어 말할 수 있는지 살펴보세요.

IH → **AL**

❶ My favorite type of weather is a warm, sunny day with a light breeze.
→ I absolutely love a warm, sunny day with a gentle breeze. It's the perfect combination of warmth and refreshing air.

❷ I love to spend time outside during this kind of weather, whether it's going for a walk, having a picnic, or simply sitting in a park.
→ I really enjoy spending time outdoors during this kind of weather, whether I'm taking a leisurely stroll, enjoying a picnic, or just relaxing in a park.

출제 가능성 ★★★☆☆

Q3 How has the weather in your country changed over the years? What was the weather like when you were a child? How different is it now?

Question Analysis 질문 분석

Answer the following questions and identify the key matter and the information to be included in your response.
다음 질문에 답하며 답변의 주제와 반드시 포함되어야 할 내용이 무엇인지 파악해 보세요.

1. What is going to be the key matter of your response?
2. What information should your response include?

Warm Your Brain Up 브레인스토밍

Answer the following questions for ideas.
다음 질문에 답하며 답변 소재를 발굴해 보세요.

Intro	• What was the weather like in the past? • How has the weather changed in recent years?
Body	• What are the causes of the changes in weather patterns? • What measures have been taken to address climate change?
Conclusion	• What is your opinion about the impact of the weather changes?

AL Booster

• What are the consequences of the weather changes?

Useful Expressions

predictable 예측 가능한   follow 뒤를 잇다, 뒤따르다   distinct 뚜렷한   seasonal pattern 계절마다 나타나는 패턴
noticeable 뚜렷한, 분명한   less predictable 예측이 어려운   extreme 극단적인   drought 가뭄   heatwave 폭염   severe storm 심한 폭풍
frequent 빈번한   have a significant impact on ~에 중요한 영향을 미치다   environment 환경   daily life 일상 생활   due to ~에 기인한
burn 연소하다   fossil fuel 화석 연료   contribute to ~에 기여하다   climate change 기후 변화   address an issue 문제를 해결하다
reduce 감소하다   greenhouse gas emission 온실 가스 배출   lessen 줄이다

Chapter 8 Weather·Season 날씨·계절

Pattern Drills 패턴 학습

Practice using the given sentence patterns to help you deliver your response clearly.
주어진 문장 패턴을 익혀 답변이 명확하게 전달될 수 있도록 연습해 보세요.

❶
These changes have had a significant impact on both _____ and _____.
- the economy / the environment
- the way we work / the way we live
- communication / relationships

❷
These changes are due to _____.
- the rapid industrialization in our country
- deforestation and the loss of natural habitats
- the increasing demand for energy

❸
To address this issue, _____.
- people can reduce their use of single-use plastic items
- individuals can reduce their reliance on cars
- people can conserve water by taking shorter showers

❹
I believe more effort is needed to _____.
- improve air and water quality in the city
- promote renewable energy
- reduce plastic waste and improve recycling

Mini Actual Test 연습 문제 🎧 16_5.mp3

Respond to the following question while keeping in mind what you have learned.
앞서 배운 내용을 떠올리면서 다음 질문에 답변해 보세요.

> How has the weather changed over the past years? Please describe these changes in detail.

Model Answer 모범 답안

Enhance your response by referring to the model answer.
다음 모범 답안을 참고하여 여러분의 답변을 발전시켜 보세요.

> In the past, the weather in my country was quite predictable and followed distinct seasonal patterns. For example, summers were usually hot and humid, while winters were cold and snowy, and there was often rain in the spring and fall. However, in recent years there have been some noticeable changes. The weather has become less predictable, with extreme events like droughts, heatwaves, and severe storms becoming more frequent. These changes have had a significant impact on both the environment and people's daily lives. These changes are due to human activities like burning fossil fuels, which contribute to climate change. To address this issue, many measures have been taken to reduce greenhouse gas emissions across various industries. However, I believe more effort is needed to lessen the impact of these changes.

Level Up to AL AL 공략하기

Read the examples below and see how IH-level sentences can be rephrased at the AL level.
다음 예시를 읽고 IH 수준의 문장을 어떻게 AL 수준으로 바꾸어 말할 수 있는지 살펴보세요.

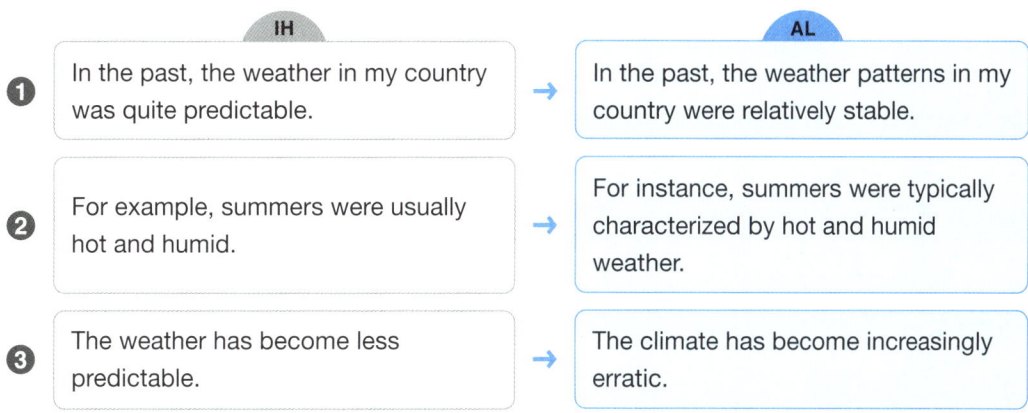

Chapter 9 Recycling 재활용

✓ Strategy Check 주제 관련 전략

Check the following strategies related to the topic of this chapter.
이 챕터의 주제와 관련된 시험 대비 전략을 확인해 보세요. AL을 목표로 하고 있다면

IH Essential

- If you choose a difficulty level of 3 or higher in the orientation, the probability of "Recycling"-related questions being presented in the exam increases.
  오리엔테이션에서 시험 난이도를 3 이상으로 선택하면, '재활용' 관련 질문이 출제될 확률이 높아집니다.

- "Recycling" is a common topic in daily life and is a frequently asked topic in the OPIc test, but many students find it challenging to respond to this topic. It is crucial to compile a list of "Recycling"-related words and expressions and become familiar with the topic by practicing your responses with the provided combo questions in this textbook.
  '재활용'은 일상적인 주제인 만큼 시험에 자주 출제되는 주제이면서도 많은 학생들이 답변을 어려워하는 주제입니다. '재활용' 관련 단어와 표현을 반드시 정리해 두고, 빈출 콤보 세트 학습을 통해 주제에 익숙해지도록 합시다.

- When "Recycling"-related questions are presented, questions that inquire about "South Korea's recycling system," "how you personally recycle," and "any special experiences related to recycling" are frequently asked in a combo format. If you set the difficulty level to 5 or higher in the orientation, there is a possibility of encountering questions about social issues related to recycling, so it is essential to be prepared for them.
  '재활용' 관련 문제가 출제되는 경우, '우리나라의 재활용 체계, 본인이 재활용하는 방법, 재활용과 관련된 특별한 경험'을 묻는 문제가 콤보로 자주 출제되었습니다. 오리엔테이션에서 시험 난이도를 5 이상으로 설정하는 경우, 재활용과 관련된 사회 문제를 묻는 문제가 출제될 수 있으니 관련하여 대비가 필요합니다.

AL Booster

- If your goal is to achieve an AL level, it is essential to respond naturally and confidently without hesitation. When you can't think of what to say, avoid silence and use filler phrases (phrases used to fill in pauses) to smoothly continue the conversation. Useful filler phrases to use during the exam include "Hold on," "Let me think," "What else," and so on.
  고득점을 목표로 하고 있다면, 머뭇거리지 않고 자연스럽게 답변하는 것이 중요합니다. 말할 내용이 생각나지 않을 때 침묵하지 않고 filler phrase(침묵을 채우기 위해 입버릇처럼 하는 말)를 사용하여 자연스럽게 대화를 이어 나가는 것이 좋습니다. 시험 중 사용할 만한 filler phrase로는 "Hold on," "Let me think," "What else," 등이 있습니다.

❓ Frequently Asked Questions 빈출 질문 유형

Here are the most frequently asked question types related to the topic. Try to identify the key matter of the question and the information that should be included in your response.
이 챕터의 주제와 관련해 자주 출제되는 질문 유형들을 확인해 보세요. 그리고 각 질문의 중심 소재와 답변에 어떤 정보를 포함시켜야 하는지 파악해 보세요.

Recycling	• I would like to know how the people in your country recycle. What items do they recycle? What is special about recycling? Tell me about it in detail. • Now, tell me about how you personally recycle. Do you separate the recycling every day? Where do you take out the recycling? Tell me everything about the ways you practice recycling in your daily life. • Tell me about a memorable or an unexpected incident regarding recycling. What exactly happened, and how did you deal with the situation? Tell me everything that you did from beginning to end. • How is recycling you practiced when you were young different from what you do today?
Role-play	• Let's assume that you have moved to a new building. You want to know about their recycling work. Ask the building manager 3 or 4 questions about the recycling policy. • You suddenly hear that the recyclables will not be picked up for a while. However, you are going to have a house party next week, and your neighbors will be unhappy about the situation. Call the building manager, explain the situation, and ask for at least two solutions to resolve the problem.
Social Issues	• Are there any issues or problems regarding recycling? Have you seen any news related to recycling recently? What was it about? Give me all the details about any issues related to recycling.

Chapter 9 · Recycling 재활용

Unit 17 · Combo Set (1)

MP3 바로가기

출제 가능성 ★★★★★

Q1 I would like to know how the people in your country recycle. What items do they recycle? What is special about recycling? Tell me about it in detail.

Question Analysis 질문 분석

Answer the following questions and identify the key matter and the information to be included in your response.
다음 질문에 답하며 답변의 주제와 반드시 포함되어야 할 내용이 무엇인지 파악해 보세요.

1. What is going to be the key matter of your response?
2. What information should your response include?

Warm Your Brain Up 브레인스토밍

Answer the following questions for ideas.
다음 질문에 답하며 답변 소재를 발굴해 보세요.

Intro	• What is the current state of recycling in your country? • What are the primary objectives and benefits of recycling in your country?
Body	• What items are commonly recycled in your country? • How do people recycle in your country? • Are there any specific recycling programs for different materials?
Conclusion	• What can you do to enhance recycling efforts?

AL Booster

• Can you provide a specific example of how to recycle?

Useful Expressions

recycling 재활용　play a vital role 중요한 역할을 하다　strive to 노력하다　promote 촉진하다　sustainability 지속 가능성
recycling system 재활용 체계　color-coded 색상별로 구분된　bin 분리수거 함　separate 분리하다　cardboard 판지
recycling center 재활용 센터　drop-off location 분리수거 장소　scatter 흩뜨리다, 퍼뜨리다　facility 시설
doorstep pickup service 집 앞 수거 서비스　engage a campaign 캠페인에 참여하다　reduce waste 폐기물을 줄이다
preserve 보존하다　resource 자원　sustainable 지속 가능한

Pattern Drills 패턴 학습

Practice using the given sentence patterns to help you deliver your response clearly.
주어진 문장 패턴을 익혀 답변이 명확하게 전달될 수 있도록 연습해 보세요.

1 _____ play(s) a vital role in my country.
- Environmental conservation
- Sports and recreation
- Volunteerism
- Technology

2 We strive to _____ and _____.
- reduce our carbon footprint / protect the environment
- achieve work-life balance / prioritize our own well-being

3 You can even recycle _____ at these facilities.
- electronic devices
- food waste
- small household appliances

4 Let's engage in recycling to _____.
- reduce greenhouse gas emissions and combat climate change
- reduce waste and minimize our impact on the environment
- support local communities and contribute to their economic development

Mini Actual Test 연습 문제   🎧 17_1.mp3

Respond to the following question while keeping in mind what you have learned.
앞서 배운 내용을 떠올리면서 다음 질문에 답변해 보세요.

> Tell me about the recycling system in your country. How is it done?

Model Answer 모범 답안

 17_2.mp3

Enhance your response by referring to the model answer.
다음 모범 답안을 참고하여 여러분의 답변을 발전시켜 보세요.

> Recycling plays a vital role in my country, South Korea, as we strive to protect the environment and promote sustainability. Knowing how to recycle properly is key to making the world greener. In Korea, we have an efficient recycling system with color-coded bins at home for separating paper, cardboard, plastic, glass, and metals. Additionally, we have recycling centers and drop-off locations conveniently scattered throughout the country. You can even recycle electronics, batteries, and clothes at these facilities. Some areas even offer doorstep pickup services for recycling. It is important to follow the local rules and guidelines for recycling, and the government and local communities actively promote recycling through engaging campaigns. Let's take part in recycling to reduce waste, preserve resources, and make our country greener and more sustainable for everyone!

Level Up to AL AL 공략하기

Read the examples below and see how IH-level sentences can be rephrased at the AL level.
다음 예시를 읽고 IH 수준의 문장을 어떻게 AL 수준으로 바꾸어 말할 수 있는지 살펴보세요.

IH → **AL**

❶ Knowing how to recycle properly is key to making the world greener. → Understanding the proper ways to recycle is essential for our daily lives and our collective efforts to create a greener world.

❷ It is important to follow the local rules and guidelines for recycling. → It is crucial to adhere to local regulations and guidelines to ensure effective recycling practices.

출제 가능성 ★★★★★

Q2 Now, tell me about how you personally recycle. Do you separate the recycling every day? Where do you take out the recycling? Tell me everything about the ways you practice recycling in your daily life.

Question Analysis 질문 분석

Answer the following questions and identify the key matter and the information to be included in your response.
다음 질문에 답하며 답변의 주제와 반드시 포함되어야 할 내용이 무엇인지 파악해 보세요.

1. What is going to be the key matter of your response?
2. What information should your response include?

Warm Your Brain Up 브레인스토밍

Answer the following questions for ideas.
다음 질문에 답하며 답변 소재를 발굴해 보세요.

Intro
- Why is recycling important to you in your everyday life?
- What are the benefits of recycling?

Body
- What specific items do you recycle at home?
- How do you recycle those items?
- Where do you take your recyclables?

Conclusion
- How do you think your recycling can contribute to society?

AL Booster
- How do you maintain cleanliness when recycling?
- Are there any specific locations where you recycle?

Useful Expressions

I'm all about 나에게는 ~이 가장 중요하다   make the world greener 세상을 더 푸르게 만들다   sustainable 지속 가능한
big deal 중요한 문제, 큰 의미   cut down on 줄이다   specifically 구체적으로, 특히   designated for ~을 위해 지정된
sort 분리하다   recyclable 재활용이 가능한   regular routine 규칙적으로 하는 일상 활동   take a moment to ~하기 위해 잠깐 시간을 내다
rinse 헹구다, 씻다   disposal 처리   maintain cleanliness 청결을 유지하다   prevent odors 악취를 방지하다   unpleasant 불쾌한
stay informed 계속 정보를 얻다(알고 있다)   procedure 절차   part with ~에 손을 떼다, ~을 분리하다   recyclables 재활용품
conveniently 편리하게   easily accessible 쉽게 접근할 수 있는   drop-off location 분리수거 장소   do one's part 자신의 역할을 하다

Chapter 9 Recycling 재활용   **187**

Pattern Drills 패턴 학습

Practice using the given sentence patterns to help you deliver your response clearly.
주어진 문장 패턴을 익혀 답변이 명확하게 전달될 수 있도록 연습해 보세요.

①
I'm all about recycling to _____.

- protect the environment
- make a positive impact on the world
- support a greener future
- adopt eco-friendly practices

②
_____ is a big deal to me because it _____.

- Reducing plastic waste / helps protect marine life
- Conserving energy / reduces carbon emissions
- Supporting renewable energy / supports a clean energy future

③
I have different bins specifically designated for _____.

- white paper, colored paper, and cardboard
- organic waste, plastic bottles, and cans
- plastics, tin cans, and glass jars

④
It's important to me to stay informed about _____.

- the effects of pollution on human health
- waste reduction strategies
- eco-friendly products and alternatives

Mini Actual Test 연습 문제 🎧 17_3.mp3

Respond to the following question while keeping in mind what you have learned.
앞서 배운 내용을 떠올리면서 다음 질문에 답변해 보세요.

> Tell me how you recycle at home. When, where, and how often do you recycle? Describe the process in detail.

Model Answer 모범 답안

🎧 17_4.mp3

Enhance your response by referring to the model answer.
다음 모범 답안을 참고하여 여러분의 답변을 발전시켜 보세요.

> In my everyday life, I'm all about recycling in order to help make the world greener and more sustainable. Recycling is a big deal to me because it cuts down on waste, saves resources, and keeps the environment happy. I have different bins at home specifically designated for paper, plastic, glass, and metals. Sorting my recyclables has become a regular and enjoyable routine for me. Additionally, I always take a moment to rinse the items before disposal to maintain cleanliness and prevent unpleasant odors. It's important to me to stay informed about the local recycling guidelines, as I strive to follow the correct procedures. When it's time to part with my recyclables, I take them to the nearby recycling center. I'm fortunate to have accessible drop-off locations in my community that even accept electronic devices, batteries, and clothing for proper recycling. By recycling every day, I believe I'm doing my part to make the world a better place.

Level Up to AL AL 공략하기

Read the examples below and see how IH-level sentences can be rephrased at the AL level.
다음 예시를 읽고 IH 수준의 문장을 어떻게 AL 수준으로 바꾸어 말할 수 있는지 살펴보세요.

IH → **AL**

❶ In my everyday life, I'm all about recycling in order to help make the world greener and more sustainable. → In my daily life, I prioritize recycling to contribute towards a more environmentally friendly and sustainable world.

❷ Recycling is a big deal to me because it cuts down on waste, saves resources, and keeps the environment happy. → Recycling holds great significance for me as it helps reduce waste, conserve valuable resources, and ensure a healthier environment.

출제 가능성 ★★★★★

Q3 Tell me about a memorable or an unexpected incident regarding recycling. What exactly happened, and how did you deal with the situation? Tell me everything that you did from beginning to end.

Question Analysis 질문 분석

Answer the following questions and identify the key matter and the information to be included in your response.
다음 질문에 답하며 답변의 주제와 반드시 포함되어야 할 내용이 무엇인지 파악해 보세요.

1. What is going to be the key matter of your response?
2. What information should your response include?

Warm Your Brain Up 브레인스토밍

Answer the following questions for ideas.
다음 질문에 답하며 답변 소재를 발굴해 보세요.

Intro	• Can you provide some context or background information for the story?
Body	• What happened during the incident? What was the problem? • How did you react to the unexpected incident? • How did you go about solving the problem?
Conclusion	• What lesson did you learn from this incident?

AL Booster

- How did you feel when the incident happened?
- Did you solve the problem alone, or did anyone assist you?

Useful Expressions

become a big part of one's life ~의 생활의 큰 부분이 되다   Let me share ... ~에 대한 이야기를 해 드릴게요   imagine 상상하다
sort 분리하다   reach into ~ ~안에 손을 넣다   catch one's attention ~의 이목을 끌다   grab 잡다   to one's surprise 놀랍게도
hidden 숨겨진   be taken aback 당황하다, 기가 차다   properly 적절하게   worry 걱정시키다   do some research 조사하다
handle 다루다   electronic waste 전자 폐기물   contact 연락하다   dispose of ~을 처리하다   follow guidelines 지침에 따르다
adventure 모험   complicated 복잡한   passionate 열정적인

Pattern Drills 패턴 학습

Practice using the given sentence patterns to help you deliver your response clearly.
주어진 문장 패턴을 익혀 답변이 명확하게 전달될 수 있도록 연습해 보세요.

1
_____ has become a big part of our lives.
- Exercise
- Reading
- Cooking

2
The idea of _____ worried me.
- being judged by others for my choices
- climate change and its impact on future generations
- not being able to find a job after graduation

3
I followed all the guidelines to _____.
- create a healthy lifestyle
- complete the project on time
- assemble the furniture correctly

4
I'm passionate about _____.
- protecting the environment
- exploring the world
- cooking and experimenting with new recipes in the kitchen

Mini Actual Test 연습 문제

🎧 17_5.mp3

Respond to the following question while keeping in mind what you have learned.
앞서 배운 내용을 떠올리면서 다음 질문에 답변해 보세요.

> Can you describe a memorable incident related to recycling? Please provide a detailed account of what occurred, including how you responded and dealt with the situation from start to finish.

Model Answer 모범 답안

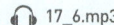 17_6.mp3

Enhance your response by referring to the model answer.
다음 모범 답안을 참고하여 여러분의 답변을 발전시켜 보세요.

> Recycling has become a big part of our lives, so let me share an interesting incident related to that. Imagine a sunny afternoon, just like any other day, when I was sorting my recyclables. As I reached into the bin, something caught my attention. I grabbed it, and to my surprise, it was an electronic device hidden among the paper and plastic. I was taken aback and thought, "Wait a minute, this doesn't belong here!" The idea of not recycling electronics properly worried me. So I quickly did some research and found a local place that handles electronic waste, and I contacted them for guidance. They were very kind and explained how to dispose of it safely. I followed all the guidelines to protect the environment. It was a bit of an adventure finding the right facility and dealing with complicated recycling rules, but it taught me a lot about being responsible. Now I'm passionate about spreading the word and making sure everyone understands recycling. Let's keep our planet green!

Level Up to AL   AL 공략하기

Read the examples below and see how IH-level sentences can be rephrased at the AL level.
다음 예시를 읽고 IH 수준의 문장을 어떻게 AL 수준으로 바꾸어 말할 수 있는지 살펴보세요.

	IH	AL
❶	Recycling has become a big part of our lives, so let me share an interesting incident related to that.	Recycling has become a significant part of our lives, so I'd like to share an interesting incident about recycling that happened to me.
❷	…, but it taught me a lot about being responsible.	…, but it taught me a valuable lesson about being responsible.
❸	Now I'm passionate about spreading the word and making sure everyone understands recycling.	Now I'm determined to spread awareness and make sure everyone understands the importance of recycling.

Chapter 9 Recycling 재활용

Unit 18 Combo Set (2)

출제 가능성 ★★★☆☆

Q1 Let's assume that you have moved to a new building. You want to know about their recycling work. Ask the building manager 3 or 4 questions about the recycling policy.

Question Analysis 질문 분석

Answer the following questions and identify the key matter and the information to be included in your response.
다음 질문에 답하며 답변의 주제와 반드시 포함되어야 할 내용이 무엇인지 파악해 보세요.

1. What is going to be the key matter of your response?
2. What information should your response include?

Warm Your Brain Up 브레인스토밍

Answer the following questions for ideas.
다음 질문에 답하며 답변 소재를 발굴해 보세요.

Intro	• How should you greet the building manager? • What is the purpose of the communication?
Body	• What questions should you ask the manager? • What information would you seek regarding the recycling policy? • How would you respond to the manager's answers?
Conclusion	• What is a suitable manner to express gratitude to the manager for providing answers? • How would you conclude the conversation?

AL Booster

- How might the answers to these questions impact your recycling habits?
- What are some polite ways to request information when you have a question?

Useful Expressions

recycling policy 재활용 정책   material 소재   specific 특정한   bin 분리수거 함   throughout 도처에   encourage 격려하다   participate in ~에 참여하다   impressive 인상적인   collaborate with ~와 협력하다   local recycling facility 지역 재활용 시설   ensure 보장하다   proper 적절한   disposal 처리   processing 과정, 절차   recyclable 재활용 가능한   be impressed with ~에 감명을 받다   effort 노력   commitment to ~에 대한 헌신   be a part of ~의 일부가 되다   sustainable 지속 가능한

Pattern Drills 패턴 학습

Practice using the given sentence patterns to help you deliver your response clearly.
주어진 문장 패턴을 익혀 답변이 명확하게 전달될 수 있도록 연습해 보세요.

❶ Can you tell me about _____?
- the materials that can be recycled
- how you encourage residents to participate in recycling
- the specific bins or areas for recycling throughout the building

❷ Are there specific _____ throughout the building?
- areas designated for recycling
- recycling stations
- locations for recycling

❸ I'm really impressed with _____.
- the building's eco-friendly initiatives
- how the building promotes recycling
- the building's focus on recycling

❹ It's great to see such a strong commitment to _____.
- reducing waste
- green initiatives
- carbon neutrality

Mini Actual Test 연습 문제   🎧 18_1.mp3

Respond to the following question while keeping in mind what you have learned.
앞서 배운 내용을 떠올리면서 다음 질문에 답변해 보세요.

> I'd like to give you a situation to act out. You just moved into a new apartment complex and you have several inquiries regarding the recycling system in the complex. Call the maintenance office and ask three to four questions pertaining to your inquiries.

Model Answer 모범 답안

 18_2.mp3

Enhance your response by referring to the model answer.
다음 모범 답안을 참고하여 여러분의 답변을 발전시켜 보세요.

> Good morning, Mr. Johnson! I'm excited to be living in this new building. Can you tell me about the recycling policy here? What materials can be recycled? That's great! Are there specific bins or areas for recycling throughout the building? Excellent! How do you encourage residents to participate in recycling? That's impressive! Do you collaborate with local recycling facilities to ensure proper disposal and processing of recyclables? Based on the information you've given me, Mr. Johnson, I'm really impressed with the building's recycling efforts. It's great to see such a strong commitment to the environment. I'm excited to be a part of it and contribute to a more sustainable future. Thank you for answering my questions, Mr. Johnson. Have a great day!

Level Up to AL AL 공략하기

Read the examples below and see how IH-level sentences can be rephrased at the AL level.
다음 예시를 읽고 IH 수준의 문장을 어떻게 AL 수준으로 바꾸어 말할 수 있는지 살펴보세요.

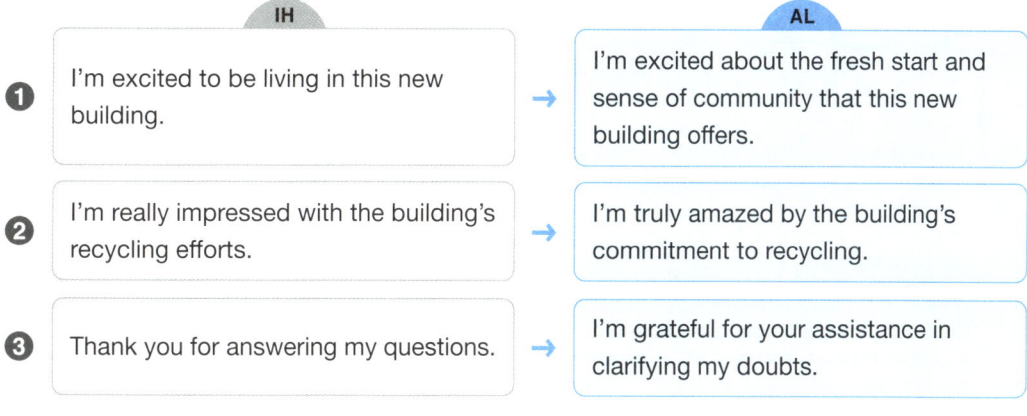

출제 가능성 ★★★☆☆

Q2 You suddenly hear that the recyclables will not be picked up for a while. However, you are going to have a house party next week, and your neighbors will be unhappy about the situation. Call the building manager, explain the situation, and ask for at least two solutions to resolve the problem.

Question Analysis 질문 분석

Answer the following questions and identify the key matter and the information to be included in your response.
다음 질문에 답하며 답변의 주제와 반드시 포함되어야 할 내용이 무엇인지 파악해 보세요.

1. What is going to be the key matter of your response?
2. What information should your response include?

Warm Your Brain Up 브레인스토밍

Answer the following questions for ideas.
다음 질문에 답하며 답변 소재를 발굴해 보세요.

Intro
- How would you start the conversation?
- What is the purpose of the phone call?
- What is the situation you need to address?

Body
- What is the situation and what do you think can be a problem?
- What are your suggestions for resolving the problem?
- How will you communicate these suggestions to the building manager?

Conclusion
- What is an appropriate way to make an apology?
- How would you end the conversation before hanging up?

AL Booster

- How would you feel if you realized that your neighbors would be unhappy because of you?
- How will you make sure your neighbors are satisfied with the solution?

Useful Expressions

come up 생기다, 발생하다   recycling pickup 재활용 수거   temporarily 일시적으로   suspended 중단된   accumulated 축적된, 쌓인   inconvenience 불편함   explore a solution 해결책을 탐구하다   temporary 임시의   additional 추가적인   suggestion 제안   ease concerns 우려를 완화시키다   halt 중단   inform A about B A에게 B에 대해 알리다   resident 거주자   coordinate with ~와 협력하다   special pickup 비정기 수거   support 지원

196 Compact OPIc 컴팩트 오픽

Pattern Drills 패턴 학습

Practice using the given sentence patterns to help you deliver your response clearly.
주어진 문장 패턴을 익혀 답변이 명확하게 전달될 수 있도록 연습해 보세요.

❶ I just learned that _____ will be temporarily interrupted.
- the electricity supply
- the bus service
- the library services

❷ I'm concerned about _____ causing inconvenience to our neighbors.
- the late-night parties
- the parking situation
- the excessive garbage disposal

❸ It would certainly ease the concerns and inconvenience caused by _____.
- the frequent power outages
- the construction noise
- the unreliable internet connection

❹ I will inform the residents about _____.
- the recycling pickup suspension
- the new recycling regulations
- the upcoming renovation plans

Mini Actual Test 연습 문제

🎧 18_3.mp3

Respond to the following question while keeping in mind what you have learned.
앞서 배운 내용을 떠올리면서 다음 질문에 답변해 보세요.

> You learn that recyclables won't be picked up for a while. You have a house party soon, and your neighbors won't be happy about the situation. Call the building manager, explain the problem, and ask for two solutions to resolve it.

Model Answer 모범 답안

Enhance your response by referring to the model answer.
다음 모범 답안을 참고하여 여러분의 답변을 발전시켜 보세요.

> Hello, Mr. Johnson, I hope you're doing well. I wanted to talk to you about an issue that has come up recently. I just learned that recycling pickup in our building will be temporarily suspended. Unfortunately, I have a house party next week and I'm concerned about the accumulated recyclables causing inconvenience to our neighbors. Is there a solution we can explore? Thank you for suggesting the temporary additional recycling bins. Any other ideas? Excellent suggestion! It would certainly ease the concerns and inconvenience caused by the temporary halt in recycling services. Thank you, Mr. Johnson. I will inform the other residents about the temporary additional recycling bins and coordinate with you for the special pickup before the party. Thank you for your time and support. Have a great day!

Level Up to AL AL 공략하기

Read the examples below and see how IH-level sentences can be rephrased at the AL level.
다음 예시를 읽고 IH 수준의 문장을 어떻게 AL 수준으로 바꾸어 말할 수 있는지 살펴보세요.

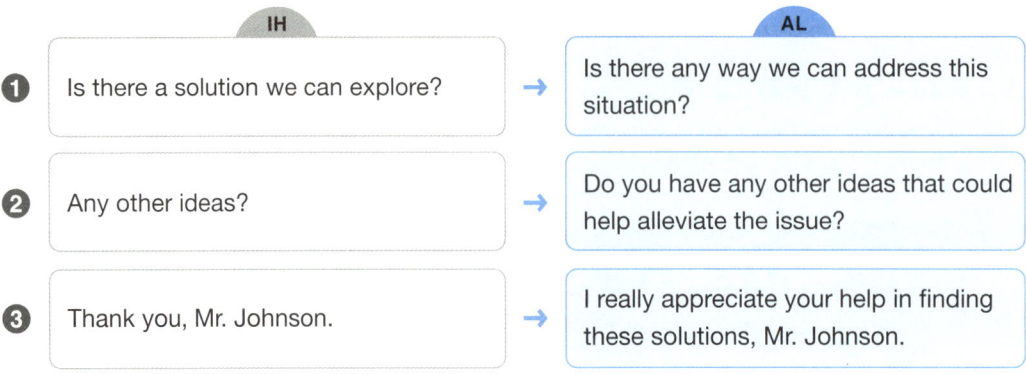

출제 가능성 ★★★☆☆

Q3 Are there any issues or problems regarding recycling? Have you seen any news related to recycling recently? What was it about? Give me all the details about any issues related to recycling.

Question Analysis 질문 분석

Answer the following questions and identify the key matter and the information to be included in your response.
다음 질문에 답하며 답변의 주제와 반드시 포함되어야 할 내용이 무엇인지 파악해 보세요.

1. What is going to be the key matter of your response?
2. What information should your response include?

Warm Your Brain Up 브레인스토밍

Answer the following questions for ideas.
다음 질문에 답하며 답변 소재를 발굴해 보세요.

Intro	Are there any problems or challenges related to recycling?
Body	• What are some specific problems in recycling that you are aware of? • How do these problems impact the recycling process? • What is the significance of news stories that discuss recycling problems?
Conclusion	• How can you improve recycling practices?

AL Booster

- What causes the problems in recycling?
- What is the purpose of discussing recycling problems in the news?

Useful Expressions

be aware of ~을 알고 있다　highlight 강조하다　concern 우려, 문제　get contaminated 오염되다　be mixed with ~와 섞이다　recyclable item 재활용 가능한 물품　process 처리하다　reuse 재사용하다　material 물질, 재료　collect 모으다　properly 제대로, 적절히　correctly 올바르게, 정확하게　raise 높이다　awareness 인식　solution 해결책　deal with ~을 다루다　take care of ~을 돌보다

Pattern Drills 패턴 학습

Practice using the given sentence patterns to help you deliver your response clearly.
주어진 문장 패턴을 익혀 답변이 명확하게 전달될 수 있도록 연습해 보세요.

1

There are problems with _____ that we need to be aware of.

- waste management
- water contamination
- deforestation

2

One problem occurs when _____.

- food is wasted and thrown away
- plastic is improperly disposed of
- energy is wasted through inefficient practices

3

This makes it difficult for people to _____.

- maintain a healthy lifestyle
- communicate effectively
- achieve their goals

4

If we understand and deal with these issues, we can _____.

- improve the situation
- create a better future
- make a positive change

Mini Actual Test 연습 문제

🎧 18_5.mp3

Respond to the following question while keeping in mind what you have learned.
앞서 배운 내용을 떠올리면서 다음 질문에 답변해 보세요.

> Do you know of any challenges or problems related to recycling? Have you seen any news recently related to recycling? Please provide a detailed description of any issues or problems related to recycling that you are aware of.

Model Answer 모범 답안

 18_6.mp3

Enhance your response by referring to the model answer.
다음 모범 답안을 참고하여 여러분의 답변을 발전시켜 보세요.

> Yes, there are problems with recycling that we need to be aware of. Recently, there have been several news articles highlighting these concerns. One problem is when recyclables get contaminated. This happens when things that can't be recycled are mixed with recyclable items. It makes it difficult to process and reuse the materials. Another issue is that some places don't have enough areas to recycle or collect recyclables. This makes it difficult for people to recycle properly. Also, there's a problem with not enough people knowing about recycling or doing it correctly. The news is discussing these problems to raise awareness and find solutions. If we understand and deal with these issues, we can make recycling better and take better care of our environment.

Level Up to AL AL 공략하기

Read the examples below and see how IH-level sentences can be rephrased at the AL level.
다음 예시를 읽고 IH 수준의 문장을 어떻게 AL 수준으로 바꾸어 말할 수 있는지 살펴보세요.

IH		AL
❶ This happens when things that can't be recycled are mixed with recyclable items.	→	This happens when non-recyclable items are improperly sorted and end up in recycling streams.
❷ Also, there's a problem with not enough people knowing about recycling or doing it correctly.	→	Additionally, there have been discussions about the challenges posed by low public awareness and participation in recycling practices.

Chapter 10

Fashion·Industry 패션·산업

✓ Strategy Check 주제 관련 전략

Check the following strategies related to the topic of this chapter.
이 챕터의 주제와 관련된 시험 대비 전략을 확인해 보세요.

IH Essential

- There are over 20 topics that could be randomly asked in the OPIc test. Therefore, it is not advisable to try to prepare and memorize individual answers for all these random topics. Instead, it is better to prepare common storytelling materials or response structures that can be used universally and be ready to handle various types of questions.
  오픽에서 돌발 질문으로 출제될 수 있는 주제는 20여 가지가 넘습니다. 따라서 모든 돌발 주제의 답변을 각각 준비하여 암기하는 것은 바람직하지 않습니다. 공용으로 사용할 수 있는 이야기 소재나 답변 구조를 준비해 다양한 질문에 대비하도록 합시다.

- "Fashion" and "Industry" are topics that can seem quite similar in terms of storytelling materials. Try selecting a few materials and practice utilizing them to respond to questions.
  '패션'과 '산업'은 이야기 소재를 연계할 수 있는 주제들입니다. 몇 가지 소재를 정해 그를 활용하여 답변하는 연습을 해 보세요.

- "Fashion" and "Industry" are topics that have a higher probability of being presented when you set the difficulty level to 3 or higher in the orientation. Therefore, if your goal is to achieve an IH level or higher, you must be prepared for both topics.
  '패션'과 '산업'은 오리엔테이션에서 시험 난이도를 3 이상으로 설정하면 출제 확률이 높아지는 주제들입니다. 따라서 목표 등급이 IH 이상이라면 반드시 두 주제를 대비해 놓아야 합니다.

AL Booster

- If you are not particularly interested in "Fashion" and "Industry," you might feel flustered if questions related to these topics are presented. Remember, it's not necessary to answer with personal experiences, so it's important to practice using your imagination to create stories. The accuracy of your answers is not being evaluated, so feel free to be creative and imaginative when responding to such questions.
  평소 '패션'과 '산업'에 크게 관심이 없다면, 이 주제들과 관련된 문제가 출제되었을 경우 당황할 수 있습니다. 꼭 본인의 경험담을 답변할 필요는 없으니, 상상력을 동원하여 이야기를 만들어 내는 연습이 필요합니다. 답변의 진실 여부는 채점 대상이 아니기 때문입니다.

❓ Frequently Asked Questions 빈출 질문 유형

Here are the most frequently asked question types related to the topic. Try to identify <u>the key matter</u> of the question and <u>the information</u> that should be included in your response.
이 챕터의 주제와 관련해 자주 출제되는 질문 유형들을 확인해 보세요. 그리고 각 질문의 중심 소재와 답변에 어떤 정보를 포함시켜야 하는지 파악해 보세요.

Fashion	• I'd like to know about fashion in your country. <u>What clothes do people wear in everyday life</u>? Describe the fashion in your country in detail. • Fashion trends have changed a lot over time. How have <u>fashion trends in your country changed</u> over the years? What was <u>the fashion trend when you were a child</u> and <u>how has it changed now</u>? • <u>Did you buy some clothes recently?</u> <u>What kind of clothes</u> did you purchase and <u>why</u>? <u>How</u> did you buy them?
Industry	• I'd like to know about the most promising industries in your country. Please <u>explain the reason why</u> that industry is successful. • Describe a well-known company in the industry you just mentioned. What are <u>the characteristics of the company</u>? <u>Why do you think that company is so famous</u>? • Describe the benefits offered by the industry or company you mentioned before. <u>What types of benefits</u> are there? • <u>Compare</u> the current situation of the industry or company you are interested in <u>with</u> the situation three years ago.

Chapter 10 — Fashion·Industry 패션·산업

Unit 19 Combo Set (1)

MP3 바로가기

출제 가능성 ★★★★☆

Q1 I'd like to know about fashion in your country. What clothes do people wear in everyday life? Describe the fashion in your country in detail.

Question Analysis 질문 분석

Answer the following questions and identify the key matter and the information to be included in your response.
다음 질문에 답하며 답변의 주제와 반드시 포함되어야 할 내용이 무엇인지 파악해 보세요.

1. What is going to be the key matter of your response?
2. What information should your response include?

Warm Your Brain Up 브레인스토밍

Answer the following questions for ideas.
다음 질문에 답하며 답변 소재를 발굴해 보세요.

Intro	• What is the typical clothing style for everyday life in your country? • What are the factors that affect people's clothing style?
Body	• What do people usually wear in a casual setting? • What are the customary clothing choices for special events or formal occasions? • In a professional environment, what is the typical attire that people generally wear?
Conclusion	• What are the overall influences and factors that shape clothing choices in your country?

AL Booster

- What are some examples of clothing commonly worn by people in your country?
- How do the clothing choices in your country contribute to its overall identity?

Useful Expressions

everyday clothing style 일상복 스타일   vary 다양하다   based on ~을 기반으로   region 지역   cultural factor 문화적 요인
typically 일반적으로   casually 캐주얼하게   favor 선호하다   special occasion 특별한 경우   ethnic attire 민족 의상
when it comes to ~에 관한 경우   distinction 구별   professional setting 직업적인 환경   formal 격식을 차린   outfit 의상, 복장
be suitable for ~에 적합하다   opt for ~을 선택하다   globalization 세계화   influence 영향을 주다   embrace 받아들이다
reflect 반영하다   a blend of 혼합된   uniqueness 독특함

Pattern Drills 패턴 학습

Practice using the given sentence patterns to help you deliver your response clearly.
주어진 문장 패턴을 익혀 답변이 명확하게 전달될 수 있도록 연습해 보세요.

❶ In my country, everyday clothing style varies based on _____.
- profession
- social occasions
- personal preference

❷ Professional settings require _____.
- a professional dress code
- punctuality and professionalism
- clear communication and teamwork

❸ _____ are suitable for creative or informal workplaces.
- Casual outfits
- Informal clothes
- Jeans and a nice blouse
- Skirts and sweaters

❹ Overall, clothing in my country reflects _____.
- cultural diversity and regional styles
- a mix of Western and ethnic fashion
- a balance between comfort and style

Mini Actual Test 연습 문제 🎧 19_1.mp3

Respond to the following question while keeping in mind what you have learned.
앞서 배운 내용을 떠올리면서 다음 질문에 답변해 보세요.

> I'd like to know about what kinds of clothes people in your country typically wear. Is it different for work as opposed to leisure? If so, how different is it?

Model Answer 모범 답안

 19_2.mp3

Enhance your response by referring to the model answer.
다음 모범 답안을 참고하여 여러분의 답변을 발전시켜 보세요.

> In my country, everyday clothing style varies and is based on climate, region, and cultural factors. People typically dress casually and comfortably, favoring Western-style clothing like jeans, t-shirts, and dresses. However, during festivals and special occasions, traditional or ethnic attire becomes important. When it comes to work, there is often a distinction in clothing choices. Professional settings require formal or business attire like suits and dresses, while more relaxed outfits are suitable for creative or informal workplaces. During leisure activities, individuals opt for relaxed clothing such as shorts, skirts, and casual tops. Fashion trends and globalization have also influenced clothing preferences, with young people embracing international styles. Overall, clothing in my country reflects a blend of traditional, cultural, and modern influences, allowing individuals to express their uniqueness and personal style.

Level Up to AL AL 공략하기

Read the examples below and see how IH-level sentences can be rephrased at the AL level.
다음 예시를 읽고 IH 수준의 문장을 어떻게 AL 수준으로 바꾸어 말할 수 있는지 살펴보세요.

IH → **AL**

❶ In my country, everyday clothing style varies and is based on climate, region, and cultural factors. → In my country, the clothing style for everyday life varies depending on different factors like climate, region, and cultural practices.

❷ People typically dress casually and comfortably. → People usually dress in a casual and comfortable manner.

Q2 Fashion trends have changed a lot over time. How have fashion trends in your country changed over the years? What was the fashion trend when you were a child and how has it changed?

Question Analysis 질문 분석

Answer the following questions and identify the key matter and the information to be included in your response.
다음 질문에 답하며 답변의 주제와 반드시 포함되어야 할 내용이 무엇인지 파악해 보세요.

1. What is going to be the key matter of your response?
2. What information should your response include?

Warm Your Brain Up 브레인스토밍

Answer the following questions for ideas.
다음 질문에 답하며 답변 소재를 발굴해 보세요.

Intro	How have fashion trends in Korea changed over the years?
Body	• What were the characteristics of fashion trends during your childhood? • What is the current fashion trend in Korea, and how does it differ from the past? • What factors have influenced these changes in fashion?
Conclusion	• What does the reflection of fashion trends reveal about cultural identity?

AL Booster

- What role has mass media played in shaping Korean fashion trends?
- Who are the influential figures in shaping Korean fashion trends?

Useful Expressions

notable change 주목할 만한 변화   reflect 반영하다   dynamic nature 동적인 특성   vibrant color 생동감 넘치는 색상
playful pattern 재미있는 패턴   a blend of 조합된   element 요소   as time goes on 시간이 흐름에 따라   a shift towards ~으로의 전환
minimalistic 미니멀한   monochromatic 단색의   influenced by ~의 영향을 받은   impact 영향을 주다
known worldwide 전 세계적으로 알려진   significant 중요한   spread 퍼뜨리다   broad audience 넓은 관객층   emerge 등장하다
influential figure 영향력 있는 인물   shape trends 트렌드를 형성하다   inspire 영감을 주다   cultural identity 문화적 정체성
creativity 창의성

Chapter 10 Fashion·Industry 패션·산업

Pattern Drills 패턴 학습

Practice using the given sentence patterns to help you deliver your response clearly.
주어진 문장 패턴을 익혀 답변이 명확하게 전달될 수 있도록 연습해 보세요.

❶ When I was a child, the popular fashion trend in Korea featured _____.

- oversized clothing and funky accessories
- bright and eye-catching prints
- unique hairstyles and experimental fashion combinations

❷ There has been a shift towards _____.

- minimalistic home decor and decluttered spaces
- remote work and flexible working arrangements
- plant-based diets and conscious eating

❸ _____ has/have greatly impacted Korean fashion.

- Social media
- Korean celebrities
- Western fashion trends

❹ _____ have played a significant role in promoting Korean fashion.

- Fashion influencers
- Fashion events and shows
- Magazines and fashion publications

Mini Actual Test 연습 문제

🎧 19_3.mp3

Respond to the following question while keeping in mind what you have learned.
앞서 배운 내용을 떠올리면서 다음 질문에 답변해 보세요.

> Describe fashion trends in your country. How have fashion trends evolved in your country over the years? What was the fashion trend during your childhood, and how has it evolved since then?

Model Answer 모범 답안

 19_4.mp3

Enhance your response by referring to the model answer.
다음 모범 답안을 참고하여 여러분의 답변을 발전시켜 보세요.

> Fashion trends in Korea have experienced notable changes over time, reflecting the dynamic nature of the fashion industry. When I was a child, the fashion trend in Korea featured vibrant colors, playful patterns, and a blend of traditional and modern elements. Over time, however, there has been a shift towards more minimalistic and monochromatic styles, due to the influence of global fashion trends. The popularity of K-pop music and Korean dramas has greatly impacted Korean fashion, making it known worldwide. Social media platforms have also played a significant role in spreading and promoting Korean fashion, making it more accessible to a broader audience. Korean fashion designers and celebrities have emerged as influential figures, shaping trends and inspiring new fashion directions. As fashion continues to evolve in Korea, it reflects not only personal style but also the cultural identity and creativity of the country.

Level Up to AL AL 공략하기

Read the examples below and see how IH-level sentences can be rephrased at the AL level.
다음 예시를 읽고 IH 수준의 문장을 어떻게 AL 수준으로 바꾸어 말할 수 있는지 살펴보세요.

IH		AL
❶ Fashion trends in Korea have experienced notable changes over time.	→	Fashion trends in Korea have undergone significant transformations over the years.
❷ The popularity of K-pop music and Korean dramas has greatly impacted Korean fashion, making it known worldwide.	→	The rise of K-pop and Korean dramas has played a significant role in promoting Korean fashion trends worldwide.

출제 가능성 ★★★☆☆

Q3 Have you bought clothes recently? What kind of clothes did you purchase and why? How did you buy them?

Question Analysis 질문 분석

Answer the following questions and identify the key matter and the information to be included in your response.
다음 질문에 답하며 답변의 주제와 반드시 포함되어야 할 내용이 무엇인지 파악해 보세요.

1. What is going to be the key matter of your response?
2. What information should your response include?

Warm Your Brain Up 브레인스토밍

Answer the following questions for ideas.
다음 질문에 답하며 답변 소재를 발굴해 보세요.

Intro	• Have you made any recent clothing purchases? • What motivated you to buy new clothes?
Body	• What types of clothing did you buy? • What factors influenced your decisions when choosing clothes? • Did you make your purchases online or in brick-and-mortar stores?
Conclusion	• What was your overall shopping experience like?

AL Booster

• What benefits did you experience from your chosen shopping method?

Useful Expressions

update 갱신하다　wardrobe 옷장　comfortable 편안한　versatile 다용도의　piece 하나, 한 벌　comfort 편안함
top priority 최우선 사항　look for ~을 찾다　made from ~으로부터 만들어진　breathable fabrics 통기성이 좋은 원단
pay attention to ~에 주의를 기울이다　latest 최신의　modern 현대적인　shop online 온라인 쇼핑하다　browse 둘러보다
a wide range of 폭넓은　compare prices 가격을 비교하다　customer review 고객 후기　convenient 편리한
match one's style ~의 스타일과 어울리다　be even happier with ~에 훨씬 더 만족하다　purchase 구매

Pattern Drills 패턴 학습

Practice using the given sentence patterns to help you deliver your response clearly.
주어진 문장 패턴을 익혀 답변이 명확하게 전달될 수 있도록 연습해 보세요.

1 _____ was a top priority for me.
- Quality
- Functionality
- Affordability

2 I looked for clothes made from _____.
- organic cotton
- lightweight and moisture-wicking fabrics
- high-quality silk
- stretchy and flexible fabrics

3 To make shopping easier, I decided to _____.
- use a shopping application
- use a price comparison website
- follow my favorite brands on social media
- set a budget

4 Overall, I'm happy with the clothes I bought because _____.
- they fit perfectly and flatter my body shape
- they are high quality and made to last.
- they were on sale, and I got great value for my money

Mini Actual Test 연습 문제   🎧 19_5.mp3

Respond to the following question while keeping in mind what you have learned.
앞서 배운 내용을 떠올리면서 다음 질문에 답변해 보세요.

> **Have you purchased any clothes recently? If so, what type of clothing did you buy and for what reason? How did you make your purchase?**

Model Answer 모범 답안

Enhance your response by referring to the model answer.
다음 모범 답안을 참고하여 여러분의 답변을 발전시켜 보세요.

> I recently bought some new clothes to update my wardrobe. I chose comfortable and versatile pieces that I can wear every day. Comfort was a top priority for me, so I looked for clothes made from soft and breathable fabrics. I also paid attention to the latest fashion trends to make sure my choices were modern. To make shopping easier, I decided to shop online. It allowed me to browse a wide range of options, compare prices, and read customer reviews. I found online shopping convenient and it saved me time. Overall, I'm happy with the clothes I bought because they match my style and are comfortable to wear. Shopping online was a good experience and gave me more choices, which made me even happier with my purchases.

Level Up to AL AL 공략하기

Read the examples below and see how IH-level sentences can be rephrased at the AL level.
다음 예시를 읽고 IH 수준의 문장을 어떻게 AL 수준으로 바꾸어 말할 수 있는지 살펴보세요.

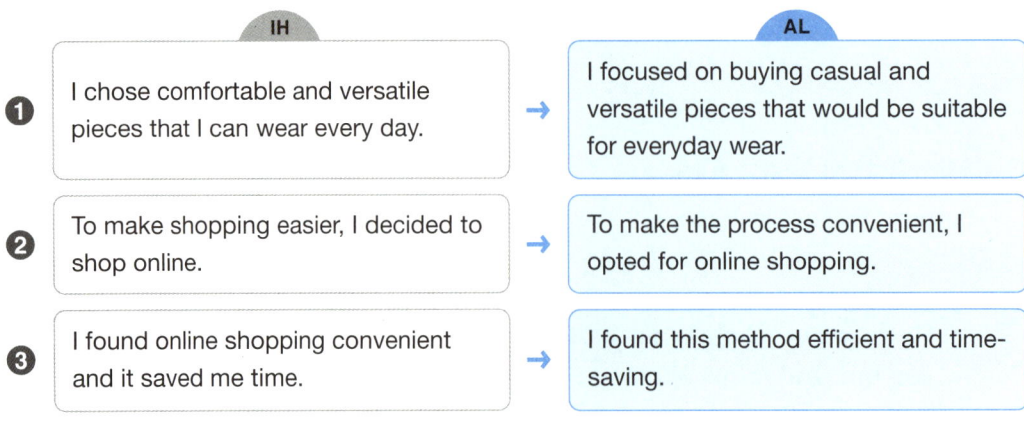

IH	AL
① I chose comfortable and versatile pieces that I can wear every day.	I focused on buying casual and versatile pieces that would be suitable for everyday wear.
② To make shopping easier, I decided to shop online.	To make the process convenient, I opted for online shopping.
③ I found online shopping convenient and it saved me time.	I found this method efficient and time-saving.

Chapter 10 Fashion·Industry 패션·산업

Unit 20 Combo Set (2)

MP3 바로가기

출제 가능성 ★★★☆☆

Q1 I'd like to know about the most promising industries in your country. Please explain the reason why that industry is successful.

 Question Analysis 질문 분석

Answer the following questions and identify the key matter and the information to be included in your response.
다음 질문에 답하며 답변의 주제와 반드시 포함되어야 할 내용이 무엇인지 파악해 보세요.

1. What is going to be the key matter of your response?
2. What information should your response include?

Warm Your Brain Up 브레인스토밍

Answer the following questions for ideas.
다음 질문에 답하며 답변 소재를 발굴해 보세요.

Intro	• What is the significance of fashion in Korea?
Body	• How have the fashion trends in Korea gained worldwide recognition? • What are the factors contributing to the success of the fashion industry in Korea?
Conclusion	• What does fashion in Korea represent beyond personal style? • What is the overall outlook for the fashion industry in Korea?

AL Booster

- How has the popularity of K-pop music and Korean dramas influenced Korean fashion?
- How has social media contributed to the popularity of Korean fashion?
- What role do famous designers and popular celebrities play in shaping fashion trends?

Useful Expressions

big deal 큰 문제   promising 유망한   popularity 인기   dress like ~처럼 옷을 입다   capture the same style 같은 스타일을 녹여 내다(구현하다)   character 등장인물   inspire 영감을 주다   recreate 재창조하다   play a big part 큰 역할을 하다   discover 발견하다   latest trend 최신 트렌드   showcase 소개하다; 시연 행사   have a big impact on ~에 큰 영향을 미치다   cultural identity 문화적 정체성   be a part of ~의 일부가 되다

Chapter 10 Fashion·Industry 패션·산업   **213**

Pattern Drills 패턴 학습

Practice using the given sentence patterns to help you deliver your response clearly.
주어진 문장 패턴을 익혀 답변이 명확하게 전달될 수 있도록 연습해 보세요.

❶
_____ is a big deal and it's always changing.
- Keeping up with technology
- Maintaining a healthy lifestyle
- Environmental sustainability

❷
_____ has made Korean fashion popular around the world.
- The influence of Korean celebrities
- The global success of Korean fashion brands
- The widespread use of social media

❸
_____ has / have played a big part in making Korean fashion popular worldwide.
- The fashion influencers on social media
- The online communities dedicated to Korean fashion
- The sharing of fashion content on platforms like Instagram

❹
Fashion in Korea is not just about personal style, it also shows _____.
- the fashion trends of the country
- the influence of K-pop and Korean dramas
- the cultural identity of the country

Mini Actual Test 연습 문제 🎧 20_1.mp3

Respond to the following question while keeping in mind what you have learned.
앞서 배운 내용을 떠올리면서 다음 질문에 답변해 보세요.

> Please tell us about a promising business field in your country. Why do you think this business field is promising? Describe it in as much detail as possible.

Model Answer 모범 답안

Enhance your response by referring to the model answer.
다음 모범 답안을 참고하여 여러분의 답변을 발전시켜 보세요.

> In Korea, fashion is a big deal and it's always changing. The fashion trends here have become famous worldwide. There are a few reasons why the fashion industry in Korea is successful. First, the popularity of K-pop music and Korean dramas has made Korean fashion popular around the world. For example, many people like to dress like their favorite K-pop idols or characters from popular Korean dramas. They might wear similar outfits, hairstyles, or accessories to capture the same style. If a character in a Korean drama becomes popular, their fashion choices might inspire viewers to recreate those looks. Additionally, social media has played a big part in making Korean fashion popular worldwide. Platforms like Instagram, TikTok, and YouTube have made it easy for people who love fashion to discover and share the latest trends from Korea. When famous designers and popular celebrities showcase their outfits on social media, it has a big impact on what people want to wear. Fashion in Korea is not just about personal style, it also shows the creativity and cultural identity of the country. It's an exciting and promising industry to be a part of.

Level Up to AL AL 공략하기

Read the examples below and see how IH-level sentences can be rephrased at the AL level.
다음 예시를 읽고 IH 수준의 문장을 어떻게 AL 수준으로 바꾸어 말할 수 있는지 살펴보세요.

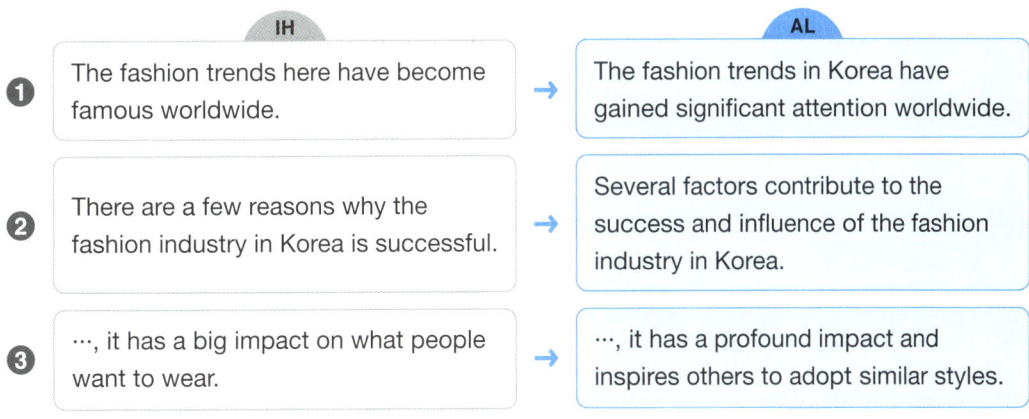

IH → **AL**

❶ The fashion trends here have become famous worldwide. → The fashion trends in Korea have gained significant attention worldwide.

❷ There are a few reasons why the fashion industry in Korea is successful. → Several factors contribute to the success and influence of the fashion industry in Korea.

❸ ⋯, it has a big impact on what people want to wear. → ⋯, it has a profound impact and inspires others to adopt similar styles.

출제 가능성 ★★★☆☆

Q2 Describe a well-known company in the industry you just mentioned. What are the characteristics of the company? Why do you think that company is so famous?

Question Analysis 질문 분석

Answer the following questions and identify the key matter and the information to be included in your response.
다음 질문에 답하며 답변의 주제와 반드시 포함되어야 할 내용이 무엇인지 파악해 보세요.

1. What is going to be the key matter of your response?
2. What information should your response include?

Warm Your Brain Up 브레인스토밍

Answer the following questions for ideas.
다음 질문에 답하며 답변 소재를 발굴해 보세요.

Intro	• What is the name of the well-known company? • What makes this company stand out among others in the industry?
Body	• What are the distinctive characteristics of this company? • What is the reputation of this company in Korea and abroad? • How has this company gained significant fame in the fashion industry?
Conclusion	• What factors have contributed to the overall success of the company?

AL Booster

• How have the company's marketing and branding strategies played a role in its success?

Useful Expressions

well-known 유명한 gain fame 명성을 얻다 abroad 해외에서 be famous for ~로 유명하다 creative design 창의적인 디자인
blend A with B A와 B를 조합하다 focus on ~에 대한 집중 small details 세밀한 디테일 high-quality 고품질의
visually appealing 시각적으로 매력적인 digital marketing 디지털 마케팅 reach a wider audience 보다 넓은 범위의 관중에 도달하다
build a strong brand 강력한 브랜드를 구축하다 collaborate with ~와 협력하다 influential 영향력이 있는 boost 증진하다
reputation 명성 popularity 인기 participation 참여 major 주요한 showcase 시연 행사; 소개하다

Pattern Drills 패턴 학습

Practice using the given sentence patterns to help you deliver your response clearly.
주어진 문장 패턴을 익혀 답변이 명확하게 전달될 수 있도록 연습해 보세요.

①

One well-known company in the _____ industry is _____.

- automotive / "AutoMasters"
- food and beverage / "TastyBites"
- entertainment industry / "StarStudios"

②

This company is famous for _____.

- its exceptional customer service
- its high-quality craftsmanship
- its diverse range of products

③

One special thing about the company is its focus on _____.

- customer satisfaction
- innovation and continuous improvement
- research and development

④

The company has effectively used _____.

- data analytics
- influencer marketing
- customer feedback

Mini Actual Test 연습 문제

🎧 20_3.mp3

Respond to the following question while keeping in mind what you have learned.
앞서 배운 내용을 떠올리면서 다음 질문에 답변해 보세요.

> Can you tell me about a well-known company in the industry you mentioned? What are the distinctive characteristics of this company? Please explain why this company has gained significant fame.

Chapter 10 Fashion·Industry 패션·산업   **217**

Model Answer 모범 답안

 20_4.mp3

Enhance your response by referring to the model answer.
다음 모범 답안을 참고하여 여러분의 답변을 발전시켜 보세요.

> One well-known company in the fashion industry is "MZ Fashion," which has gained significant fame in Korea and abroad. This company is famous for its unique and creative designs that blend traditional Korean elements with modern styles. One special thing about MZ Fashion is its focus on craftsmanship and attention to small details, which results in visually appealing, high-quality products. Additionally, the company has effectively used digital marketing and social media to reach a wider audience and build a strong brand. MZ Fashion has also collaborated with influential fashion designers and celebrities, further boosting its reputation and popularity. Its successful participation in major fashion events and showcases has also contributed to the company's fame.

Level Up to AL AL 공략하기

Read the examples below and see how IH-level sentences can be rephrased at the AL level.
다음 예시를 읽고 IH 수준의 문장을 어떻게 AL 수준으로 바꾸어 말할 수 있는지 살펴보세요.

	IH	→	AL
❶	One well-known company in the fashion industry is "MZ Fashion."	→	One widely recognized company in the fashion industry is "MZ Fashion."
❷	One special thing about MZ Fashion is its focus on craftsmanship and attention to small details, which results in visually appealing, high-quality products.	→	One distinctive characteristic of MZ Fashion is its commitment to craftsmanship and attention to detail, resulting in high-quality and visually stunning products.

출제 가능성 ★★★☆☆

Q3
Compare the current situation of the industry or company you are interested in with the situation three years ago.

Question Analysis 질문 분석

Answer the following questions and identify the key matter and the information to be included in your response.
다음 질문에 답하며 답변의 주제와 반드시 포함되어야 할 내용이 무엇인지 파악해 보세요.

1. What is going to be the key matter of your response?
2. What information should your response include?

Warm Your Brain Up 브레인스토밍

Answer the following questions for ideas.
다음 질문에 답하며 답변 소재를 발굴해 보세요.

Intro	• How has the popularity of Korean fashion changed over the past three years? • What were the main characteristics or trends in the fashion industry three years ago? • How is the fashion industry different now compared to three years ago?
Body	• What factors have contributed to the global expansion of Korean fashion brands? • What are some notable changes that have occurred in the Korean fashion industry? • How have K-fashion influencers and celebrities influenced the growth of the industry?
Conclusion	• What are the overall features or traits in the Korean fashion industry these days?

AL Booster

- How have consumer behavior or fashion preferences changed in the fashion industry?
- How has the fashion industry in Korea used digital platforms and social media?

Useful Expressions

significant change 중요한 변화   international recognition 국제적 인정   soar to new heights 새로운 정점으로 도약하다   embrace 받아들이다   digital platform 디지털 플랫폼   growing 성장하는   sustainability 지속 가능성   ethical practice 윤리적 실천   eco-friendly material 친환경 재료   adopt 채택하다   responsible 책임 있는   influencer 인플루언서(인기 등을 바탕으로 대중이나 업계에 영향을 미치는 사람)   celebrity 유명 인사   make an impact 영향을 미치다   globally 전 세계적으로   with a strong emphasis on ~을 강조하여   influential 영향력이 있는   personality 인물

Pattern Drills 패턴 학습

Practice using the given sentence patterns to help you deliver your response clearly.
주어진 문장 패턴을 익혀 답변이 명확하게 전달될 수 있도록 연습해 보세요.

①
The industry has embraced _____.
- technological advancements
- e-commerce and customization
- innovative design techniques

②
There is also a growing focus on _____.
- ethical fashion
- slow fashion
- local production

③
Influencers and celebrities have played a big role in _____.
- shaping consumer preferences
- setting fashion trends
- driving brand awareness and exposure

④
The Korean fashion industry has continued to _____.
- evolve and innovate
- expand its reach and influence
- collaborate with international brands and designers

Mini Actual Test 연습 문제

🎧 20_5.mp3

Respond to the following question while keeping in mind what you have learned.
앞서 배운 내용을 떠올리면서 다음 질문에 답변해 보세요.

> Compare how things are currently in the industry or company you find interesting to how they were three years ago.

Model Answer 모범 답안

🎧 20_6.mp3

Enhance your response by referring to the model answer.
다음 모범 답안을 참고하여 여러분의 답변을 발전시켜 보세요.

> Over the past three years, the fashion industry in Korea has experienced significant changes. Three years ago, Korean fashion was already gaining international recognition, but since then its popularity has soared to new heights. Now you can find Korean clothing and accessories in many places around the world. The industry has embraced digital platforms and social media to reach more people and promote their products. There is also a growing focus on sustainability and ethical practices, with Korean fashion brands using eco-friendly materials and adopting responsible production methods. Influencers and celebrities who wear Korean fashion have played a big role in its popularity. Overall, the Korean fashion industry has continued to grow and make an impact globally, with a strong emphasis on sustainability and a wide reach through digital platforms and influential personalities.

Level Up to AL   AL 공략하기

Read the examples below and see how IH-level sentences can be rephrased at the AL level.
다음 예시를 읽고 IH 수준의 문장을 어떻게 AL 수준으로 바꾸어 말할 수 있는지 살펴보세요.

IH	AL
❶ ···, the fashion industry in Korea has experienced significant changes.	→ ···, the fashion industry in Korea has witnessed significant changes and developments.
❷ Influencers and celebrities who wear Korean fashion have played a big role in its popularity.	→ The rise of K-fashion influencers and celebrities has further contributed to the industry's growth, as their fashion choices inspire and influence consumers.

Chapter 11
Geography · Environmental Issues 지형·환경 문제

✓ Strategy Check 주제 관련 전략

Check the following strategies related to the topic of this chapter.
이 챕터의 주제와 관련된 시험 대비 전략을 확인해 보세요.

IH Essential

- Among the random topics, "Geography" and "Environmental issues" are the most challenging ones to respond to, so thorough preparation is necessary.
  돌발 주제 중 '지형' 및 '환경 이슈'는 가장 답변하기 까다로운 주제들이므로, 꼼꼼한 대비가 필요합니다.

- If the test difficulty is set to 3 or higher during the orientation, two questions on a single topic will be presented as a pair for questions 14 and 15. If the difficulty is set to 5 or higher, there is a higher probability of "Geography" or "Environmental issues" being chosen as the topic for the pair question.
  오리엔테이션에서 시험 난이도를 3 이상으로 설정할 경우, 하나의 주제에 대한 2개의 질문이 14번과 15번에 걸쳐 페어로 출제됩니다. 난이도를 5 이상으로 설정할 경우, '지형' 또는 '환경 이슈'가 페어 질문의 주제로 출제될 확률이 높아집니다.

- Among the questions related to "Environmental issues," the question about global warming may also be presented for "Weather" or "Seasons" topics covered in the Chapter 8.
  '환경 이슈'에 관한 질문 중 '지구 온난화'를 묻는 질문은 8번째 대단원(Chapter)에서 다루었던 '날씨' 또는 '계절' 주제와 연계하여서도 출제될 수 있습니다.

AL Booster

- If you aim to achieve a IH level or higher, it is recommended to set the test difficulty to 5 or higher. However, even if you are not confident in the topics related to social issues and set the difficulty to 3-4, there is still a probability of around 30% to achieve the aimed level. The main difference between difficulty levels 3-4 and 5 or higher is the likelihood of questions related to social issues being presented. Therefore, it is crucial to understand your strengths and weaknesses and strategically choose the difficulty level accordingly.
  오픽에서 IH 이상을 득점하고자 한다면 시험 난이도를 5 이상으로 설정할 것을 권장합니다. 다만, '사회 문제' 주제에 자신이 없어 난이도를 3~4로 설정한다 하더라도 30% 전후의 확률로 목표 등급이 나올 수 있습니다. 난이도 3~4와 5 이상의 차이는 '사회 문제'와 관련된 질문의 출제 여부이니, 자신의 강점과 약점을 잘 파악하여 난이도를 전략적으로 선택하시기 바랍니다.

❓ Frequently Asked Questions 빈출 질문 유형

Here are the most frequently asked question types related to the topic. Try to identify the key matter of the question and the information that should be included in your response.
이 챕터의 주제와 관련해 자주 출제되는 질문 유형들을 확인해 보세요. 그리고 각 질문의 중심 소재와 답변에 어떤 정보를 포함시켜야 하는지 파악해 보세요.

Geography	• I would like to know about the geographic features of the country that you live in now. What makes them different from other countries? Please describe them in as much detail as possible. • Describe the last place you visited related to the geography of your country. What was special about that place? What did you do there? Tell me everything about the landscape and why you went there. • Can you tell me about outdoor activities that the people in your country do, and where do they do them? What do you usually do? Give me all the details. • Tell me about a country that has similar geographical features to your country. Tell me about the people and traditions of the country. Please describe the country in as much detail as possible.
Pollution	• I'd like to know about the problems or issues related to the environment that people have recently discussed. What things are people discussing the most and why are they so important in your society? • In every country, clean water and air are essential for everyone. However, some areas do not have enough clean air due to environmental pollution. Please give your opinion about this issue. • A lot of people volunteer in programs to improve the environment in the community. Have you ever participated in such a program? Tell me what you did and why you got involved in that program.
Global Warming	• These days we have many environmental issues, such as global warming and climate change. Global warming is the greatest challenge facing our planet. Please tell me about it in as much detail as possible. • How has the weather changed over the years? What do you think causes climate change? How has it affected the lives of people in your country?

Chapter 11 Geography·Environmental Issues 지형·환경 문제

Unit 21 Combo Set (1)

MP3 바로가기

출제 가능성 ★★★★☆

Q1 I would like to know about the geographic features of the country that you live in now. What makes them different from those of other countries? Please describe them in as much detail as possible.

Question Analysis 질문 분석

Answer the following questions and identify the key matter and the information to be included in your response.
다음 질문에 답하며 답변의 주제와 반드시 포함되어야 할 내용이 무엇인지 파악해 보세요.

1. What is going to be the key matter of your response?
2. What information should your response include?

Warm Your Brain Up 브레인스토밍

Answer the following questions for ideas.
다음 질문에 답하며 답변 소재를 발굴해 보세요.

Intro	• How does your country look when looking at it on the map? • What are some distinct geographic features of your country?
Body	• What are some notable mountain ranges in your country? • What does the coastline of your country look like? • How does your country's geography impact its culture and economy?
Conclusion	• What unique geographical features does your country have that cannot be found in other countries? • Have you ever had an experience where you thought that your country is special due to its geographical features?

AL Booster

- Is the territory of the country you live in elongated vertically or horizontally? Does such topography influence the weather in each region?
- Is your country composed of several islands? Tell me about some of the most famous islands in your country.

Useful Expressions

geography 지리, 지형   mountains 산맥   coastline 해안   diverse 다양한   stunning 아름다운   landscape 경관   have an amazing view 놀라운 경치를 갖고 있다   the East Sea 동해   the West Sea 서해   surrounding 주변의   Korean Peninsula 한반도   volcanic terrain 화산 지형   hot and humid 덥고 습한   forest 숲   economy 경제   locals 지역 주민들   appreciate nature 자연을 감상하다   seafood industry 수산업   tourism 관광

224   Compact OPIc 컴팩트 오픽

Pattern Drills 패턴 학습

Practice using the given sentence patterns to help you deliver your response clearly.
주어진 문장 패턴을 익혀 답변이 명확하게 전달될 수 있도록 연습해 보세요.

1 _____ has a special geography that has _____.
- Korea / the east side high and the west side low
- China / become a major draw for tourism
- The United States / shaped its economy

2 It has mountains and beautiful coastlines that offer _____.
- a playground for beach lovers and mountain explorers
- a refreshing escape from the hustle and bustle of city life
- a gateway to adventure

3 _____'s geography is important for _____.
- Korea / its logistics networks and diplomatic relations
- China / its tourism industry
- America / understanding its culture

4 Understanding the geography of your country helps you _____.
- explore the diverse natural attractions
- plan and organize outdoor activities and trips
- analyze and interpret the impact of climate and weather patterns

Mini Actual Test 연습 문제

🎧 21_1.mp3

Respond to the following question while keeping in mind what you have learned.
앞서 배운 내용을 떠올리면서 다음 질문에 답변해 보세요.

> Tell me about your country's geography. What distinctive geographical features does your country have compared to other countries? I'd like to know all the details about your country's geography.

Model Answer 모범 답안

 21_2.mp3

Enhance your response by referring to the model answer.
다음 모범 답안을 참고하여 여러분의 답변을 발전시켜 보세요.

> Korea has a special geography that makes it unique. It has mountains and beautiful coastlines that offer a diverse and stunning landscape. The mountains, like Mount Seorak and Mount Hallasan, are great for outdoor activities and have amazing views. Korea also has a long coastline with pretty beaches along the East and West Seas. There are many islands surrounding the Korean Peninsula, such as Jeju Island, which has unique volcanic terrain and natural beauty. The climate in Korea has distinct seasons, with hot and humid summers and cold winters. This creates different kinds of plants and forests. Korea's geography is important for its culture and economy. People love hiking and skiing in the mountains, which attract tourists and encourage locals to appreciate nature. The coastlines are good for fishing, seafood industries, and tourism. Understanding Korea's geography helps us appreciate its beauty and culture. It adds to the world's diversity and reminds us to protect these special places.

Level Up to AL AL 공략하기

Read the examples below and see how IH-level sentences can be rephrased at the AL level.
다음 예시를 읽고 IH 수준의 문장을 어떻게 AL 수준으로 바꾸어 말할 수 있는지 살펴보세요.

	IH	→	AL
❶	Korea has special geography that makes it unique.	→	Korea has special geography that makes it different from other places in the world.
❷	Korea's geography is important for its culture and economy.	→	The unique geographic features of Korea contribute to its cultural and economic aspects.
❸	The coastlines are good for fishing, seafood industries, and tourism.	→	The coastlines not only provide excellent fishing opportunities but also play a significant role in the development of the fishing industry and tourism.

출제 가능성 ★★★★☆

Q2 Describe the last place you visited in your country. What was the geography like? What was special about that place? What did you do there? Tell me everything about the landscape and why you went there.

Question Analysis 질문 분석

Answer the following questions and identify the key matter and the information to be included in your response.
다음 질문에 답하며 답변의 주제와 반드시 포함되어야 할 내용이 무엇인지 파악해 보세요.

1. What is going to be the key matter of your response?
2. What information should your response include?

Warm Your Brain Up 브레인스토밍

Answer the following questions for ideas.
다음 질문에 답하며 답변 소재를 발굴해 보세요.

Intro	• Have you ever been to an area in your country that has unique geographical features? • Where was the unique area located?
Body	• Why did you get to go to that area? • What were the distinctive geographical features of the area? • What activities did you do during your visit to the area?
Conclusion	• Did any geographical aspect add to your overall experience during your visit to the area?

AL Booster

- Did you have any expectations before going to that area?
- How did the area and its geographical features live up to your expectations?

explore geographically unique eastern range valley pristine extend as far as embark on exhilarating ascending steep trail be rewarded with panoramic vistas sandy shore gentle breeze soothing sound wave crash against peacefulness

Pattern Drills 패턴 학습

Practice using the given sentence patterns to help you deliver your response clearly.
주어진 문장 패턴을 익혀 답변이 명확하게 전달될 수 있도록 연습해 보세요.

❶
I have had the opportunity to _____.
- study abroad in France
- attend a music festival in Busan

❷
The region had _____.
- breathtaking natural landscapes
- a well-developed transportation system
- a comfortable climate

❸
During my visit, I embarked on _____.
- a captivating city tour
- a scenic boat tour
- an exciting hiking expedition

❹
This unique place left a strong impression on me because (of) _____.
- the vibrant colors and aromas
- the fascinating blend of traditional and modern elements
- its bustling atmosphere energized me

Mini Actual Test 연습 문제   🎧 21_3.mp3

Respond to the following question while keeping in mind what you have learned.
앞서 배운 내용을 떠올리면서 다음 질문에 답변해 보세요.

> Have you ever been to a geographically unique area in your country? Where was it and what did the place look like? What did you see and do there? What was special about that place? Please tell me in as much detail as possible.

Model Answer 모범 답안

🎧 21_4.mp3

Enhance your response by referring to the model answer.
다음 모범 답안을 참고하여 여러분의 답변을 발전시켜 보세요.

> Yes, I had the opportunity to explore a geographically unique area last summer. It was in the eastern part of Korea, surrounded by the Taebaek Mountain range. This area has big mountains like Mount Seorak with amazing views of valleys and forests. The region also has beautiful coastlines along the East Sea, with pristine beaches that extend as far as you can see. During my visit, I embarked on exhilarating hikes, ascending the steep trails of Mount Seorak and being rewarded with panoramic vistas. I also enjoyed peaceful moments on the sandy shores, feeling the gentle breeze and listening to the soothing sound of waves crashing against the rocks. This unique place left a strong impression on me because it combined the beauty of mountains and the peacefulness of the sea in one amazing spot.

Level Up to AL AL 공략하기

Read the examples below and see how IH-level sentences can be rephrased at the AL level.
다음 예시를 읽고 IH 수준의 문장을 어떻게 AL 수준으로 바꾸어 말할 수 있는지 살펴보세요.

IH → **AL**

① It was in the eastern part of Korea, surrounded by the Taebaek Mountain range. → It was in the eastern part of the country, nestled within the Taebaek Mountain range.

② This area has big mountains like Mount Seorak with amazing views of valleys and forests. → This area boasts towering mountains, such as Mount Seorak, which offers breathtaking vistas of sprawling valleys and lush forests.

출제 가능성 ★★★★☆

Q3 Tell me about a country that has similar geographical features to your country. Tell me about the people and traditions of the country. Please describe the country in as much detail as possible.

Question Analysis 질문 분석

Answer the following questions and identify the key matter and the information to be included in your response.
다음 질문에 답하며 답변의 주제와 반드시 포함되어야 할 내용이 무엇인지 파악해 보세요.

1. What is going to be the key matter of your response?
2. What information should your response include?

Warm Your Brain Up 브레인스토밍

Answer the following questions for ideas.
다음 질문에 답하며 답변 소재를 발굴해 보세요.

Intro	• Can you tell me about a country that shares similar geographical features with your country? • What is the biggest similarity between that country and your country?
Body	• What are some notable geographical features of that country? • How do you think those geographical features have affected the country's people and its culture? • Are there any similarities in terms of people and culture between that country and your country?
Conclusion	• Do you agree that similar geographical features are the most influential factors in shaping a country's culture and its people?

AL Booster

• Can you describe the landscapes, such as mountains, coastlines, or rivers, that are similar in both countries?

Useful Expressions

fascinating culture 매력적인 문화   diverse landscape 다양한 지형   unique tradition 독특한 전통   peak 정상, 봉우리
special meaning 특별한 의미   busy port 붐비는 항구   breathtaking view 숨막히는 경치   coastal tourism 해안 관광
be known for ~로 알려져 있다   abundant 풍부한   similarity 유사성   bring ~ together ~를 함께 모이게 하다
shape one's tradition 전통을 형성하다   value 가치를 두다, 소중히 여기다

Pattern Drills 패턴 학습

Practice using the given sentence patterns to help you deliver your response clearly.
주어진 문장 패턴을 익혀 답변이 명확하게 전달될 수 있도록 연습해 보세요.

❶

South Korea and _____ share similar geographical features and _____.

- China / rich historical connections
- Vietnam / vibrant culinary traditions
- Australia / a love for outdoor activities and sports

❷

Both countries have _____.

- a strong work ethic
- traditional festivals and celebrations
- a rich cultural heritage

❸

The coastlines of both countries have _____.

- charming coastal villages
- ferry services and scenic cruises
- vibrant seaside towns

❹

These similarities _____.

- create a sense of familiarity
- foster respect for each other's traditions
- serve as a foundation for building strong diplomatic relationships

Mini Actual Test 연습 문제   🎧 21_5.mp3

Respond to the following question while keeping in mind what you have learned.
앞서 배운 내용을 떠올리면서 다음 질문에 답변해 보세요.

> Can you share information about a country that shares similar geographical characteristics with your own? Please provide detailed descriptions of the country's people, traditions, and any other relevant details.

Model Answer 모범 답안

 21_6.mp3

Enhance your response by referring to the model answer.
다음 모범 답안을 참고하여 여러분의 답변을 발전시켜 보세요.

> South Korea and Japan share similar geographical features and fascinating cultures. They both have diverse landscapes, long histories, and unique traditions. Both countries have mountains with famous peaks, like Mount Seorak in South Korea and Mount Fuji in Japan. People love these mountains and they have special meaning in their cultures. The coastlines of both countries have beautiful beaches and busy ports. In South Korea, the coastline along the East Sea offers breathtaking views and opportunities for coastal tourism. Similarly, Japan's coastlines along the Pacific Ocean are known for their beauty and abundant seafood. These similarities bring the people together and shape their traditions. Learning about their customs shows how much they value nature and their geography.

Level Up to AL AL 공략하기

Read the examples below and see how IH-level sentences can be rephrased at the AL level.
다음 예시를 읽고 IH 수준의 문장을 어떻게 AL 수준으로 바꾸어 말할 수 있는지 살펴보세요.

IH → **AL**

❶ People love these mountains and they have special meaning in their cultures. → These mountains hold profound cultural significance and are deeply cherished by the people in both countries.

❷ Learning about their customs shows how much they value nature and their geography. → Exploring their customs provides insights into their deep appreciation for nature and the value they place on their geographical features.

Chapter 11 Geography·Environmental Issues 지형·환경 문제

Unit 22 Combo Set (2)

출제 가능성 ★★★☆☆

Q1 I'd like to know about problems or issues related to the environment that people have recently discussed. What things are people discussing the most and why are they so important in your society?

Question Analysis 질문 분석

Answer the following questions and identify the key matter and the information to be included in your response.
다음 질문에 답하며 답변의 주제와 반드시 포함되어야 할 내용이 무엇인지 파악해 보세요.

1. What is going to be the key matter of your response?
2. What information should your response include?

Warm Your Brain Up 브레인스토밍

Answer the following questions for ideas.
다음 질문에 답하며 답변 소재를 발굴해 보세요.

Intro	What are the environmental problems being discussed in our society?
Body	• What is the impact of climate change on ecosystems and humans? • Why are pollution and waste management a concern for the environment and human health? • Why is deforestation and habitat destruction a problem? • What are the dangers of plastic pollution in oceans and rivers?
Conclusion	• Why is it important to take action to solve these environmental problems?

AL Booster

- What are some specific examples of how each environmental issue affects our lives?
- What are the underlying causes of each environmental problem?

Useful Expressions

society 사회   environmental 환경의   big issue 큰 문제   ecosystem 생태계   waste 폐기물   big concern 큰 걱정거리
harm 해를 입히다   come up 나타나다, 제기되다   deforestation 산림 벌채   destroy 파괴하다   habitat 서식지
put ~ at risk ~을 위험에 빠뜨리다   polluted 오염된   harmful chemical 유해한 화학 물질   farming 농업   damage 손상시키다
grow 재배하다   plastic pollution 플라스틱으로 인한 환경 오염   marine life 해양 생물   take action 조치를 취하다

Chapter 11 Geography·Environmental Issues 지형·환경 문제   **233**

Pattern Drills 패턴 학습

Practice using the given sentence patterns to help you deliver your response clearly.
주어진 문장 패턴을 익혀 답변이 명확하게 전달될 수 있도록 연습해 보세요.

One of the big issues is _____.

❶
- waste management
- the loss of biodiversity
- the depletion of natural resources

Pollution and waste management are also big concerns because _____.

❷
- they have long-term consequences
- they can lead to the emergence of diseases
- they can contaminate air, water, and soil

Another topic that comes up a lot is _____.

❸
- the importance of raising awareness
- the reduction of single-use plastics
- the need for eco-friendly waste management

_____ is another issue because it can damage the environment.

❹
- Chemical pollution
- Deforestation
- Industrial waste

Mini Actual Test 연습 문제 🎧 22_1.mp3

Respond to the following question while keeping in mind what you have learned.
앞서 배운 내용을 떠올리면서 다음 질문에 답변해 보세요.

> What are the current environmental problems or issues being widely discussed in your society? Please highlight the key topics of discussion and explain their significance.

Model Answer 모범 답안  22_2.mp3

Enhance your response by referring to the model answer.
다음 모범 답안을 참고하여 여러분의 답변을 발전시켜 보세요.

> In our society, there are several important environmental problems that people are talking about right now. One of the big issues is climate change, which is causing a lot of problems for our ecosystems and for us humans. Pollution and waste management are also big concerns because they can harm the environment and our health. Another topic that comes up a lot is deforestation and the destruction of habitats, which is a problem because it puts many different plants and animals at risk. We also worry about not having enough clean water to drink and about water being polluted. Using harmful chemicals and practices in farming is another issue because it can damage the environment and make it difficult for us to grow enough food. Lastly, we talk about the problem of plastic pollution in our oceans and rivers, which is dangerous for marine life and for us. We need to take action now to solve these problems and protect our environment for the future.

Level Up to AL AL 공략하기

Read the examples below and see how IH-level sentences can be rephrased at the AL level.
다음 예시를 읽고 IH 수준의 문장을 어떻게 AL 수준으로 바꾸어 말할 수 있는지 살펴보세요.

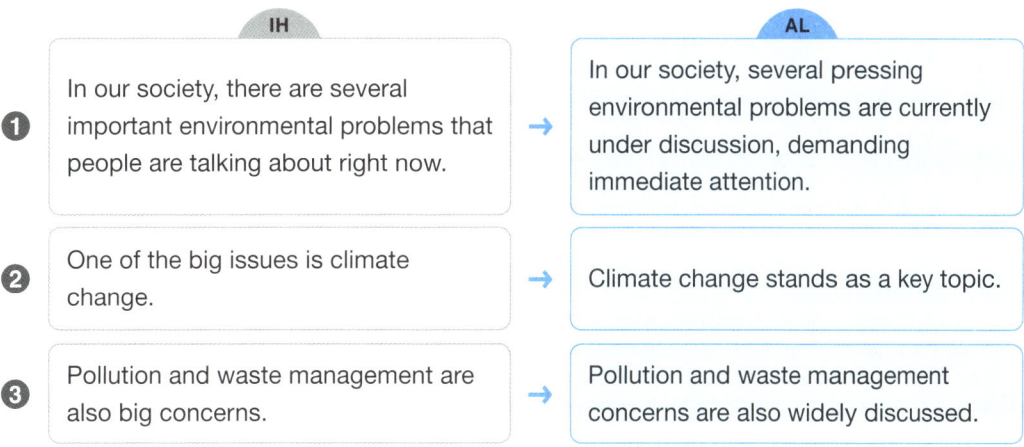

출제 가능성 ★★★★☆

Q2 These days we have many environmental issues, such as global warming and climate change. Global warming is the greatest challenge facing our planet. Please tell me about it in as much detail as possible.

Question Analysis 질문 분석

Answer the following questions and identify the key matter and the information to be included in your response.
다음 질문에 답하며 답변의 주제와 반드시 포함되어야 할 내용이 무엇인지 파악해 보세요.

1. What is going to be the key matter of your response?
2. What information should your response include?

Warm Your Brain Up 브레인스토밍

Answer the following questions for ideas.
다음 질문에 답하며 답변 소재를 발굴해 보세요.

Intro	• Why has global warming become a major environmental problem? • What is global warming?
Body	• What causes global warming, particularly in relation to human activities? • What are the consequences of global warming? • What challenges exist in combating global warming, including political and economic obstacles?
Conclusion	• How can we contribute to solving the problem of global warming?

AL Booster

- How does global warming impact ecosystems, including melting ice and rising sea levels?
- What are the risks associated with global warming for human health, agriculture, and food security?

Useful Expressions

global warming 지구 온난화   major 주요한   face 직면하다   greenhouse gas 온실 가스   burn 태우다   fossil fuel 화석 연료
cut down forest 산림을 벌채하다   consequence 결과   lead to ~을 초래하다, ~로 이어지다   rainfall pattern 강수 패턴
extreme weather event 극단적인 기상 (이변으로 인한) 사건   melting ice 녹고 있는 빙하   rising sea levels 상승하는 해수면
at risk 위험에 처한   overcome 극복하다   raise awareness 인식을 고취시키다   gas emission 가스 배출   adapt to ~에 적응하다
next generation 다음 세대

Pattern Drills 패턴 학습

Practice using the given sentence patterns to help you deliver your response clearly.
주어진 문장 패턴을 익혀 답변이 명확하게 전달될 수 있도록 연습해 보세요.

①
Global warming is a major environmental problem that _____.
- challenges us to rethink our consumption patterns
- calls for widespread awareness and education
- demands innovative solutions to reduce its impacts

②
Global warming leads to _____.
- the spread of diseases
- increased energy demands
- social and geopolitical challenges

③
To solve this problem, we need everyone to _____.
- take collective action
- prioritize environmental conservation
- engage in meaningful discussions

④
By taking action now, we can _____.
- reduce greenhouse gas emissions
- make a positive difference
- adapt to a changing climate

Mini Actual Test 연습 문제

🎧 22_3.mp3

Respond to the following question while keeping in mind what you have learned.
앞서 배운 내용을 떠올리면서 다음 질문에 답변해 보세요.

> Currently, there are numerous environmental concerns, including global warming and climate change. What are your thoughts on global warming? Please provide a detailed explanation of its causes, impacts, and any other relevant information.

Model Answer 모범 답안

 22_4.mp3

Enhance your response by referring to the model answer.
다음 모범 답안을 참고하여 여러분의 답변을 발전시켜 보세요.

> Global warming is a major environmental problem that our planet is currently facing. It happens when there are more greenhouse gasses in the air, mostly because of things people do. Burning fossil fuels and cutting down forests are some of the main reasons for this. Global warming has many consequences. It leads to higher temperatures, changes in rainfall patterns, and more extreme weather events. It also affects ecosystems, such as melting ice and rising sea levels, which harm plants and animals. Human health, agriculture, and food security are also at risk. The world has agreements like the Paris Agreement to try and stop global warming. However, there are challenges to overcome, especially those related to politics and money. To solve this problem, we need everyone to work together and raise awareness about reducing greenhouse gas emissions and adapting to a changing climate. By taking action now, we can create a better future for our planet and the next generations.

Level Up to AL AL 공략하기

Read the examples below and see how IH-level sentences can be rephrased at the AL level.
다음 예시를 읽고 IH 수준의 문장을 어떻게 AL 수준으로 바꾸어 말할 수 있는지 살펴보세요.

IH → **AL**

❶ It happens when there are more greenhouse gasses in the air, mostly because of things people do. → It occurs when there is an increase in greenhouse gasses in the Earth's atmosphere, mostly caused by human activities.

❷ The world has agreements like the Paris Agreement to try and stop global warming. → International agreements like the Paris Agreement aim to reduce global warming by using more renewable energy sources.

출제 가능성 ★★★★☆

Q3 How has the weather changed over the years? What do you think causes climate change? How has it affected the lives of people in your country?

Question Analysis 질문 분석

Answer the following questions and identify the key matter and the information to be included in your response.
다음 질문에 답하며 답변의 주제와 반드시 포함되어야 할 내용이 무엇인지 파악해 보세요.

1. What is going to be the key matter of your response?
2. What information should your response include?

Warm Your Brain Up 브레인스토밍

Answer the following questions for ideas.
다음 질문에 답하며 답변 소재를 발굴해 보세요.

Intro	Have you observed any changes in the weather patterns over the years?
Body	• What are the notable changes in weather patterns over the years? • What factors do you believe contribute to climate change? • How has climate change impacted the lives of people in your country?
Conclusion	• What are the potential implications of weather changes on various aspects of life? • How can we contribute to resolving the problem?

AL Booster

- What impact does climate change have on the seasons of your country?
- Are there any climate phenomena you are currently experiencing that you never encountered during your childhood?

Useful Expressions

notice 주목하다   be connected to ~와 연결되다   all around the world 전 세계적으로   heatwave 폭염   extremely hot 극도로 더운   on the other hand 반면에   milder 더 온화한   freezing temperature 꽁꽁 얼게 추운 기온   be caused by ~에 의해 야기되다   trap 가두다   heat from the sun 태양의 열   as a result 과학적 연구 결과로   rainfall pattern 강수 패턴   typhoon 태풍   combine A with B A와 B를 결합하다   observe 관찰하다   scientific research   spread awareness 인식을 확산시키다   lessen 줄이다, 경감시키다

Pattern Drills 패턴 학습

Practice using the given sentence patterns to help you deliver your response clearly.
주어진 문장 패턴을 익혀 답변이 명확하게 전달될 수 있도록 연습해 보세요.

❶ In Korea, we have noticed some big changes in _____.
- the amount of snowfall during the winter season
- the duration of heatwaves
- the intensity of rainfall

❷ In summer, we have been experiencing _____.
- hotter temperatures than usual
- longer and more intense heat waves
- more frequent and intense thunderstorms

❸ These changes are caused by _____.
- industrialization and the expansion of urban areas
- the excessive burning of fossil fuels
- the inefficient use of energy

❹ By _____, we can learn more about the climate.
- monitoring greenhouse gas concentrations
- conducting scientific research
- studying climate data and trends

Mini Actual Test 연습 문제 🎧 22_5.mp3

Respond to the following question while keeping in mind what you have learned.
앞서 배운 내용을 떠올리면서 다음 질문에 답변해 보세요.

> What significant changes in weather patterns have been observed over the years? How have people in your country been affected by climate change?

Model Answer 모범 답안 🎧 22_6.mp3

Enhance your response by referring to the model answer.
다음 모범 답안을 참고하여 여러분의 답변을 발전시켜 보세요.

> In Korea, we have noticed some big changes in the weather, and these changes are connected to climate change happening all around the world. Summers have become hotter and longer, and we have been experiencing more heatwaves and extremely hot days. On the other hand, winters have become milder, with less snow and shorter periods of freezing temperatures. These changes are caused by the increase in greenhouse gasses in the air, which trap heat from the sun. As a result, temperatures are going up, rainfall patterns are changing, and we are seeing stronger typhoons. By combining what we personally observe with scientific research, we can learn more about climate change in Korea. It's important to spread awareness about it and take action to lessen its impact.

Level Up to AL AL 공략하기

Read the examples below and see how IH-level sentences can be rephrased at the AL level.
다음 예시를 읽고 IH 수준의 문장을 어떻게 AL 수준으로 바꾸어 말할 수 있는지 살펴보세요.

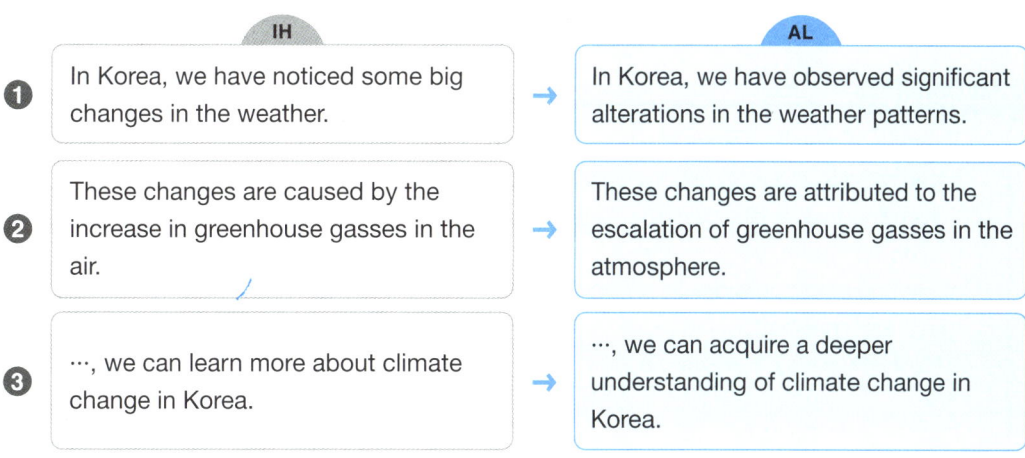

IH		AL
❶ In Korea, we have noticed some big changes in the weather.	→	In Korea, we have observed significant alterations in the weather patterns.
❷ These changes are caused by the increase in greenhouse gasses in the air.	→	These changes are attributed to the escalation of greenhouse gasses in the atmosphere.
❸ ···, we can learn more about climate change in Korea.	→	···, we can acquire a deeper understanding of climate change in Korea.

Chapter 12 Transportation · Health 교통·건강

✓ Strategy Check 주제 관련 전략

Check the following strategies related to the topic of this chapter.
이 챕터의 주제와 관련된 시험 대비 전략을 확인해 보세요.

IH Essential

- "Transportation" is one of the most frequently presented topics. Take some time to think about various transportation methods around you and choose the ones you often use. It's essential to create your own stories and examples related to your chosen transportation methods.
'교통'은 가장 자주 출제되는 돌발 주제 중 하나입니다. 주변 교통수단을 잘 떠올려 보고, 본인이 평소 자주 이용하는 교통수단을 골라 자신만의 이야기를 만들어 놓을 필요가 있습니다.

- When questions related to "Transportation" are presented, they are most likely to follow the sequence of "preferred method of transportation and reasons, changes in transportation methods from childhood to the present, and issues encountered while using transportation."
'교통' 관련 문제가 출제되는 경우, 주로 '선호하는 교통 수단과 이유,' '어릴 때와 지금의 교통수단 변화,' '교통수단을 이용하면서 생긴 문제' 순서로 콤보가 전개될 확률이 높습니다.

- "Health" is also a topic that quite frequently appears in the test. When faced with questions related to "Health," it is recommended to approach them with ease and confidence. Think about someone you consider healthy and create stories related to their characteristics, habits, etc. It is important to prepare stories in connection with topics previously covered, such as "Walking," "Jogging," "Hiking," and more.
'건강' 또한 시험에서 꽤 자주 마주치게 되는 주제입니다. '건강' 관련 문제가 출제되었을 때, 쉽게 접근하여 답변을 풀어나갈 것을 권장합니다. 평소 본인이 건강하다고 생각하는 사람을 떠올리며, 그 사람의 특성이나 습관 등과 관련해 이야기를 만들어 놓는 것이 중요합니다. 또한 앞서 다루었던 '걷기,' '조깅,' '하이킹' 등의 주제와 연계해 답변을 준비할 수도 있습니다.

AL Booster

- To achieve a high score in the test, the most crucial aspect to focus on is the well-organized structure of responses. When faced with questions that require in-depth thinking, consider discussing only two aspects. For example, if asked about activities you do for health, you can focus on 'exercise' and 'diet' in your response. Similarly, for questions about changes in transportation methods, you can compare and contrast the 'past' and 'present'.
본시험에서 높은 등급을 얻기 위해 가장 신경 써야 할 부분은 짜임새 있는 답변의 구성입니다. 복잡한 사고를 요하는 문제가 출제되었을 경우, 두 가지 측면만 이야기할 것이라고 생각해 보십시오. 예를 들어, 평소 건강을 위해 하는 활동을 묻는 질문에는 '운동'과 '식단'에 초점을 맞추어 답변할 수 있고, 교통수단의 변화를 묻는 질문에는 '과거'와 '현재'를 대조하여 답변할 수 있습니다.

❓ Frequently Asked Questions 빈출 질문 유형

Here are the most frequently asked question types related to the topic. Try to identify <u>the key matter</u> of the question and <u>the information</u> that should be included in your response.
이 챕터의 주제와 관련해 자주 출제되는 질문 유형들을 확인해 보세요. 그리고 각 질문의 중심 소재와 답변에 어떤 정보를 포함시켜야 하는지 파악해 보세요.

Transportation	• I would like to know about public transportation in your country. What kind of transportation do people use to get around? Do you use public transportation, or do you drive? Which one do you prefer to take and why? • Tell me about a time when you had trouble due to a certain mode of transportation. What exactly happened, and how did you deal with the situation? Give me all the details. • Sometimes riding the subway or bus can be uncomfortable. Have you ever had any problems related to transportation? Were there traffic jams, or did something uncomfortable happen? What was the problem, and how did you deal with the situation? • Transportation systems have improved. Have there been any changes to transportation in your country since you were young? What are the changes between the past and the present?
Health	• Tell me about a healthy person you have met. What does he or she look like? What kind of food does he or she usually eat? Please explain in detail. • What do you do to stay healthy? What kind of exercise do you usually do? Explain what you do in detail. • Have you ever had to stop doing something because of your health? What was it that you had to give up? What about now? Give as many details as you can.

Chapter 12 Transportation · Health 교통·건강

Unit 23 Combo Set (1)

MP3 바로가기

출제 가능성 ★★★★☆

Q1 I would like to know about public transportation in your country. What kind of transportation do people use to get around? Do you use public transportation, or do you drive? Which one do you prefer to take and why?

▶ Question Analysis 질문 분석

Answer the following questions and identify the key matter and the information to be included in your response.
다음 질문에 답하며 답변의 주제와 반드시 포함되어야 할 내용이 무엇인지 파악해 보세요.

1. What is going to be the key matter of your response?
2. What information should your response include?

▶ Warm Your Brain Up 브레인스토밍

Answer the following questions for ideas.
다음 질문에 답하며 답변 소재를 발굴해 보세요.

Intro
- What kind of transportation do people use to get around in your country?
- How essential is public transportation in the daily lives of people?

Body
- What are the advantages of using public transportation?
- What are the challenges or drawbacks of public transportation?
- Which public transportation modes do you prefer using and why?

Conclusion
- What factors influence your choice between public transportation and private driving?
- What improvements have been made to the public transportation system?

▣ AL Booster

- How reliable and efficient is the public transportation system?
- How affordable is public transportation compared to private transportation options?

▣ Useful Expressions

public transportation 대중교통 convenient 편리한 efficient 효율적인 travel 이동하다 extensive 광범위한
reduce traffic 교통량을 감소시키다 be better for ~에게 유리하다, 더 좋다 affordable 경제적인, 가격이 합리적인 delay 지연
crowded 혼잡한 during busy times 붐비는 시간 동안 personally 개인적으로 cheaper 더 저렴한 less stressful 덜 스트레스 받는
get better 더 나아지다 different modes of 다양한 방식의 passenger 승객

Pattern Drills 패턴 학습

Practice using the given sentence patterns to help you deliver your response clearly.
주어진 문장 패턴을 익혀 답변이 명확하게 전달될 수 있도록 연습해 보세요.

1 Public transportation is a _____ way for people to travel.
- time-saving
- cost-effective
- convenient

2 However, there can sometimes be _____.
- limited seating
- schedule changes
- overcrowding

3 I prefer using public transportation because _____.
- it reduces my carbon footprint
- it allows me to avoid the stress of driving
- it allows me to read or work during my commute

4 It is easier to _____.
- reach my destination
- explore new places
- avoid traffic congestion

Mini Actual Test 연습 문제

23_1.mp3

Respond to the following question while keeping in mind what you have learned.
앞서 배운 내용을 떠올리면서 다음 질문에 답변해 보세요.

> Tell me about public transportation in your country. What kind of transportation do people use to travel around? Do you personally rely on public transportation or do you drive? Why?

Model Answer 모범 답안

🎧 23_2.mp3

Enhance your response by referring to the model answer.
다음 모범 답안을 참고하여 여러분의 답변을 발전시켜 보세요.

> Public transportation is very important in Korea, especially in big cities like Seoul, where I live. It is a convenient and efficient way for people to travel. We have an extensive network of buses, subways, and trains, allowing people to travel easily. Public transportation in Korea has many benefits. It helps reduce traffic and is better for the environment. It is also affordable for people who use it every day. However, sometimes there can be delays, and the buses or trains can be very crowded during busy times. Personally, I prefer using public transportation in Seoul because it is cheaper and less stressful than driving, and it helps protect the environment. Recently, the public transportation system in Seoul has gotten better. It is easier to connect to different modes of transportation, and there are new technologies and services that make it more convenient for passengers.

Level Up to AL AL 공략하기

Read the examples below and see how IH-level sentences can be rephrased at the AL level.
다음 예시를 읽고 IH 수준의 문장을 어떻게 AL 수준으로 바꾸어 말할 수 있는지 살펴보세요.

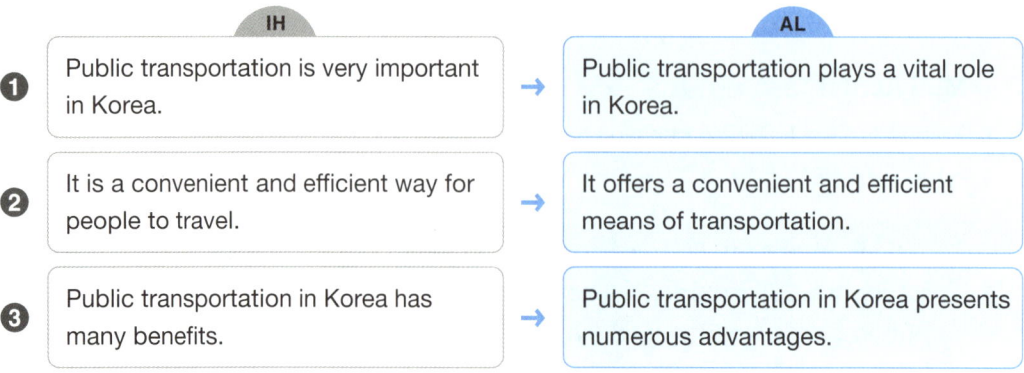

	IH	→	AL
❶	Public transportation is very important in Korea.	→	Public transportation plays a vital role in Korea.
❷	It is a convenient and efficient way for people to travel.	→	It offers a convenient and efficient means of transportation.
❸	Public transportation in Korea has many benefits.	→	Public transportation in Korea presents numerous advantages.

출제 가능성 ★★★★☆

Q2 Sometimes riding the subway or bus can be uncomfortable. Have you ever had any problems related to transportation? Were there traffic jams, or did something uncomfortable happen? What was the problem, and how did you deal with the situation?

Question Analysis 질문 분석

Answer the following questions and identify the key matter and the information to be included in your response.
다음 질문에 답하며 답변의 주제와 반드시 포함되어야 할 내용이 무엇인지 파악해 보세요.

1. What is going to be the key matter of your response?
2. What information should your response include?

Warm Your Brain Up 브레인스토밍

Answer the following questions for ideas.
다음 질문에 답하며 답변 소재를 발굴해 보세요.

Intro	How often do you rely on subways or buses? Have you ever encountered any uncomfortable situation while using public transportation?
Body	• Where and when did it happen? • Could you give me more details about the situation where you faced the problem? • What made the experience uncomfortable and how did you deal with the situation?
Conclusion	• Reflecting on your experience, how did it impact your perception of public transportation?

AL Booster
• Did you seek assistance from any authority or fellow passengers?

Useful Expressions

indeed 정말로   encounter 마주치다, 경험하다   stand out 두드러지다   board 탑승하다   crowded 혼잡한
during rush hour 붐비는 시간에   packed 가득찬   cramped aisle 좁은 통로   for the entire journey 이동하는 내내
maintain one's balance 균형을 유지하다   hold onto ~을 꽉 붙잡다   handrail 손잡이   stability 안정성
immediate solution 즉각적인 해결책   at maximum capacity 수용 인원으로   peak hours 가장 수요가 많은 시간대
occasional 가끔의   discomfort 불편함   appreciate 감사하게 여기다   affordability 가격 대비 이익

Chapter 12 Transportation·Health 교통·건강   247

Pattern Drills 패턴 학습

Practice using the given sentence patterns to help you deliver your response clearly.
주어진 문장 패턴을 익혀 답변이 명확하게 전달될 수 있도록 연습해 보세요.

①
I have personally encountered a few problems while _____.
- attempting to assemble the furniture
- cooking a complicated recipe
- troubleshooting technical issues on my computer

②
One incident that stands out was when _____.
- I lost my wallet on the bus
- my car broke down in the middle of nowhere
- I got locked out of my house

③
However, I learned from this experience and now try to _____.
- plan my vacations in advance
- prioritize self-care
- seek assistance when facing challenging situations

④
Despite occasional discomfort, I still _____.
- make time for regular exercise
- recognize the significance of helping others
- cherish the moments of joy

Mini Actual Test 연습 문제

🎧 23_3.mp3

Respond to the following question while keeping in mind what you have learned.
앞서 배운 내용을 떠올리면서 다음 질문에 답변해 보세요.

> Sometimes using the transportation system can cause discomfort. Have you ever had any problems while taking public transportation? What happened? How did you deal with it?

Model Answer 모범 답안

Enhance your response by referring to the model answer.
다음 모범 답안을 참고하여 여러분의 답변을 발전시켜 보세요.

> Sometimes riding the subway or bus can indeed be uncomfortable. I have personally encountered a few problems while taking public transportation. One incident that stands out was when I boarded a crowded bus during rush hour. The bus was packed, and I had to stand in the cramped aisle for the entire journey. It was hot, stuffy, and uncomfortable. To deal with it, I tried to maintain my balance and hold on to the handrails for stability. Unfortunately, there was no immediate solution at that moment, as the bus was already at maximum capacity. However, I learned from this experience and now try to avoid peak hours whenever possible. I also bring a book or listen to music to make the journey more enjoyable. Despite occasional discomfort, I still appreciate the convenience and affordability of public transportation in my daily life.

Level Up to AL AL 공략하기

Read the examples below and see how IH-level sentences can be rephrased at the AL level.
다음 예시를 읽고 IH 수준의 문장을 어떻게 AL 수준으로 바꾸어 말할 수 있는지 살펴보세요.

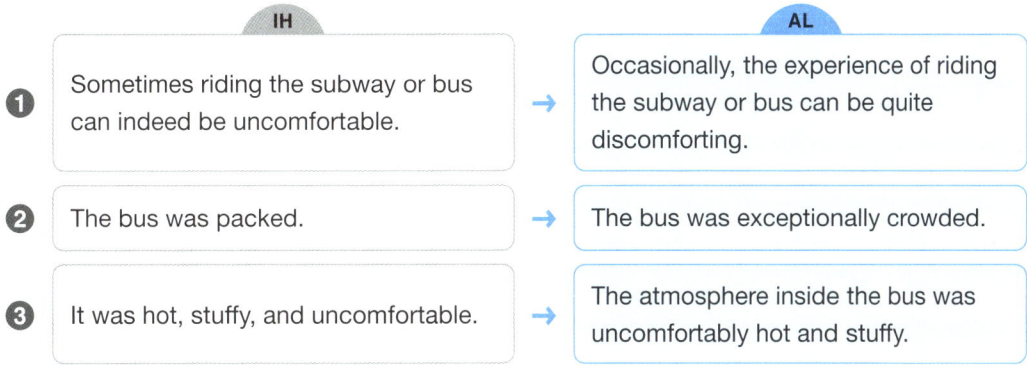

출제 가능성 ★★★★☆

Q3 Transportation systems have definitely improved. Have there been any changes to transportation in your country since you were young? What are the changes between the past and the present?

> ### Question Analysis 질문 분석

Answer the following questions and identify the key matter and the information to be included in your response.
다음 질문에 답하며 답변의 주제와 반드시 포함되어야 할 내용이 무엇인지 파악해 보세요.

1. What is going to be the key matter of your response?
2. What information should your response include?

> ### Warm Your Brain Up 브레인스토밍

Answer the following questions for ideas.
다음 질문에 답하며 답변 소재를 발굴해 보세요.

Intro	Do you think transportation systems in your country have changed a lot? Why do you think so?
Body	• What were the main modes of transportation in the past? • What are some alternative options available now, for instance, e-bikes and e-kickboards? • How have cities improved their transportation infrastructure?
Conclusion	• What benefits have resulted from these changes? • What future improvements are you excited to see?

AL Booster

• How has public transportation become more convenient and accessible?

Useful Expressions

mainly 주로   rely on 의존하다   ride-sharing service 카풀 서비스   electric vehicle 전기차   completely 완전히   transform 변화시키다   travel 이동하다   additionally 추가로   e-bike 전동 자전거   e-kickboard 전동 킥보드   transportation infrastructure 교통 인프라   implement 도입하다, 실행하다   smart system 스마트 시스템   better manage 더 잘 관리하다   traffic flow 교통 흐름   environmentally friendly 환경 친화적인   accessible 접근 가능한   get around 이동하다, 다니다   improvement 개선, 발전   happen 일어나다, 발생하다

Pattern Drills 패턴 학습

Practice using the given sentence patterns to help you deliver your response clearly.
주어진 문장 패턴을 익혀 답변이 명확하게 전달될 수 있도록 연습해 보세요.

① In the past, people mainly relied on _____.
- trains for long-distance travel
- traditional taxis for their transportation needs
- bicycles or walking to get to places

② We have new technologies like _____ that _____.
- smart home devices / allow us to control our household appliances
- smartphones and mobile apps / have revolutionized communication
- virtual reality headsets / provide immersive entertainment experiences

③ These changes have made transportation _____.
- safer and more secure
- more interconnected and seamless
- more reliable and punctual

④ Personally, I think these changes are great because _____.
- they make commuting more convenient and time-efficient
- they provide a wider range of choices for getting around
- they enhance the overall quality of transportation services

Mini Actual Test 연습 문제   🎧 23_5.mp3

Respond to the following question while keeping in mind what you have learned.
앞서 배운 내용을 떠올리면서 다음 질문에 답변해 보세요.

> Tell me about the transportation you used in the past and what you use now.

Model Answer 모범 답안

 23_6.mp3

Enhance your response by referring to the model answer.
다음 모범 답안을 참고하여 여러분의 답변을 발전시켜 보세요.

> Transportation systems in my country have changed a lot since I was young. In the past, people mainly relied on their own cars and regular buses for transportation. But now, things are very different. We have new technologies like ride-sharing services and electric vehicles that have completely transformed how we travel. Additionally, there are other options like e-bikes and e-kickboards that we can rent and use anywhere in the city. Moreover, our cities have made improvements in transportation infrastructure by implementing smart systems to better manage traffic flow. These changes have made transportation more efficient and environmentally friendly. Public transportation has also become more convenient and accessible for everyone. Personally, I think these changes are great because they make it easier to get around and they're better for our planet. I'm excited to see what other improvements will happen in the future.

Level Up to AL AL 공략하기

Read the examples below and see how IH-level sentences can be rephrased at the AL level.
다음 예시를 읽고 IH 수준의 문장을 어떻게 AL 수준으로 바꾸어 말할 수 있는지 살펴보세요.

	IH	→	AL
①	Transportation systems in my country have changed a lot since I was young.	→	Transportation systems in my country have undergone significant changes since I was young.
②	But now, things are very different.	→	However, things have greatly evolved.
③	These changes have made transportation more efficient and environmentally friendly.	→	These changes have resulted in more efficient and eco-friendly transportation options.

Chapter 12 Transportation·Health 교통·건강

Unit 24 Combo Set (2)

Q1 Tell me about a healthy person you have met. What does he or she look like? What kind of food does he or she usually eat to stay healthy? Please explain in detail.

출제 가능성 ★★★☆☆

Question Analysis 질문 분석

Answer the following questions and identify the key matter and the information to be included in your response.
다음 질문에 답하며 답변의 주제와 반드시 포함되어야 할 내용이 무엇인지 파악해 보세요.

1. What is going to be the key matter of your response?
2. What information should your response include?

Warm Your Brain Up 브레인스토밍

Answer the following questions for ideas.
다음 질문에 답하며 답변 소재를 발굴해 보세요.

Intro	• Who is a healthy person you know? • Could you describe their physical appearance and overall well-being?
Body	• How does this person's appearance reflect their commitment to health? • What kind of food do they usually eat for their well-being?
Conclusion	• How does this person's healthy lifestyle affect your own?

AL Booster

• Could you tell me about the time when you realized that this person is very healthy?

Useful Expressions

take good care of 잘 돌보다 well-being 건강과 안녕 both A and B A와 B 둘 다 energetic 활기찬 appearance 외모
fit body 건강한 몸 vibrant skin 생기 넘치는 피부 even considering one's age ~의 나이를 고려하더라도
when it comes to ~에 관해서 이야기하면 focus on 집중하다 balanced 균형 잡힌 lean protein 저지방 단백질
consciously 의식적으로 processed food 가공 식품 sugary drink 당분이 많은 음료 herbal tea 허브 차 portion control 양 조절
strong commitment to ~에 대한 강한 몰두 lead a healthy lifestyle 건강한 삶을 살다 serve as ~로서 기능하다 motivation 동기
inspire ~ to … ~에게 …하도록 영감을 주다 top priority 최우선 사항

Pattern Drills 패턴 학습

Practice using the given sentence patterns to help you deliver your response clearly.
주어진 문장 패턴을 익혀 답변이 명확하게 전달될 수 있도록 연습해 보세요.

①
> I know a very healthy person who _____.

- maintains a balanced diet
- inspires others to make their own well-being a top priority
- consciously chooses water over sugary drinks

②
> When it comes to food, he/she focuses on _____.

- choosing nutrient-dense options
- including a variety of colors on their plate
- cooking at home and using fresh ingredients

③
> Additionally, he/she engages in _____.

- outdoor activities such as hiking
- regular cardiovascular exercise
- strength training exercises
- flexibility exercises like yoga

④
> Their strong commitment to _____ serves as _____.

- regular exercise / a model for others to lead an active life
- healthy lifestyle / an inspiration for others to prioritize their well-being
- self-care / a reminder for others to take care of their mental and physical health

Mini Actual Test 연습 문제 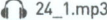 24_1.mp3

Respond to the following question while keeping in mind what you have learned.
앞서 배운 내용을 떠올리면서 다음 질문에 답변해 보세요.

> Do you know anyone who maintains good health? How would you describe their appearance? What types of food do they typically consume to prioritize their well-being? Please provide a detailed explanation.

Model Answer 모범 답안

🎧 24_2.mp3

Enhance your response by referring to the model answer.
다음 모범 답안을 참고하여 여러분의 답변을 발전시켜 보세요.

> I know a very healthy couple who takes good care of their well-being: my parents. They both have a healthy and energetic appearance, with fit bodies and vibrant skin, especially considering their age. When it comes to food, they focus on eating a balanced diet that includes lots of fruits, vegetables, lean proteins like eggs and fish, and whole grains. They consciously avoid processed foods and sugary drinks, preferring water and herbal teas instead. Portion control is also important to them. They prefer eating smaller meals throughout the day. Additionally, they engage in regular physical exercise, such as hiking and yoga. Their strong commitment to leading a healthy lifestyle serves as a source of motivation not just for me but also for other members of our family. It inspires us to make our own well-being a top priority.

Level Up to AL AL 공략하기

Read the examples below and see how IH-level sentences can be rephrased at the AL level.
다음 예시를 읽고 IH 수준의 문장을 어떻게 AL 수준으로 바꾸어 말할 수 있는지 살펴보세요.

IH	→	AL
❶ Portion control is also important to them.	→	They also pay attention to portion control, ensuring they eat appropriate serving sizes.
❷ Their strong commitment to leading a healthy lifestyle serves as a source of motivation not just for me but also for other members of our family. It inspires us to make our own well-being a top priority.	→	Their dedication to a healthy lifestyle serves as an inspiration not only to me but also to other family members, encouraging us to prioritize our own well-being.

Chapter 12 Transportation·Health 교통·건강 **255**

출제 가능성 ★★★☆☆

Q2 What do you do to stay healthy? What kind of exercise do you usually do? What kind of food do you eat? Explain what you do in detail.

Question Analysis 질문 분석

Answer the following questions and identify the key matter and the information to be included in your response.
다음 질문에 답하며 답변의 주제와 반드시 포함되어야 할 내용이 무엇인지 파악해 보세요.

1. What is going to be the key matter of your response?
2. What information should your response include?

Warm Your Brain Up 브레인스토밍

Answer the following questions for ideas.
다음 질문에 답하며 답변 소재를 발굴해 보세요.

Intro	• How do you prioritize your health in your daily life? • Why is it important for you to stay healthy?
Body	• What kind of exercise do you typically engage in to stay fit? • How frequently do you exercise and for how long? • What does a typical meal plan look like for you? • How do you ensure that you have a balanced diet that includes essential nutrients?
Conclusion	• How do your exercise and dietary choices contribute to your overall well-being?

AL Booster

- When did you realize that your health is important and prioritize it?
- What advice or recommendations would you give to others who want to maintain a healthy lifestyle?

Useful Expressions

prioritize 우선순위를 정하다   regular exercise 규칙적인 운동   balanced diet 균형 잡힌 식단   engage in ~에 참여하다, 관여하다
strength training 근력 훈련   aim to ~를 목표로 하다   at least 최소한   rich 풍부한   whole grain 도정 안 된 곡물, 전곡
lean protein 저지방 단백질   processed food 가공 식품   sugary snack 당분이 많은 간식   opt for ~을 선택하다
alternative 대안   portion control 양 조절   maintain a healthy weight 건강한 체중을 유지하다
have a positive impact on ~에 긍정적인 영향을 미치다   energetic 활기찬   improve stamina 체력을 향상시키다
ongoing 지속적인   dedication 헌신   worth 가치가 있는

Pattern Drills 패턴 학습

Practice using the given sentence patterns to help you deliver your response clearly.
주어진 문장 패턴을 익혀 답변이 명확하게 전달될 수 있도록 연습해 보세요.

❶
To stay healthy, I prioritize _____.
- getting enough sleep each night
- stress management by practicing meditation
- staying hydrated by drinking plenty of water

❷
I try to avoid _____.
- fried foods
- excessive caffeine consumption
- skipping meals and prioritize regular eating patterns

❸
Portion control is important to me to _____.
- avoid feeling overly full
- balance my nutrient intake
- prevent overeating and promote digestion

❹
These choices have had a positive impact on _____.
- preventing food waste
- maintaining consistent energy levels throughout the day
- preventing the temptation of overeating

Mini Actual Test 연습 문제 🎧 24_3.mp3

Respond to the following question while keeping in mind what you have learned.
앞서 배운 내용을 떠올리면서 다음 질문에 답변해 보세요.

> Please explain how you maintain your health. What type of physical exercise do you typically engage in, and what kind of food do you usually eat?

Model Answer 모범 답안

Enhance your response by referring to the model answer.
다음 모범 답안을 참고하여 여러분의 답변을 발전시켜 보세요.

> To stay healthy, I prioritize my well-being through regular exercise and a balanced diet. For exercise, I engage in activities like jogging, hiking, and strength training. I aim to exercise for at least 30 minutes, five times a week. When it comes to food, I focus on a balanced diet rich in fruits, vegetables, whole grains, and lean proteins like chicken and fish. I try to avoid processed foods and sugary snacks, opting for healthier alternatives instead. Portion control is important for me to maintain a healthy weight. These choices have had a positive impact on my physical and mental well-being. I feel more energetic, have improved stamina, and experience better overall health. It's an ongoing journey that requires dedication, but the benefits are worth it.

Level Up to AL AL 공략하기

Read the examples below and see how IH-level sentences can be rephrased at the AL level.
다음 예시를 읽고 IH 수준의 문장을 어떻게 AL 수준으로 바꾸어 말할 수 있는지 살펴보세요.

IH	AL
❶ To stay healthy, I prioritize my well-being through regular exercise and a balanced diet.	→ To maintain my health, I try to focus on two important things: regular exercise and a balanced diet.
❷ I feel more energetic, have improved stamina, and experience better overall health.	→ By following these practices, I've noticed improvements in my energy levels, stamina, and overall well-being.

출제 가능성 ★★☆☆☆

Q3 Have you ever had to stop doing something for your health? What was it that you had to give up? What about now? Give as many details as you can.

Question Analysis 질문 분석

Answer the following questions and identify the key matter and the information to be included in your response.
다음 질문에 답하며 답변의 주제와 반드시 포함되어야 할 내용이 무엇인지 파악해 보세요.

1. What is going to be the key matter of your response?
2. What information should your response include?

Warm Your Brain Up 브레인스토밍

Answer the following questions for ideas.
다음 질문에 답하며 답변 소재를 발굴해 보세요.

Intro	• What did you have to give up for the sake of your health? • Why did you have to give it up?
Body	• Was it easy for you to give it up? • What challenges did you face and how did you deal with them? • What positive changes did you experience in your well-being after you gave it up?
Conclusion	• What did you learn from your experience?

AL Booster

• How do you hope your experience will inspire others to make positive changes for their health?

Useful Expressions

for the sake of ~을 위해서   give up 포기하다   processed sugar 가공 설탕   have a big impact on ~에 큰 영향을 미치다
require 요구하다   cut out 제거하다, 끊다   have cravings 갈망을 느끼다   stay committed to ~에 꾸준히 헌신하다
satisfy one's cravings ~의 갈망을 충족하다   natural sweetener 천연 감미료   improve one's energy level ~의 체력 수준을 향상시키다
manage one's weight ~의 체중을 관리하다   mindful 의식하는, 염두에 두는   inspire ~ to … ~에게 …하도록 영감을 주다
positive 긍정적인   diet 식단

Chapter 12 Transportation·Health 교통·건강

Pattern Drills 패턴 학습

Practice using the given sentence patterns to help you deliver your response clearly.
주어진 문장 패턴을 익혀 답변이 명확하게 전달될 수 있도록 연습해 보세요.

❶
There have been times when I decided to _____.
- take a break from social media
- challenge myself and participate in a marathon
- prioritize my well-being over work commitments

❷
This decision had a big impact on _____.
- my physical health and fitness level
- my overall well-being and quality of life
- my mental and emotional state

❸
I learned the importance of _____.
- gratitude and appreciating the little things in life
- embracing change in life
- effective communication in building strong relationships

❹
I hope my experience inspires others to _____.
- prioritize their mental health
- embrace self-love and practice self-care
- engage in acts of kindness in their communities

Mini Actual Test 연습 문제 🎧 24_5.mp3

Respond to the following question while keeping in mind what you have learned.
앞서 배운 내용을 떠올리면서 다음 질문에 답변해 보세요.

> **Tell me about the times when you had to stop doing certain activities because of your health. What were the things you had to give up? And how are things for you now? Please provide a detailed explanation.**

Model Answer 모범 답안

 24_6.mp3

Enhance your response by referring to the model answer.
다음 모범 답안을 참고하여 여러분의 답변을 발전시켜 보세요.

> There were times when I decided to stop eating a certain type of food for the sake of my health. One memory that stands out is when I chose to give up processed sugar. This decision had a big impact on how I felt and required changing my eating habits. I realized that eating too much processed sugar was bad for me, so I chose to cut it out. It wasn't easy, especially when I had cravings or was around sugary snacks. However, I stayed committed to my well-being. I found healthier ways to satisfy my sweet cravings, like eating fruits or making treats with natural sweeteners. Cutting processed sugar out of my diet helped improve my energy levels, helped manage my weight, and made me feel better overall. It took some effort, but the positive effects were worth it. I learned the importance of being mindful of what I eat and making choices that support my health goals. I hope my experience inspires others to make positive changes in their diet for their own well-being.

Level Up to AL AL 공략하기

Read the examples below and see how IH-level sentences can be rephrased at the AL level.
다음 예시를 읽고 IH 수준의 문장을 어떻게 AL 수준으로 바꾸어 말할 수 있는지 살펴보세요.

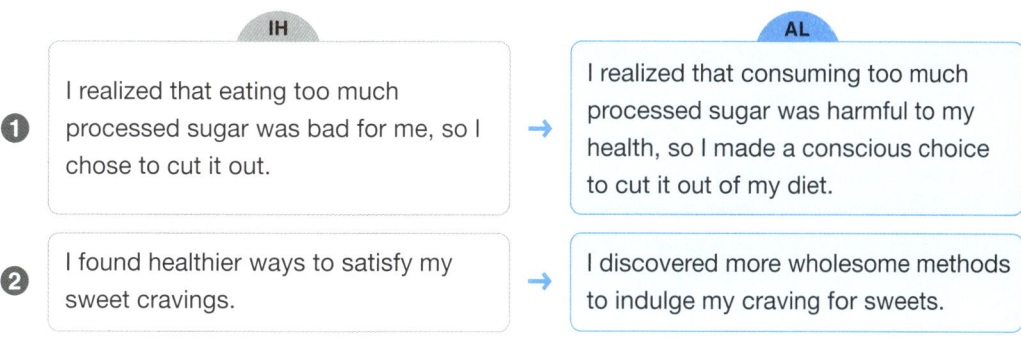

Chapter 13 Bank 은행

✓ Strategy Check 주제 관련 전략

Check the following strategies related to the topic of this chapter.
이 챕터의 주제와 관련된 시험 대비 전략을 확인해 보세요.

IH Essential

- As in the previous chapter, "Bank" is also one of the most frequently presented topics. Specially, questions that require to narrate your experiences or do a role-play are very frequently presented, so it is important to thoroughly prepare for various types of questions.
  이전 단원과 마찬가지로, '은행' 또한 가장 자주 출제되는 돌발 주제 중 하나입니다. 특히 경험 등을 '서술'하라는 문제와 '역할극'을 요하는 문제가 매우 빈번하게 출제되기 때문에, 여러 유형의 문제에 꼼꼼하게 대비해 두는 것이 중요합니다.

- If "Bank" related questions are presented in the test, there is a high probability that the questions requiring you to describe a typical bank in Korea, explain the tasks you do at a bank, and compare banks in the past and present (or describe a memorable experience at a bank) will be presented in a row.
  본시험에서 '은행' 관련 문제가 출제된다면 '한국의 보편적인 은행을 설명하라,' '은행에 가서 하는 업무를 설명하라,' '과거와 현재의 은행을 비교하라(또는 '인상 깊은 은행에서의 일을 설명하라')'는 문제가 콤보로 전개될 확률이 높습니다.

- Some of the questions related to "Bank" can be answered using a similar response structure as the one related to "Technology," which will be covered in the next chapter. For example, in a question that asks you to compare banks in the past with those of the present day, you can prepare your response by saying, "In the past, people had to physically go to the bank to handle their transactions, but now, with the use of mobile phones, they can access financial services remotely."
  '은행' 관련 문제 중 다음 챕터에서 다루게 될 '기술' 주제와 연계하여 답변할 수 있는 문제들이 있습니다. 예를 들어, 은행의 과거와 현재를 비교하라는 질문에 대해서는 '예전에는 은행에 직접 가서 업무를 처리했지만, 지금은 휴대 전화를 이용해서 원격으로 금융 업무를 볼 수 있다'는 흐름으로 답변을 준비할 수 있습니다.

AL Booster

- One of the most frequently presented types of role-play questions is "ask questions." In this "ask questions" type, you will ask questions related to the given situation and topic. In this case, instead of simply listing questions, if you incorporate your own stories or explanations into the questions, you can receive a higher score. For example, after asking a question, if you add the reason why you are asking that particular question or provide additional context, your response can be evaluated as a more advanced one.
  본시험에서 가장 자주 출제되는 역할극 문제 유형 중 하나는 '질문하기'입니다. 이 '질문하기' 유형에서는 주어진 상황을 바탕으로 주제와 관련된 질문을 하라는 문제가 출제됩니다. 이때, 단순히 질문만 나열하기보다 질문 속에 본인의 이야기를 추가로 녹여 답변하면 높은 점수를 받을 수 있습니다. 예를 들어, 질문을 한 뒤 본인이 그와 같은 질문을 하는 이유나 상황을 추가적으로 설명한다면 더 수준 높은 답변으로 평가 받을 수 있습니다.

❓ Frequently Asked Questions 빈출 질문 유형

Here are the most frequently asked question types related to the topic. Try to identify the key matter of the question and the information that should be included in your response.
이 챕터의 주제와 관련해 자주 출제되는 질문 유형들을 확인해 보세요. 그리고 각 질문의 중심 소재와 답변에 어떤 정보를 포함시켜야 하는지 파악해 보세요.

Bank	• Let's talk about a bank in your country. What does it look like? What are the people like who work there? Provide as many details as you can. • Tell me about what you usually do at a bank. What do you do from the moment you walk into the bank until you walk out? • When was the last time you went to a bank? What did you do? Why did you go there? Please describe your experience in detail. • You may have a memorable experience related to a bank. When was it? What exactly happened? Please tell me about your experience in detail.
Role-play	• You want to open a bank account, so you decide to make a call to the bank's sales person but get a voicemail. Leave a message making three to four inquiries about opening a new account. • I'd like to give you a situation to act out. Your bank statement says that you spent one million won last month. However, you didn't spend that amount of money. Call customer service and ask three or four questions to find out what happened. • I am sorry, but there is a problem that I need you to resolve. You just got your credit card but found out that there is something wrong with it. Call the bank, explain the situation, and solve the problem.

Chapter 13 · Bank 은행

Unit 25 · Combo Set (1)

MP3 바로가기

출제 가능성 ★★★★★

Q1 Let's talk about a bank in your country. What does it look like? How are the people who work there? Provide as many details as you can.

Question Analysis 질문 분석

Answer the following questions and identify the key matter and the information to be included in your response.
다음 질문에 답하며 답변의 주제와 반드시 포함되어야 할 내용이 무엇인지 파악해 보세요.

1. What is going to be the key matter of your response?
2. What information should your response include?

Warm Your Brain Up 브레인스토밍

Answer the following questions for ideas.
다음 질문에 답하며 답변 소재를 발굴해 보세요.

Intro	• Which bank do people in your country mainly use?
Body	• Does the bank have offline branches? If so, how does the bank usually look from the outside and what are the different areas inside the bank? • What are the people who work there like? What roles do they have, and how are they dressed?
Conclusion	• What kind of feeling do you get when you think about the appearance of the bank or the attire of the staff?

AL Booster

- What are the typical features or characteristics of the buildings where banks are located?
- Is there any specific etiquette or behavior expected from the bank staff while interacting with customers?

Useful Expressions

financial service 금융 서비스   professional 전문적인; 전문가   from the outside 외부에서   sleek 매끄러운   architecture 건축
clear sign 명확한 표지판   be divided into ~로 나누어지다   teller counter 창구   customer service zone 고객 서비스 구역
private office 개인 사무실   knowledgeable 지식이 있는   skilled 숙련된   bank teller 은행원   representative 대표
loan officer 대출 담당자   branch manager 지점 관리자   polite 예의 바른   appearance 외모   dedication to ~에 대한 전념
professionalism 전문성   reliability 신뢰성   customer satisfaction 고객 만족도

Pattern Drills 패턴 학습

Practice using the given sentence patterns to help you deliver your response clearly.
주어진 문장 패턴을 익혀 답변이 명확하게 전달될 수 있도록 연습해 보세요.

1
When you look at a bank, it looks _____ from the outside.
- imposing
- professional
- inviting
- secure

2
The buildings are well-designed with _____.
- attractive exteriors and eye-catching details
- functional layouts and efficient use of space
- accessible entrances and user-friendly features

3
Inside, the bank is divided into _____.
- individual offices and workstations for employees
- well-defined areas to facilitate smooth customer flow
- distinct zones catering to different services and functions

4
The bank employees are always _____.
- friendly and approachable
- attentive and responsive
- customer-oriented and focused
- punctual and organized

Mini Actual Test 연습 문제

25_1.mp3

Respond to the following question while keeping in mind what you have learned.
앞서 배운 내용을 떠올리면서 다음 질문에 답변해 보세요.

> I'd like to learn about a bank in your country. Could you describe its appearance and provide detailed information about the people who work there?

Model Answer 모범 답안

 25_2.mp3

Enhance your response by referring to the model answer.
다음 모범 답안을 참고하여 여러분의 답변을 발전시켜 보세요.

> Banks in my country are very important for the economy. They help with financial services that people need. When you look at a bank, it looks modern and professional from the outside. The buildings are well-designed with sleek architecture, glass walls, and clear signs. Inside, the bank is divided into different areas, such as teller counters, customer service zones, and private offices. The employees at the bank are highly knowledgeable and skilled professionals. They have various roles, including bank tellers, customer service representatives, loan officers, and branch managers. They dress nicely in formal clothes to look professional. The bank employees are always polite and helpful when they talk to customers. They want to make sure everyone feels good and gets the help they need. Overall, the appearance and the people working at banks reflect a dedication to professionalism, reliability, and customer satisfaction.

Level Up to AL AL 공략하기

Read the examples below and see how IH-level sentences can be rephrased at the AL level.
다음 예시를 읽고 IH 수준의 문장을 어떻게 AL 수준으로 바꾸어 말할 수 있는지 살펴보세요.

IH		AL
❶ Banks in my country are very important for the economy.	→	In my country, banks play a vital role in the economy.
❷ When you look at a bank, it looks modern and professional from the outside.	→	A typical bank stands out with its modern and professional look.
❸ They dress nicely in formal clothes to look professional.	→	The bank staff dress formally in business attire to maintain a professional appearance.

출제 가능성 ★★★★★

Q2 Tell me about what you usually do at a bank. What do you do from the moment you walk into the bank until you walk out?

Question Analysis 질문 분석

Answer the following questions and identify the key matter and the information to be included in your response.
다음 질문에 답하며 답변의 주제와 반드시 포함되어야 할 내용이 무엇인지 파악해 보세요.

1. What is going to be the key matter of your response?
2. What information should your response include?

Warm Your Brain Up 브레인스토밍

Answer the following questions for ideas.
다음 질문에 답하며 답변 소재를 발굴해 보세요.

Intro
- What are the usual operating hours of banks in your country?
- When you enter a bank, what is the first thing you do?

Body
- What tasks do you typically perform at the teller counter?
- Are there any additional areas or services you utilize within the bank?
- Have the banking transactions you've tried to get done so far been generally well handled?

Conclusion
- What do you think are the benefits of visiting a bank in person to get your tasks done?

AL Booster

- How do you ensure the security of your transactions at the bank?
- What are the most memorable experiences where you realized the benefits of visiting a bank in person to get your tasks done?

Useful Expressions

involve 포함하다   from the moment ~하는 순간부터   customer service area 고객 서비스 구역   wait in line 줄 서서 기다리다
once it's my turn 내 차례가 되면   purpose 목적   withdrawal 인출   deposit 입금   inquiry 조회   teller counter 출납 창구
necessary document 필요한 서류   transaction 거래   loan department 대출 부서   investment advisory 투자 상담
depending on ~에 따라   prioritize 우선순위를 정하다; 우선으로 처리하다   security 보안   ensure 확실히 하다   required 필요한, 요구되는
authentication 인증   identification 본인 인증   procedure 절차   interact with ~와 상호 작용하다   query 질문   guidance 안내

Pattern Drills 패턴 학습

Practice using the given sentence patterns to help you deliver your response clearly.
주어진 문장 패턴을 익혀 답변이 명확하게 전달될 수 있도록 연습해 보세요.

Once it's my turn, I _____ .

①
- approach the teller and make a deposit
- explain my inquiry to the customer service representative
- request a withdrawal from the teller
- discuss my investment options with the financial advisor

At the teller counter, I _____ .

②
- complete my withdrawal transaction
- update my personal information
- discuss loan options with the bank representative
- check my account balance

During my visit, I prioritize _____ .

③
- efficient and timely service
- the privacy of my personal and financial information
- resolving any issues or concerns I may have

Throughout the process, I may interact with _____ .

④
- bank tellers who assist me with my transaction
- loan officers who help me with loan applications
- the technology personnel, who help me reset my password

Mini Actual Test 연습 문제

🎧 25_3.mp3

Respond to the following question while keeping in mind what you have learned.
앞서 배운 내용을 떠올리면서 다음 질문에 답변해 보세요.

> **What are your typical activities at a bank? What tasks do you typically perform from the moment you enter the bank until the moment you leave?**

Model Answer 모범 답안

🎧 25_4.mp3

Enhance your response by referring to the model answer.
다음 모범 답안을 참고하여 여러분의 답변을 발전시켜 보세요.

> At a bank, my typical activities involve several steps from the moment I enter until I leave. First, I go to the customer service area and wait in line or get a ticket. Once it's my turn, I communicate with the bank staff, explaining the purpose of my visit, whether it's a withdrawal, deposit, or inquiry. At the teller counter, I provide the necessary documents and complete the transaction. Sometimes I might go to other places in the bank, like the loan department or investment advisory, depending on what I need. During my visit, I prioritize the security of my transactions, being sure to follow any required authentication or identification procedures. Throughout the process, I may interact with bank staff who assist me with my queries or offer guidance. Overall, these things show how important it is for banks to offer us different financial services and to make it easy to do our transactions.

Level Up to AL AL 공략하기

Read the examples below and see how IH-level sentences can be rephrased at the AL level.
다음 예시를 읽고 IH 수준의 문장을 어떻게 AL 수준으로 바꾸어 말할 수 있는지 살펴보세요.

IH	→	AL
❶ First, I go to the customer service area and wait in line or get a ticket.	→	Firstly, I approach the customer service area, where I may wait in a queue or take a ticket.
❷ Sometimes I might go to other places in the bank, like the loan department or investment advisory, depending on what I need.	→	Depending on my needs, I may also visit other areas, such as the loan department or investment advisory.
❸ Overall, these things show how important it is for banks to offer us different financial services and to make it easy to do our transactions.	→	Overall, these activities highlight the essential role of banks in providing a range of financial services and facilitating smooth transactions for customers.

출제 가능성 ★★★★☆

Q3 When was the last time you went to a bank? Why did you go there? What did you do? Please describe your experience in detail.

Question Analysis 질문 분석

Answer the following questions and identify the key matter and the information to be included in your response.
다음 질문에 답하며 답변의 주제와 반드시 포함되어야 할 내용이 무엇인지 파악해 보세요.

1. What is going to be the key matter of your response?
2. What information should your response include?

Warm Your Brain Up 브레인스토밍

Answer the following questions for ideas.
다음 질문에 답하며 답변 소재를 발굴해 보세요.

Intro	• When did you visit the bank? • Why did you go to the bank? • What tasks did you have to do during your visit?
Body	• What process did you go through to get your tasks done?
Conclusion	• Did the bank meet your financial needs? • How would you describe your overall experience at the bank?

AL Booster

• How was your interaction with the bank staff?
• How did they help you and how did you feel about it?

Useful Expressions

branch 지점　**recently** 최근에　**take care of** 처리하다　**make a deposit** 입금하다　**wait for one's turn** ~의 차례를 기다리다　**friendly** 친절한　**greet ~ with a smile** ~에게 미소로 인사하다　**fill out** 작성하다　**deposit slip** 입금 신청서　**along with** ~와 함께　**process** 처리하다; 처리 과정　**receipt** 영수증　**get a loan** 대출 받다　**direct A to B** A를 B로 안내하다　**different options** 다양한 선택지　**loan application** 대출 신청　**go smoothly** 원활하게 진행되다　**leave feeling satisfied with** ~에 만족한 채로 떠나다

Pattern Drills 패턴 학습

Practice using the given sentence patterns to help you deliver your response clearly.
주어진 문장 패턴을 익혀 답변이 명확하게 전달될 수 있도록 연습해 보세요.

1 When I entered the bank, I went to _____.
- the teller counter to deposit some cash
- the customer service desk to inquire about opening a new account
- the ATM section to withdraw some money

2 I filled out _____ with the necessary information.
- the withdrawal slip
- the credit card application
- the address change form

3 They directed me to _____.
- the new accounts' section
- online banking support
- the loan department

4 I left feeling satisfied with _____.
- their level of professionalism
- the efficiency of the transactions
- my overall experience
- the resolution of my concerns

Mini Actual Test 연습 문제

🎧 25_5.mp3

Respond to the following question while keeping in mind what you have learned.
앞서 배운 내용을 떠올리면서 다음 질문에 답변해 보세요.

> **Can you recall your most recent visit to a bank? What was the reason for your visit and what tasks did you perform during your visit? Please provide a detailed description of your experience.**

Model Answer 모범 답안

 25_6.mp3

Enhance your response by referring to the model answer.
다음 모범 답안을 참고하여 여러분의 답변을 발전시켜 보세요.

> I visited a branch of ABC Bank recently to deal with some important business. It happened about two weeks ago, and I had a few things to take care of. First, I needed to make a deposit. When I entered the bank, I went to the customer service area and waited for my turn. The bank staff was friendly and greeted me with a smile. I filled out a deposit slip with the necessary information and gave it to the teller along with the cash I had. The teller processed everything quickly and gave me a receipt. I also had some questions about getting a loan for a future project. They directed me to the loan department, where a friendly loan officer explained different options and helped me with the loan application. Overall, my experience at the bank was good. The staff was helpful, and everything went smoothly. It met my financial needs, and I left feeling satisfied with their services.

Level Up to AL AL 공략하기

Read the examples below and see how IH-level sentences can be rephrased at the AL level.
다음 예시를 읽고 IH 수준의 문장을 어떻게 AL 수준으로 바꾸어 말할 수 있는지 살펴보세요.

IH	AL
① When I entered the bank, I went to the customer service area and waited for my turn.	Upon entering the bank, I proceeded to the customer service area and waited patiently for my turn.
② The bank staff was friendly and greeted me with a smile.	The bank staff greeted me with friendly smiles, creating a welcoming atmosphere.
③ The staff was helpful, and everything went smoothly.	The staff members were extremely helpful and made the whole process smooth and efficient.

Chapter 13 Bank 은행

Unit 26 Combo Set (2)

MP3 바로가기

출제 가능성 ★★★★☆

Q1 You want to open a bank account, so you decide to make a call to the bank's sales person but get voicemail. Leave a message with three to four inquiries about opening a new account.

Question Analysis 질문 분석

Answer the following questions and identify the key matter and the information to be included in your response.
다음 질문에 답하며 답변의 주제와 반드시 포함되어야 할 내용이 무엇인지 파악해 보세요.

1. What is going to be the key matter of your response?
2. What information should your response include?

Warm Your Brain Up 브레인스토밍

Answer the following questions for ideas.
다음 질문에 답하며 답변 소재를 발굴해 보세요.

Intro	Why are you leaving a voice message for the bank? How would you explain the purpose of your message?
Body	• What are the specific things you would like to ask the bank? • What additional information are you seeking from them?
Conclusion	• How would you request that the bank return your call? • How will you address them before ending the call?

AL Booster

- What factors should you consider before proceeding with the account creation process?
- What information or documents may be required to open an account?

Useful Expressions

bank account 은행 계좌   representative 대표자   get a voicemail 음성 메시지를 받다   leave a message 메시지를 남기다   process 과정   open a new account 새 계좌를 개설하다   available 이용할 수 있는   specific 특정한, 구체적인   feature 특징   benefit 혜택   document 문서   provide A with B A에게 B를 제공하다   required 필요한   be aware of ~을 알다   fee 수수료   charge 요금   associated with ~와 관련된   look forward to ~을 기대하다   response 답변

Pattern Drills 패턴 학습

Practice using the given sentence patterns to help you deliver your response clearly.
주어진 문장 패턴을 익혀 답변이 명확하게 전달될 수 있도록 연습해 보세요.

① I'm leaving a message to _____.
- request more information about a bank account
- inquire about the status of my order

② Could you please explain _____?
- the process for opening a deposit account
- how the new security features on the website work

③ What documents and information do I need to bring in order to _____?
- open a business bank account
- apply for a loan

④ Are there any fees or charges associated with _____?
- opening a business bank account
- withdrawing cash from an ATM

Mini Actual Test 연습 문제

🎧 26_1.mp3

Respond to the following question while keeping in mind what you have learned.
앞서 배운 내용을 떠올리면서 다음 질문에 답변해 보세요.

> I'd like to give you a situation and ask you to act it out. You decided to create an account with the bank and contact their sales representative via phone. However, when you call, you reach their voicemail instead. You leave a message and ask three to four questions regarding the process of setting up a new account.

Model Answer 모범 답안

🎧 26_2.mp3

Enhance your response by referring to the model answer.
다음 모범 답안을 참고하여 여러분의 답변을 발전시켜 보세요.

> Hello, I want to open a bank account, but when I called the bank's representative they didn't answer and I got their voicemail. So I'm leaving a message to ask about the process of opening a new account. I have a few questions that I would like to ask. Firstly, could you please explain the different types of accounts available and their specific features and benefits? Next, what documents and information do I need to bring in order to open an account? Can you provide me with a list of the specific documents required and any important requirements I should be aware of? Lastly, are there any fees or charges associated with opening a bank account? Would you please call me back soon to discuss these questions? Thank you, and I look forward to your response.

Level Up to AL AL 공략하기

Read the examples below and see how IH-level sentences can be rephrased at the AL level.
다음 예시를 읽고 IH 수준의 문장을 어떻게 AL 수준으로 바꾸어 말할 수 있는지 살펴보세요.

IH → **AL**

❶ Firstly, could you please explain the different types of accounts available and their specific features and benefits?
→ Firstly, could you please explain the different types of accounts available and their specific features and benefits? This will help me choose the account that aligns with my financial goals.

❷ Lastly, are there any fees or charges associated with opening a bank account?
→ Lastly, are there any fees or charges associated with opening a bank account? I would appreciate understanding the costs involved as well as any minimum deposit requirements for each type of account.

Chapter 13 Bank 은행 **275**

출제 가능성 ★★★★☆

Q2 I am sorry, but there is a problem that I need you to resolve. You just got your credit card but found out that there is something wrong with it. Call the bank, explain the situation, and solve the problem.

Question Analysis 질문 분석

Answer the following questions and identify the key matter and the information to be included in your response.
다음 질문에 답하며 답변의 주제와 반드시 포함되어야 할 내용이 무엇인지 파악해 보세요.

1. What is going to be the key matter of your response?
2. What information should your response include?

Warm Your Brain Up 브레인스토밍

Answer the following questions for ideas.
다음 질문에 답하며 답변 소재를 발굴해 보세요.

Intro	• How would you explain the purpose of the call? • What situation would you assume there is if you have a problem with your credit card?
Body	• How would you describe the situation? • How would you respond to the bank representative's answers?
Conclusion	• What is a suitable manner to express gratitude to the representative for helping you solve the problem? • How would you conclude the conversation?

AL Booster

• What are the possible responses that the bank representative might give you?

Useful Expressions

recently 최근에   receive 받다   unfortunately 불행히도   discover 발견하다   issue 문제   assist 돕다   resolve 해결하다
matter 문제   look into ~을 살피다   every time 매번, ~할 때마다   attempt to ~하려고 시도하다   make a purchase 구매하다
get declined 거절 당하다   despite ~에도 불구하고   sufficient 충분한   funds 자금   available 이용 가능한   account 계좌
multiple times 여러 번   occur 발생하다   activation sticker 활성화 스티커   appreciate 감사하다   address an issue 문제를 해결하다
prompt 신속한   assistance 도움

Pattern Drills 패턴 학습

Practice using the given sentence patterns to help you deliver your response clearly.
주어진 문장 패턴을 익혀 답변이 명확하게 전달될 수 있도록 연습해 보세요.

Unfortunately, I've discovered that _____ .

①
- there is an unauthorized transaction in my checking account
- my credit card statement shows incorrect charges
- my online banking login credentials are not working

Thank you for your help in _____ .

②
- understanding the process
- guiding me through the steps
- taking prompt action
- clarifying the situation

Every time I attempt to _____ , _____ .

③
- withdraw cash from the ATM / it shows an error message
- transfer funds online / the transaction fails
- check my account balance / the system displays an incorrect figure

This has happened multiple times, and I'm _____ .

④
- frustrated
- starting to lose patience
- at a loss for an explanation
- getting quite annoyed

Mini Actual Test 연습 문제

🎧 26_3.mp3

Respond to the following question while keeping in mind what you have learned.
앞서 배운 내용을 떠올리면서 다음 질문에 답변해 보세요.

> I'd like to give you a situation and ask you to act it out. You received your new credit card, but you've just found out that there is something wrong with it. Contact the bank, describe the situation, and ask the bank for the solution to your situation.

Model Answer 모범 답안

Enhance your response by referring to the model answer.
다음 모범 답안을 참고하여 여러분의 답변을 발전시켜 보세요.

> Hello, I recently received my new credit card, but, unfortunately, I've discovered that there is an issue with it. I was hoping you could assist me in resolving this matter. Every time I attempt to make a purchase using the card, it gets declined, despite having sufficient funds available in my account. This has happened multiple times, and I'm unsure why it's occurring. Yes, I removed the activation sticker when I received the card. Alright, I understand. Sure, I will wait. Yes, I'm still here. Thank you for finding the cause of the problem. I appreciate your help in resolving this issue. That sounds great. I'm glad we could address this issue quickly. Thank you for your prompt assistance. No, that's all for now. I appreciate your help and excellent customer service.

Level Up to AL AL 공략하기

Read the examples below and see how IH-level sentences can be rephrased at the AL level.
다음 예시를 읽고 IH 수준의 문장을 어떻게 AL 수준으로 바꾸어 말할 수 있는지 살펴보세요.

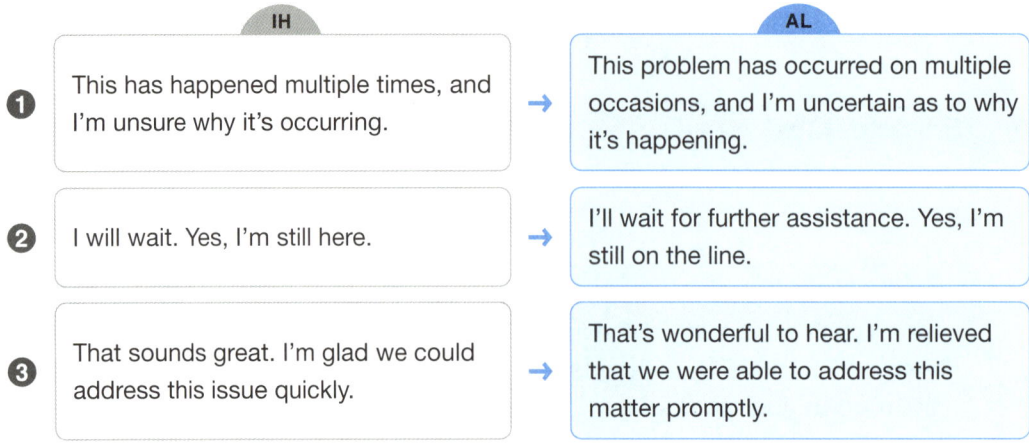

출제 가능성 ★★★★☆

Q3 You may have a memorable experience in a bank. When was it? What exactly happened? Please tell me about your experience in detail.

Question Analysis 질문 분석

Answer the following questions and identify the key matter and the information to be included in your response.
다음 질문에 답하며 답변의 주제와 반드시 포함되어야 할 내용이 무엇인지 파악해 보세요.

1. What is going to be the key matter of your response?
2. What information should your response include?

Warm Your Brain Up 브레인스토밍

Answer the following questions for ideas.
다음 질문에 답하며 답변 소재를 발굴해 보세요.

Intro	Have you ever had a memorable experience in a bank? When and where did it happen?
Body	• Can you describe the situation? • What was the reaction of the bank like? How did they assist you to handle the situation?
Conclusion	• How did the experience affect your perception of the bank's customer service? • What would you do if you encounter a similar situation in the future?

AL Booster

• How did you feel throughout the process of solving the problem?

memorable deposit be down cause a delay process transaction frustrating anticipate encounter bank staff handle assure work on fix an issue alternative option online banking nearby branch longer than expected ease patient adaptable

Pattern Drills 패턴 학습

Practice using the given sentence patterns to help you deliver your response clearly.
주어진 문장 패턴을 익혀 답변이 명확하게 전달될 수 있도록 연습해 보세요.

❶
> This was frustrating because _____.

- I couldn't withdraw cash from the ATM
- the bank charged me an unexpected fee
- the bank's online banking system was inaccessible

❷
> They suggested alternative options like _____.

- transferring funds through mobile banking applications
- visiting a different branch of the bank
- using a prepaid debit card for making purchases

❸
> This experience taught me _____.

- the value of maintaining open communication with bank staff
- to be more patient when facing unexpected challenges
- the need to regularly review my bank statements

❹
> I would advise others to _____.

- maintain a backup payment method
- stay informed about the various online banking features and available services
- keep a record of important banking information

Mini Actual Test 연습 문제

🎧 26_5.mp3

Respond to the following question while keeping in mind what you have learned.
앞서 배운 내용을 떠올리면서 다음 질문에 답변해 보세요.

> Talk about a memorable experience you've personally had at a bank. What happened and how did you deal with the situation?

> **Model Answer** 모범 답안

Enhance your response by referring to the model answer.
다음 모범 답안을 참고하여 여러분의 답변을 발전시켜 보세요.

> Last year, I had a memorable experience at a bank when I went to deposit some cash. Unfortunately, the bank's system was down, causing a delay in processing transactions. This was frustrating because I never anticipated such an issue at the bank. However, the bank staff handled the situation professionally and assured me they were working on fixing the issue. They suggested alternative options like using online banking or visiting a nearby branch to solve my problem. I chose online banking and was able to complete the transaction successfully, although it took longer than expected. The bank's quick response and helpfulness in offering alternatives eased my frustration. This experience taught me the importance of being patient and adaptable when unexpected problems occur. I would advise others to consider different banking options and maintain open communication with the bank's staff during similar situations.

> **Level Up to AL** AL 공략하기

Read the examples below and see how IH-level sentences can be rephrased at the AL level.
다음 예시를 읽고 IH 수준의 문장을 어떻게 AL 수준으로 바꾸어 말할 수 있는지 살펴보세요.

IH → **AL**

❶ Unfortunately, the bank's system was down, causing a delay in processing transactions. → Unfortunately, the bank's system experienced a technical failure, rendering it temporarily inaccessible to process transactions.

❷ They suggested alternative options. → The bank personnel proposed alternative options.

Chapter 14

Technology · Internet 기술·인터넷

✓ Strategy Check 주제 관련 전략

Check the following strategies related to the topic of this chapter.
이 챕터의 주제와 관련된 시험 대비 전략을 확인해 보세요.

IH Essential

- If we analyze recent past exam questions related to "Technology," we can see that not only descriptive questions but also role-play type questions are frequently being asked. Therefore, it is recommended to prepare your response for this question type using various devices such as smartphones, computers, and laptops as a subject.
  최근 '기술' 관련 기출 문제를 분석해 보면, 서술을 요하는 문제뿐만 아니라 역할극 유형의 문제 또한 자주 출제되고 있습니다. 따라서 스마트폰, 컴퓨터, 노트북과 같이 다양한 기기를 소재로 해당 문제 유형에 대비해 놓는 것을 권장합니다.

- One of the topics that can be easily related to "Technology" is the "Internet." By recalling your experiences of using the Internet on different electronic devices, you can efficiently prepare for the test. Think about the websites you frequently visit or the applications you often use and prepare your responses accordingly.
  '기술'과 쉽게 연계할 수 있는 주제로는 '인터넷'이 있습니다. 다양한 전자 기기로 인터넷을 한 경험을 떠올리며 답변을 준비해 놓으면 효율적으로 시험에 대비할 수 있습니다. 본인이 평소 자주 방문하는 웹 사이트나 즐겨 찾는 어플리케이션을 떠올리면서 답변을 준비해 보세요.

AL Booster

- The most challenging question among those related to "Technology" is the one that asks you to explain the development of a specific technology by comparing the present to the past. In this case, the content of your response does not necessarily have to be factual. Also, it is important to pay attention to the use of tenses such as past, present, and present perfect to avoid losing points.
  '기술'과 관련하여 출제되는 문제 중 가장 까다로운 것은 특정 기술이 어떻게 발달하고 있는지 과거와 현재를 비교하여 설명하라는 문제입니다. 이때, 답변 내용이 반드시 사실일 필요는 없음을 유념하면서 과거, 현재, 현재 완료 등 시제 사용에 주의를 기울여 감점을 받지 않도록 하는 것이 중요합니다.

❓ Frequently Asked Questions 빈출 질문 유형

Here are the most frequently asked question types related to the topic. Try to identify the key matter of the question and the information that should be included in your response.
이 챕터의 주제와 관련해 자주 출제되는 질문 유형들을 확인해 보세요. 그리고 각 질문의 중심 소재와 답변에 어떤 정보를 포함시켜야 하는지 파악해 보세요.

Technology	• What piece of technology do people use every day? How do people use it? Why is it so widely used? • Can you describe all the technologies, such as a cell phone or computer, that you enjoy using most these days? What are they? How do you use them? • How has technology changed our lives over the years? What is the difference between technology in the past and the present? Do you think this change has been beneficial? • Tell me about a time when you had trouble using a piece of technology or an electronic device. When was it? What happened? How did you deal with the situation? Tell me about the incident from the beginning to the end. • You want to write a technology industry report. Call your friend and ask three questions about the report. • Learning a new technology is often very difficult and frustrating. Have you had an experience when you were frustrated with trying to use a new technology? Please tell me all the details.
Internet	• What do you normally do on the internet? What are your internet habits? Do you shop for things online? ? Talk about the things you do when you surf the internet. • What websites do you frequently visit? What activities do you do on these websites? Also, tell me the reason you are interested in these websites. • When was the first time you used the internet? What did you do on the internet? How did you use it? What was your first impression while surfing the internet? • What made you interested in internet surfing? How has your interest changed since then? • Can you describe an interesting or unforgettable experience that you had while surfing the internet? Maybe you found a really good website or maybe you met a new friend. Tell me about that experience in as much detail as possible.

Chapter 14 Technology · Internet 기술·인터넷

Unit 27 Combo Set (1)

MP3 바로가기

출제 가능성 ★★★★☆

Q1 What piece of technology do people use every day? How do people use it? Why is it so widely used?

Question Analysis 질문 분석

Answer the following questions and identify the key matter and the information to be included in your response.
다음 질문에 답하며 답변의 주제와 반드시 포함되어야 할 내용이 무엇인지 파악해 보세요.

1. What is going to be the key matter of your response?
2. What information should your response include?

Warm Your Brain Up 브레인스토밍

Answer the following questions for ideas.
다음 질문에 답하며 답변 소재를 발굴해 보세요.

Intro	• What is a piece of technology that people use every day and that they have become dependent on? • What are the different functions and purposes of it?
Body	• How does it facilitate communication with others? • In what ways does it provide access to entertainment? • How does it enable people to do a search, check emails, and use social media? • How does it contribute to remote work and distance learning?
Conclusion	• Why is it widely popular and extensively used?

AL Booster

• Could you tell me about a time when you experienced the convenience of technology?

Useful Expressions

dependent 의존하는　**gadget** 기기, 장치　**such as** ~와 같은　**stay in touch with** ~와 연락을 유지하다　**app** 앱, 어플리케이션　**allow A to-v** A가 ~할 수 있게 하다　**entertainment** 오락, 엔터테인먼트　**whenever** 언제든지　**additionally** 게다가　**serve as** ~로 사용되다　**convenient tool** 편리한 도구　**browse the internet** 인터넷을 둘러보다　**access** 접근하다, 이용하다　**social media platform** 소셜 미디어 플랫폼　**accomplish** 성취하다, 완료하다　**convenient** 편리한　**versatile** 다용도의, 다재다능한　**feature** 기능, 특징　**advancement** 발전, 진보

284　Compact OPIc 컴팩트 오픽

Pattern Drills 패턴 학습

Practice using the given sentence patterns to help you deliver your response clearly.
주어진 문장 패턴을 익혀 답변이 명확하게 전달될 수 있도록 연습해 보세요.

❶

_____ is/are technology that people use every day and that they have become dependent on.

- The internet
- Social media
- Smartphones

❷

We use _____ for various activities, such as _____ and _____.

- smartphones / communication / entertainment
- computers / work / research
- social media platforms / connecting with friends / sharing updates

❸

_____ serve as a convenient tool for _____.

- Search engines / finding information
- Online banking platforms / making transactions
- Translation apps / understanding different languages

❹

_____ allow us to _____ whenever we want.

- Streaming services / watch TV shows
- Online shopping platforms / shop for products
- Food delivery apps / order food

Mini Actual Test 연습 문제

🎧 27_1.mp3

Respond to the following question while keeping in mind what you have learned.
앞서 배운 내용을 떠올리면서 다음 질문에 답변해 보세요.

> What are some of the technologies that people use on a daily basis? How do people use it? What do they use it for? Give as many details as you can.

Model Answer 모범 답안

 27_2.mp3

Enhance your response by referring to the model answer.
다음 모범 답안을 참고하여 여러분의 답변을 발전시켜 보세요.

> The smartphone is a technology that people use every day and one that they have become dependent on. It's a small gadget that can do many things, and we can't imagine our lives without it. We use smartphones for various activities, such as talking to others, watching videos, listening to music, and playing games. They make it easy to stay in touch with our friends, family, and coworkers through calls, texts, and messaging apps. Smartphones also allow us to enjoy entertainment like movies and music whenever we want. Additionally, smartphones serve as a convenient tool for browsing the internet, checking emails, and accessing social media platforms. They are even useful for working or studying from home, as they help us connect with others and accomplish tasks. People love smartphones because they are convenient and versatile, and they are always improving with new features and advancements.

Level Up to AL AL 공략하기

Read the examples below and see how IH-level sentences can be rephrased at the AL level.
다음 예시를 읽고 IH 수준의 문장을 어떻게 AL 수준으로 바꾸어 말할 수 있는지 살펴보세요.

IH		AL
❶ It's a small gadget that can do many things, and we can't imagine our lives without it.	→	It's a small and powerful gadget that has become an essential part of our lives.
❷ They are even useful for working or studying from home, as they help us connect with others and accomplish tasks.	→	They have even become indispensable for remote work and distance learning, enabling us to connect with others and complete tasks efficiently.

출제 가능성 ★★★☆☆

Q2 Can you identify all the technologies, such as a cell phone or computer, that you enjoy using most these days? What are they? How do you use them?

Question Analysis 질문 분석

Answer the following questions and identify the key matter and the information to be included in your response.
다음 질문에 답하며 답변의 주제와 반드시 포함되어야 할 내용이 무엇인지 파악해 보세요.

1. What is going to be the key matter of your response?
2. What information should your response include?

Warm Your Brain Up 브레인스토밍

Answer the following questions for ideas.
다음 질문에 답하며 답변 소재를 발굴해 보세요.

Intro	What are the technologies that you find most enjoyable and that you frequently use in today's world?
Body	• How do you utilize these devices in your everyday activities and tasks? • In what ways do these technologies enhance your communication, productivity, and entertainment experiences? • Can you describe the specific apps, features, or functionalities that make these technologies particularly enjoyable and useful for you?
Conclusion	• Would you recommend these technologies to other? What advice would you give them?

AL Booster

- Reflecting on your experiences, how do these technologies contribute to the overall convenience, efficiency, and enjoyment in your daily life?

Useful Expressions

enjoyable 즐거운   frequently 자주, 빈번히   device 장치, 기기   essential tool 필수 도구   rely on 의지하다, 의존하다
stay connected with ~와 연락을 유지하다   quickly 빠르게   browse the internet 인터넷을 탐색하다   navigation app 내비게이션 앱
on the other hand 반면에   primarily 주로   do research 조사하다   make presentation 발표 자료를 만들다   at once 동시에, 한번에
complicated 복잡한   overall 전반적으로   productive 생산적인, 유익한

Chapter 14 Technology·Internet 기술·인터넷

Pattern Drills 패턴 학습

Practice using the given sentence patterns to help you deliver your response clearly.
주어진 문장 패턴을 익혀 답변이 명확하게 전달될 수 있도록 연습해 보세요.

I use various apps to _____.

❶
- read e-books and expand my knowledge in different subjects
- stay organized and manage my daily tasks efficiently
- track my fitness progress and maintain a healthy lifestyle

I can even find information quickly by _____.

❷
- using search engines like Google
- using mobile apps that provide instant access to research materials
- browsing reliable news websites

On the other hand, _____ is primarily used for _____.

❸
- my laptop / work-related tasks and projects
- my tablet / reading e-books and browsing the internet
- my smartwatch / tracking my fitness activities and monitoring my health

These technologies have changed the way I _____.

❹
- access financial services
- organize my tasks and schedule
- entertain myself

Mini Actual Test 연습 문제   🎧 27_3.mp3

Respond to the following question while keeping in mind what you have learned.
앞서 배운 내용을 떠올리면서 다음 질문에 답변해 보세요.

> I'd like to know about the technologies you currently enjoy using. What are they and why do you use them?

Model Answer 모범 답안

🎧 27_4.mp3

Enhance your response by referring to the model answer.
다음 모범 답안을 참고하여 여러분의 답변을 발전시켜 보세요.

> The technologies that I find most enjoyable and that I frequently use are my smartphone and computer. These devices have become essential tools that I rely on in my daily life. My smartphone is like a little computer that I can use for many things. I stay connected with friends and family through calls, text messages, and social media. It's also great for entertainment because I can watch videos, listen to music, and play games. I can even find information quickly by checking emails, browsing the internet, or using navigation apps. On the other hand, my computer is primarily used for work and studies. I can write, do research, make presentations, and work with others on it. It's better for doing lots of things at once and for more complicated tasks. Overall, these technologies have changed the way I communicate, work, learn, and have fun. They make my life easier, more productive, and more enjoyable.

Level Up to AL AL 공략하기

Read the examples below and see how IH-level sentences can be rephrased at the AL level.
다음 예시를 읽고 IH 수준의 문장을 어떻게 AL 수준으로 바꾸어 말할 수 있는지 살펴보세요.

	IH		AL
❶	My smartphone is like a little computer that I can use for many things.	→	My smartphone is like a mini-computer that serves multiple purposes.
❷	It's also great for entertainment because I can watch videos, listen to music, and play games.	→	It also provides me with entertainment options such as streaming videos, listening to music, and playing games.
❸	I can write, do research, make presentations, and work with others on it.	→	It allows me to write, conduct research, create presentations, and collaborate with others efficiently.

출제 가능성 ★★★★☆

Q3 How has technology changed our lives over the years? What is the difference between the past and the present? Do you think this change has been beneficial?

Question Analysis 질문 분석

Answer the following questions and identify the key matter and the information to be included in your response.
다음 질문에 답하며 답변의 주제와 반드시 포함되어야 할 내용이 무엇인지 파악해 보세요.

1. What is going to be the key matter of your response?
2. What information should your response include?

Warm Your Brain Up 브레인스토밍

Answer the following questions for ideas.
다음 질문에 답하며 답변 소재를 발굴해 보세요.

Intro	• How has technology brought significant changes to our lives? • Can you imagine life without the technological innovations that we have today?
Body	• In what ways has communication been revolutionized by technology? • What are the advancements in entertainment facilitated by technology? • How has technology enhanced various industries? • What benefits has technology brought to healthcare and transportation?
Conclusion	• Reflecting on the past and present, how has the evolution of technology shaped our society, and what are the potential future implications?

AL Booster

- Which type of technology do you think has had the greatest impact on people's lives? What changes has the technology brought to our lives?
- Do you agree that the emergence or advancement of new technologies always has a positive impact on human life? Why do you think so?

Useful Expressions

make a big change 큰 변화를 일으키다   reshape 재구성하다   lifestyle 생활 방식   interaction 상호 작용, 교류
be transformed with ~와 함께 변화하다   no matter 아무리 ~해도   whenever 언제라도   streaming service 스트리밍 서비스
realistic 현실적인, 사실적인   immersive 몰입감 있는   enhance 향상시키다   industry 산업, 업계   healthcare 의료, 보건
transportation 교통, 이동 수단   advanced 발전된   efficient 효율적인   along with ~와 함께   benefit 이점
pose a challenge 어려움을 야기하다   privacy concern 개인 정보 보호에 관한 우려   excessive screen time 과도한 기기 사용 시간
evolve 진화하다, 발전하다   shape one's life ~의 삶을 형성하다

Pattern Drills 패턴 학습

Practice using the given sentence patterns to help you deliver your response clearly.
주어진 문장 패턴을 익혀 답변이 명확하게 전달될 수 있도록 연습해 보세요.

①
> Over the years, _____ has made big changes in our lives, _____.

- social media / connecting people from all around the world
- transportation technology / making it faster and more convenient to travel to different places
- smart home technology / providing convenience and energy efficiency

②
> We can _____, no matter where _____.

- communicate with our loved ones / they are
- access our work documents / they are located
- receive medical consultations / the providers are based

③
> We can _____ whenever we want with _____.

- listen to a wide range of music genres / music streaming platforms
- order food from our favorite restaurants / food delivery apps
- access a variety of recipes / cooking websites

④
> However, along with the benefits, technology poses challenges, including _____.

- social isolation and digital addiction
- information overload and fake news
- the negative impact on mental health, such as decreased attention span

Mini Actual Test 연습 문제   🎧 27_5.mp3

Respond to the following question while keeping in mind what you have learned.
앞서 배운 내용을 떠올리면서 다음 질문에 답변해 보세요.

> What changes has technology brought to our lives over the years? What are the differences between past and present technology? Do you think this change has had a positive impact on our lives?

Model Answer 모범 답안

🎧 27_6.mp3

Enhance your response by referring to the model answer.
다음 모범 답안을 참고하여 여러분의 답변을 발전시켜 보세요.

> Over the years, technology has made big changes in our lives, reshaping our lifestyle, work, and interactions. Communication has been completely transformed with smartphones, social media, and instant messaging. Now we can talk to anyone quickly and easily, no matter where they are. Entertainment has also changed a lot. We can watch movies and shows whenever we want with streaming services, and video games have become more realistic and immersive. Technology has also enhanced various industries. It helps businesses work faster and better, and it has made healthcare and transportation more advanced and efficient. However, along with the benefits, technology poses challenges, including privacy concerns and excessive screen time. We need to think about the positive and negative impacts of technology as it continues to evolve and shape our lives.

Level Up to AL AL 공략하기

Read the examples below and see how IH-level sentences can be rephrased at the AL level.
다음 예시를 읽고 IH 수준의 문장을 어떻게 AL 수준으로 바꾸어 말할 수 있는지 살펴보세요.

	IH	→	AL
❶	Communication has been completely transformed with smartphones, social media, and instant messaging.	→	Communication has experienced a complete revolution with the advent of smartphones, social media, and instant messaging.
❷	Now we can talk to anyone quickly and easily, no matter where they are.	→	Nowadays, we can effortlessly connect with anyone, irrespective of their location.
❸	Entertainment has also changed a lot.	→	Entertainment has also undergone a remarkable transformation.

Chapter 14 Technology·Internet 기술·인터넷

Unit 28 Combo Set (2)

MP3 바로가기

출제 가능성 ★★★★☆

Q1 What do you normally do on the internet? What are your internet habits? Do you shop for things online? Do you read books or post videos? Talk about the things you do when you surf the internet.

Question Analysis 질문 분석

Answer the following questions and identify the key matter and the information to be included in your response.
다음 질문에 답하며 답변의 주제와 반드시 포함되어야 할 내용이 무엇인지 파악해 보세요.

1. What is going to be the key matter of your response?
2. What information should your response include?

Warm Your Brain Up 브레인스토밍

Answer the following questions for ideas.
다음 질문에 답하며 답변 소재를 발굴해 보세요.

Intro	How do you typically spend your time on the internet?
Body	• Do you shop online? If so, what kind of items do you usually purchase and why? • Do you engage in reading books or posting videos online? What topics or genres do you find most interesting? • Are there any other activities or hobbies you pursue on the internet, such as participating in online communities or learning new skills?
Conclusion	• What are the advantages and potential drawbacks of spending too much time on the internet?

AL Booster

• Reflecting on your internet habits, how have they shaped your daily life and interactions?

Useful Expressions

entertained 즐거운   connected 연결된   regular habit 일상적인 습관   conveniently 편리하게   purchase 구매하다
a wide range of 넓은 범위의   electronics 전자 제품   a greater variety of 더 다양한 종류의   expand one's knowledge ~의 지식을 확장하다
actively 적극적으로   establish a connection with ~와 관계를 형성하다   like-minded 같은 관심을 가진   integral 핵심인, 중요한
avenue 경로   self-expression 자기 표현   find a balance 균형을 찾다   possible disadvantage 가능한 단점

Pattern Drills 패턴 학습

Practice using the given sentence patterns to help you deliver your response clearly.
주어진 문장 패턴을 익혀 답변이 명확하게 전달될 수 있도록 연습해 보세요.

❶
On the internet, I engage in various activities that _____.
- allow me to express myself creatively
- help me stay connected with friends and family
- cater to my entertainment preferences

❷
One of my regular habits is online shopping, where I _____.
- read customer reviews before making a purchase
- can easily search for specific products
- take advantage of seasonal sales to save money

❸
Beyond that, I actively participate in _____.
- online surveys and provide feedback to companies
- online book clubs and engage in discussions
- online fitness communities and share workout routines

❹
Although the internet brings many benefits, I understand _____.
- the need to manage and limit screen time
- the importance of critical thinking
- the potential impact of online addiction

Mini Actual Test 연습 문제 🎧 28_1.mp3

Respond to the following question while keeping in mind what you have learned.
앞서 배운 내용을 떠올리면서 다음 질문에 답변해 보세요.

> Now, let's talk about the internet. The internet can be used for various purposes. What do you personally use it for? Tell me about your internet habits and the things you do when you are surfing the internet.

Model Answer 모범 답안

🎧 28_2.mp3

Enhance your response by referring to the model answer.
다음 모범 답안을 참고하여 여러분의 답변을 발전시켜 보세요.

> On the internet, I engage in various activities that keep me entertained and connected. One of my regular habits is online shopping, which allows me to conveniently purchase a wide range of items, from clothing to electronics. It saves me time and offers a greater variety of products to choose from. Additionally, I enjoy reading books and watching videos online. I explore different genres and topics, expanding my knowledge and entertainment options. Beyond that, I actively participate in online communities, where I can share my experiences, learn from others, and establish connections with like-minded individuals. Overall, the internet has become an integral part of my daily life, offering convenience, access to information, and avenues for self-expression. Although the internet brings many benefits, I understand the importance of finding a balance and being aware of possible disadvantages, like spending too much time on screens.

Level Up to AL AL 공략하기

Read the examples below and see how IH-level sentences can be rephrased at the AL level.
다음 예시를 읽고 IH 수준의 문장을 어떻게 AL 수준으로 바꾸어 말할 수 있는지 살펴보세요.

IH	AL
❶ On the internet, I engage in various activities that keep me entertained and connected.	→ When I go online, I find myself engaged in various activities that bring me entertainment and help me connect with others.
❷ Although the internet brings many benefits, I understand the importance of finding a balance and being aware of possible disadvantages, like spending too much time on screens.	→ While the internet offers numerous advantages, I recognize the significance of maintaining a healthy balance and being mindful of potential drawbacks, such as excessive screen time.

출제 가능성 ★★★★☆

Q2 What websites do you frequently visit? What activities do you do on these websites? Also, tell me the reason you are interested in the websites.

Question Analysis 질문 분석

Answer the following questions and identify the key matter and the information to be included in your response.
다음 질문에 답하며 답변의 주제와 반드시 포함되어야 할 내용이 무엇인지 파악해 보세요.

1. What is going to be the key matter of your response?
2. What information should your response include?

Warm Your Brain Up 브레인스토밍

Answer the following questions for ideas.
다음 질문에 답하며 답변 소재를 발굴해 보세요.

Intro	• Which websites do you visit frequently? • What draws you to these particular websites?
Body	• Do you primarily use the websites for communication, entertainment, information, or other purposes? • What features or contents of the websites keep you engaged?
Conclusion	• How do these websites contribute to your personal growth or other aspects of your life?

AL Booster

• Would you recommend that others use these websites? Why?

Useful Expressions

cater to ~에 맞춤화하다   various needs 다양한 요구   regularly access 정기적으로 접속하다   share updates 업데이트를 공유하다
explore 탐색하다   connected 연결된   entertained 즐거운
stay informed about 계속해서 ~에 관한 최신 정보를 알다   current event 최근 사건
a wide range of 다양한   article 기사   feature 특징   capture one's attention ~의 이목을 끌다   marketplace 온라인 마켓
shop for 쇼핑하다   find a great deal 좋은 구매가를 찾다   provide convenience 편의를 제공하다   valuable 가치 있는
daily routine 일상에서 늘 하는 일   enrich 풍요롭게 하다   satisfy 만족시키다

Pattern Drills 패턴 학습

Practice using the given sentence patterns to help you deliver your response clearly.
주어진 문장 패턴을 익혀 답변이 명확하게 전달될 수 있도록 연습해 보세요.

① The websites that I frequently visit cater to _____ .

- my educational needs by offering online courses
- my fashion sense by highlighting the latest trends
- my music passion by providing music streaming

② One of the websites I regularly access is _____ , where _____ .

- a recipe-sharing platform / I can find a vast collection of delicious recipes
- a travel blog / I can read inspiring travel stories
- a book recommendation website / I can discover new books

③ This website offers a wide range of _____ .

- articles, covering topics such as technology and lifestyle
- a wide range of electronic gadgets, such as smartphones and tablets
- pet products, such as pet food and toys

④ The reason I am interested in these websites is that _____ .

- they provide convenience
- they offer a wide variety of options
- they keep me informed and up-to-date
- they save me time and effort

Mini Actual Test 연습 문제 🎧 28_3.mp3

Respond to the following question while keeping in mind what you have learned.
앞서 배운 내용을 떠올리면서 다음 질문에 답변해 보세요.

> I'd like to know if there's any website you frequently visit. What is this website, and what do you do on the website? What interests you about that website?

Model Answer 모범 답안

 28_4.mp3

Enhance your response by referring to the model answer.
다음 모범 답안을 참고하여 여러분의 답변을 발전시켜 보세요.

> The websites that I frequently visit cater to my various needs and interests. One of the websites I regularly access is a social media platform where I connect with friends, share updates, and explore interesting content. It keeps me connected and entertained. Additionally, I often browse an online news website to stay informed about current events and expand my knowledge. This website offers a wide range of articles and features that capture my attention. Another website I visit is an online marketplace, where I can conveniently shop for a variety of products and find great deals. The reason I am interested in these websites is that they provide convenience, entertainment, and valuable information. They allow me to stay connected with others, access news from around the world, and easily purchase items I need. These websites have become an integral part of my daily routine, enriching my online experience and satisfying my specific interests.

Level Up to AL AL 공략하기

Read the examples below and see how IH-level sentences can be rephrased at the AL level.
다음 예시를 읽고 IH 수준의 문장을 어떻게 AL 수준으로 바꾸어 말할 수 있는지 살펴보세요.

IH	**AL**
❶ One of the websites I regularly access is a social media platform where I connect with friends, share updates, and explore interesting content.	→ A social media platform that enables me to connect with friends, share updates, and explore captivating content is one of my regular destinations.
❷ They allow me to stay connected with others, access news from around the world, and easily purchase items I need.	→ They facilitate my social connections, grant access to global news, and simplify my shopping experience.

출제 가능성 ★★★★☆

Q3 When was the first time you used the internet? What did you do on the internet? How did you use it? What was your first impression while surfing the internet?

Question Analysis 질문 분석

Answer the following questions and identify the key matter and the information to be included in your response.
다음 질문에 답하며 답변의 주제와 반드시 포함되어야 할 내용이 무엇인지 파악해 보세요.

1. What is going to be the key matter of your response?
2. What information should your response include?

Warm Your Brain Up 브레인스토밍

Answer the following questions for ideas.
다음 질문에 답하며 답변 소재를 발굴해 보세요.

Intro	When was the first time you used the internet? How did you first encounter the internet?
Body	• What did you do on the internet during your first experience? • How did the internet work at that time?
Conclusion	• What was your first impression while surfing the internet? • How has your perception or use of the internet evolved over time?

AL Booster

- How did you learn to use the internet? Did you get any help from others?
- What was the internet speed like, and how did the screen look?

Useful Expressions

early teenage years 10대 초반　open up 열다　whole new world 완전히 새로운 세계　possibility 가능성　vividly 생생하게
in front of ~의 앞에　desktop computer 데스크탑 컴퓨터　dial-up internet 전화로 연결하는 인터넷　distinct sound 독특한 소리
modem 모뎀　be amazed by ~에 놀라다　available at one's fingertips ~의 손끝에서 이용할 수 있는
have a library of ~의 서고를 보유하다; ~에 대한 방대한 양의 정보를 가지고 있다　instantly 즉시　first impression 첫인상
surf the internet 인터넷을 서핑하다　delightful mix of ~의 즐거운 혼합　curiosity 호기심　wonder 놀라움
be captivated by ~에 매료되다　diverse culture 다양한 문화　spark one's curiosity 호기심을 자극하다　turning point 전환점
motivate 동기를 부여하다

Chapter 14 Technology·Internet 기술·인터넷　299

Pattern Drills 패턴 학습

Practice using the given sentence patterns to help you deliver your response clearly.
주어진 문장 패턴을 익혀 답변이 명확하게 전달될 수 있도록 연습해 보세요.

❶
The first time I used the internet was _____.
- a turning point in my life
- a milestone in my technological journey
- an eye-opening experience

❷
As a beginner, my main activity on the internet was _____.
- browsing websites
- watching videos
- playing online games
- listening to music

❸
I was captivated by _____.
- the ease of discovering new books
- the power of online communities
- the speed and efficiency of online research

❹
This exciting experience sparked _____.
- my passion for technology
- my desire to stay up-to-date with the latest trends
- my interest in connecting with people from different backgrounds

Mini Actual Test 연습 문제   🎧 28_5.mp3

Respond to the following question while keeping in mind what you have learned.
앞서 배운 내용을 떠올리면서 다음 질문에 답변해 보세요.

> Think about the day when you first used the internet. Describe your first experience with the internet in detail. Also, what was your first impression while surfing the internet?

Model Answer 모범 답안  28_6.mp3

Enhance your response by referring to the model answer.
다음 모범 답안을 참고하여 여러분의 답변을 발전시켜 보세요.

> The first time I used the internet was during my early teenage years. It was an exciting and memorable experience that opened up a whole new world of possibilities. I vividly remember sitting in front of a desktop computer, connecting to the dial-up internet with the distinct sound of the modem. As a beginner, my main activity on the internet was browsing websites and searching for information. I was amazed by the vast amount of knowledge and resources available at my fingertips. It was like having a library of information instantly accessible. My first impression while surfing the internet was a delightful mix of curiosity and wonder. I was also captivated by my ability to connect with people from different parts of the world, explore diverse cultures, and discover new interests. This exciting experience sparked my curiosity and led me to explore and use the internet more often. It was a turning point that opened up new opportunities and motivated me to continue exploring and using the internet in my daily life.

Level Up to AL AL 공략하기

Read the examples below and see how IH-level sentences can be rephrased at the AL level.
다음 예시를 읽고 IH 수준의 문장을 어떻게 AL 수준으로 바꾸어 말할 수 있는지 살펴보세요.

IH	→	AL
❶ As a beginner, my main activity on the internet was browsing websites and searching for information.	→	As a novice user, my primary activity on the internet was browsing websites and searching for information.
❷ It was like having a library of information instantly accessible.	→	It felt like having a vast library of information that I could access instantly.

Chapter 15

Holiday · Gathering 명절·모임

✓ Strategy Check 주제 관련 전략

Check the following strategies related to the topic of this chapter.
이 챕터의 주제와 관련된 시험 대비 전략을 확인해 보세요.

IH Essential

- Sometimes, topics like "Holiday" or "Gathering" can be overlooked because it is said that they are not frequently presented in the test. However, these topics can be randomly presented regardless of the Background Survey response. Therefore, it is advisable to be thoroughly prepared for these subjects if there is even a slight possibility of them being included in the test.
  간혹 '명절'이나 '모임' 주제가 시험에 자주 출제되지 않는다고 하여 간과하는 경우가 있습니다. 그러나 해당 주제들은 백그라운드 서베이 응답 결과와 관계 없이 돌발 출제되는 주제들로, 출제 가능성이 조금이라도 있다면 철저히 대비해 두는 편이 좋습니다.

- One of the reasons why test-takers for the OPIc get flustered when they receive questions related to "Holiday" is that there are too many holidays that immediately come to mind. If you are not prepared for this topic, you may become flustered when asked such questions. Therefore, it is recommended that you select one specific holiday in advance, and prepare your response accordingly.
  오픽 응시생들이 '명절' 주제와 관련된 질문을 받았을 때 당황하는 이유 중 하나는 당장 머릿속에 떠오르는 명절들이 너무 많기 때문입니다. 해당 주제에 대비해 놓지 않으면 이와 같이 질문을 받았을 때 당황하게 되므로, 미리 하나의 명절을 정해 놓고 그에 대한 답변을 준비하는 것이 좋습니다.

- Regarding "Holiday" and "Gathering," a topic that can be easily connected for the response is "Spending vacations at home." It is recommended to imagine scenarios where you spent the holiday or hosted a gathering at home without any special outdoor activities. By linking "Holiday" and "Gathering" to "Spending vacations at home," you can incorporate various stories that you have already created in previous chapters, such as "Watching movies," "Reading books," and "Cooking," in your response.
  '명절,' '모임,'과 쉽게 연계하여 답변할 수 있는 주제로는 '집에서 보내는 휴가'가 있습니다. 특별한 활동 없이 집에서 명절을 보냈다거나 집에서 모임을 진행했다고 가정해 둘 것을 추천합니다. 이렇게 '명절'과 '모임'을 모두 집과 연계해 놓으면 이전 대단원에서 학습했던 '영화 보기,' '독서하기,' '요리하기' 등 다양한 주제의 답변을 끌어와 소재로 사용할 수 있습니다.

AL Booster

- If you prepare your responses by interconnecting various topics, you may find yourself consistently answering related questions with similar content. Some test-takers worry that providing similar responses will result in point deductions. However, if you use different expressions while talking about the same material, you will not have any negative impact on your score. For example, let's assume you were asked about "Spending vacations at home" and then received a question about "Holiday." In this case, even if you repeatedly mention that you watched movies at home, you can still achieve your target score by rephrasing your responses with various expressions.
  답변을 연계하여 준비해 놓은 주제들이 연달아 나오면, 같은 소재를 반복하여 말하게 돼서 감점을 받는 것이 아니냐고 묻는 수험생분들이 계십니다. 동일한 소재를 가지고 이야기하더라도, 다양한 표현을 사용하여 답변한다면 점수에는 아무런 영향이 없습니다. 예를 들어, '집에서 보내는 휴가'에 관한 질문에 이어 '명절'에 관한 질문을 받았다고 가정해 봅시다. 이 경우, 비슷한 이야기더라도 다양한 표현을 사용해 답변을 바꾸어 말한다면 충분히 목표 등급을 받을 수 있습니다.

❓ Frequently Asked Questions 빈출 질문 유형

Here are the most frequently asked question types related to the topic. Try to identify the key matter of the question and the information that should be included in your response.
이 챕터의 주제와 관련해 자주 출제되는 질문 유형들을 확인해 보세요. 그리고 각 질문의 중심 소재와 답변에 어떤 정보를 포함시켜야 하는지 파악해 보세요.

National Holiday	• Tell me about holidays in your country. Which holiday is the biggest? What do people do on that day? Is there any special food for the day? • Choose a holiday and discuss how the celebrations have changed over the years. Compare the past and present. What things are the same? What things are different? • Think back to your childhood. I'd like to know about one of the most memorable holidays. Do you have any special memories? If so, what happened?
Role-play	• I'd like to give you a situation to act out. Imagine your foreign friend has invited you to celebrate a traditional holiday from his / her country. Ask him / her three or four questions about the holiday.
Gathering	• Talk about gatherings and celebrations in your country. What do people do when they get together or celebrate things? • What did you do at your last gathering or celebration? What was the occasion? Give me all the details about it. • Tell me about a memorable event that happened at a gathering or a celebration. Why was it memorable?

Chapter 15 Holiday·Gathering 명절·모임

Unit 29 Combo Set (1)

MP3 바로가기

출제 가능성 ★★★☆☆

Q1 Tell me about holidays in your country. Which holiday is the biggest? What do people do on that day? Is there any special food for the day?

▶ Question Analysis 질문 분석

Answer the following questions and identify the key matter and the information to be included in your response.
다음 질문에 답하며 답변의 주제와 반드시 포함되어야 할 내용이 무엇인지 파악해 보세요.

1. What is going to be the key matter of your response?
2. What information should your response include?

▶ Warm Your Brain Up 브레인스토밍

Answer the following questions for ideas.
다음 질문에 답하며 답변 소재를 발굴해 보세요.

Intro	• What is one of the most cherished holidays in Korea? • What is the holiday also known as?
Body	• What are some common traditions and activities associated with this holiday? • What does your family do to celebrate this holiday? • Is there a special dish or food that is typically prepared and enjoyed on this day?
Conclusion	• How does the holiday create cherished memories for families?

AL Booster

• Is there any historical or cultural significance behind this holiday?
• Are there any specific customs or rituals observed on this day?

Useful Expressions

harvest 수확   beloved 사랑 받는   hold cultural significance 문화적인 의미를 가지다   be awaited by ~가 기다리다   eagerly 열심히   ancestor 선조   decorate 장식하다   gravesite 묘지   honor 존경을 표하다   spirit 영혼   gather together 함께 모이다   either A or B A 또는 B 중 하나   designated place 지정된 장소   play a big part in ~에 큰 역할을 하다   festivity 축제   feast 잔치   seasonal fruit 계절 과일   create a joyful atmosphere 즐거운 분위기를 조성하다   express gratitude for ~에 대한 감사의 마음을 표현하다   blessing 축복   make a lasting memory 오래도록 기억에 남게 하다

Pattern Drills 패턴 학습

Practice using the given sentence patterns to help you deliver your response clearly.
주어진 문장 패턴을 익혀 답변이 명확하게 전달될 수 있도록 연습해 보세요.

❶ _____ is one of the most beloved holidays in Korea.
- Chuseok
- Lunar New Year
- Children's Day

❷ During _____, people take part in _____.
- Chuseok / traditional activities
- Lunar New Year / family gatherings and ancestral rituals
- Children's Day / events and games specifically organized for children

❸ Sharing and cooking these foods brings _____.
- families closer
- joy and togetherness
- a sense of community and bonding

❹ Overall, _____ is a special time when _____.
- Chuseok / families come together to honor their ancestors
- Lunar New Year / families reunite and celebrate the beginning of a new year
- Children's Day / various events are organized to entertain children

Mini Actual Test 연습 문제

🎧 29_1.mp3

Respond to the following question while keeping in mind what you have learned.
앞서 배운 내용을 떠올리면서 다음 질문에 답변해 보세요.

> Choose one of the biggest holidays in your country and provide a detailed description of it. What activities do you typically engage in during this holiday? What types of food are traditionally consumed on this day?

Model Answer 모범 답안

Enhance your response by referring to the model answer.
다음 모범 답안을 참고하여 여러분의 답변을 발전시켜 보세요.

> Chuseok, also known as the Harvest Moon Festival, is one of the most beloved holidays in Korea. It's a special time that holds great cultural significance and is eagerly awaited by Koreans everywhere. During Chuseok, people take part in various traditional activities. Some visit their ancestors' hometowns to clean and decorate gravesites, offering food and fruits as a way to honor their spirits. In my family's case, we gather together either at home or at a designated place to celebrate Chuseok. And of course, food plays a big part in the festivities. We enjoy a delicious feast of traditional Korean dishes like Song-pyeon (rice cakes shaped like half-moons), jeon (pan-fried dishes), and a variety of seasonal fruits. Sharing and cooking these foods bring our family closer together and create a joyful atmosphere. Overall, Chuseok is a special time when families come together to share stories, express gratitude for the blessings in our lives, and make lasting memories.

Level Up to AL AL 공략하기

Read the examples below and see how IH-level sentences can be rephrased at the AL level.
다음 예시를 읽고 IH 수준의 문장을 어떻게 AL 수준으로 바꾸어 말할 수 있는지 살펴보세요.

	IH	→	AL
❶	Chuseok, also known as the Harvest Moon Festival, is one of the most beloved holidays in Korea.	→	One of the most cherished holidays in Korea is Chuseok, also known as the Harvest Moon Festival.
❷	And of course, food plays a big part in the festivities.	→	And of course, when it comes to food, we indulge in a delightful feast of traditional Korean dishes.
❸	Sharing and cooking these foods bring our family closer together and create a joyful atmosphere.	→	This act of cooking and sharing food strengthens the bonds within my family and creates a joyous and festive atmosphere.

출제 가능성 ★★★☆☆

Q2 Choose a holiday and discuss how the celebrations have changed over the years. Compare the past and present. What things are the same? What things are different?

Question Analysis 질문 분석

Answer the following questions and identify the key matter and the information to be included in your response.
다음 질문에 답하며 답변의 주제와 반드시 포함되어야 할 내용이 무엇인지 파악해 보세요.

1. What is going to be the key matter of your response?
2. What information should your response include?

Warm Your Brain Up 브레인스토밍

Answer the following questions for ideas.
다음 질문에 답하며 답변 소재를 발굴해 보세요.

Intro	What holiday have you chosen to discuss? Why did you choose this holiday?
Body	• How did people celebrate this holiday in the past? • How have the celebrations of the holiday changed, and what do people do during the holiday?
Conclusion	• What are the key differences and similarities between past and present celebrations of the holiday?

AL Booster

• Are there any new traditions or activities that have emerged in the present celebrations?

Useful Expressions

unite 결속시키다   pay homage to ~에 경의를 표하다   ancestor 조상, 선조   engage in ~에 참여하다   traditional custom 전통적인 관습
include 포함하다   traditional attire 전통 의복   conduct a ritual 의식을 하다   partake in ~에 참여하다   traditional game 전통 놀이
modernized 현대화된   strictly 엄격히   shift toward ~로 변화하다   spend quality time with ~와 양질의 시간을 보내다
despite ~에도 불구하고   element 요소   family bonding 가족 유대감   be valued 소중히 여기다   in short 간략히 말하면
remain significant 여전히 의미가 있다

Chapter 15 Holiday·Gathering 명절·모임 307

Pattern Drills 패턴 학습

Practice using the given sentence patterns to help you deliver your response clearly.
주어진 문장 패턴을 익혀 답변이 명확하게 전달될 수 있도록 연습해 보세요.

1
In the past, the focus was on _____.
- preserving traditional customs
- wearing Hanbok and conducting ancestral rites
- maintaining strong connections with ancestors

2
The celebrations have become _____.
- more diverse and inclusive
- more modernized
- more vibrant and lively

3
Many families prefer to _____ instead of strictly following the old customs.
- travel and explore new destinations
- have a relaxing staycation at home
- engage in recreational activities

4
_____ is(are) still valued.
- The tradition of sharing delicious foods
- Respecting and honoring ancestors
- Bonding with family and passing down cultural heritage

Mini Actual Test 연습 문제

🎧 29_3.mp3

Respond to the following question while keeping in mind what you have learned.
앞서 배운 내용을 떠올리면서 다음 질문에 답변해 보세요.

> Tell me about one of the holidays that has changed over the years. How is it different from what it used to be? What remains the same?

Model Answer 모범 답안

 29_4.mp3

Enhance your response by referring to the model answer.
다음 모범 답안을 참고하여 여러분의 답변을 발전시켜 보세요.

> Seollal, the Korean Lunar New Year, has changed a lot over the years. In the past, the focus was on families uniting to pay homage to their ancestors and engaging in traditional customs. This included wearing traditional attire, conducting rituals, and partaking in traditional games. However, things are different these days; the celebrations have become more diverse and modernized, and people have more options and preferences. Many families prefer to travel or enjoy leisure activities during Seollal instead of strictly following the old customs. The focus has shifted more towards spending quality time with family and creating memorable experiences. Despite these changes, certain elements remain the same. Family bonding and the tradition of sharing delicious foods like Tteok-guk (rice cake soup) are still valued. In short, while Seollal celebrations have become more diverse and modernized, the importance of family and cultural traditions remains significant.

Level Up to AL AL 공략하기

Read the examples below and see how IH-level sentences can be rephrased at the AL level.
다음 예시를 읽고 IH 수준의 문장을 어떻게 AL 수준으로 바꾸어 말할 수 있는지 살펴보세요.

IH

❶ In Korea, Seollal, the Korean Lunar New Year, has changed a lot over the years.

→

AL

In Korea, Seollal, the Korean Lunar New Year, has undergone significant changes over the years.

❷ Many families prefer to travel or enjoy leisure activities during Seollal instead of strictly following the old customs.

→

Many families now choose to travel or engage in leisure activities during Seollal, breaking away from the traditional customs.

출제 가능성 ★★★☆☆

Q3 Think back to your childhood. I'd like to know about one of the most memorable holidays. Do you have any special memories? If so, what happened?

Question Analysis 질문 분석

Answer the following questions and identify the key matter and the information to be included in your response.
다음 질문에 답하며 답변의 주제와 반드시 포함되어야 할 내용이 무엇인지 파악해 보세요.

1. What is going to be the key matter of your response?
2. What information should your response include?

Warm Your Brain Up 브레인스토밍

Answer the following questions for ideas.
다음 질문에 답하며 답변 소재를 발굴해 보세요.

Intro	• Can you recall one of the most memorable holidays from your childhood? • When was it and who were you with?
Body	• What happened during the holiday that made it special? • Did you also receive any special gifts or surprises during the holiday?
Conclusion	• Reflecting on your childhood holiday memories, how do they make you feel?

AL Booster

• How have those memories influenced your perception of holidays now?

Useful Expressions

special holiday 특별한 휴일   traditional 전통적인   celebrate 축하하다   create special memories 특별한 추억을 만들다
beautifully decorated 아름답게 장식된   gather 모이다   exchange 교환하다   particular 특별한   stand out 두드러지다
receive 받다   unexpected 예상치 못한   brand new 새로운   unforgettable 잊지 못할   feel warm 따뜻함을 느끼다
feel nostalgic 향수(그리움)를 느끼다   loved one 사랑하는 사람   stay the same 변하지 않다

Pattern Drills 패턴 학습

Practice using the given sentence patterns to help you deliver your response clearly.
주어진 문장 패턴을 익혀 답변이 명확하게 전달될 수 있도록 연습해 보세요.

_____ was a very special holiday that I will always remember.

1
- New Year's Eve
- Thanksgiving
- Easter Sunday
- Christmas

One of my favorite memories is _____.

2
- attending a music concert
- waking up to the sound of ocean waves
- spending summer evenings with my friends

We spent the entire day together _____.

3
- hiking in the mountains
- cooking a delicious meal
- playing board games

Recalling these memories makes me feel _____.

4
- joyful and blessed
- nostalgic and content
- warm and happy

Mini Actual Test 연습 문제   🎧 29_5.mp3

Respond to the following question while keeping in mind what you have learned.
앞서 배운 내용을 떠올리면서 다음 질문에 답변해 보세요.

> I'd like you to tell me about one of your most memorable holidays from your childhood. What happened? Why is it so memorable for you? Please explain in detail.

Model Answer 모범 답안

 29_6.mp3

Enhance your response by referring to the model answer.
다음 모범 답안을 참고하여 여러분의 답변을 발전시켜 보세요.

> Christmas was a very special holiday that I will always remember. Even though Christmas isn't a traditional holiday in Korea, many families, especially those with children, celebrate it and create special memories. One of my favorite memories is waking up on Christmas morning and seeing a beautifully decorated tree with presents all around it. It was so exciting! Gathered around the tree, my family exchanged gifts with big smiles on our faces. We spent the entire day together, enjoying a delicious meal and playing fun games. One year in particular stands out: the year I received an unexpected gift—a brand new bicycle! It was such a happy and unforgettable moment for me. Recalling these memories makes me feel warm and nostalgic. Although holidays change as we get older, the importance of spending time with loved ones and making happy memories stays the same.

Level Up to AL AL 공략하기

Read the examples below and see how IH-level sentences can be rephrased at the AL level.
다음 예시를 읽고 IH 수준의 문장을 어떻게 AL 수준으로 바꾸어 말할 수 있는지 살펴보세요.

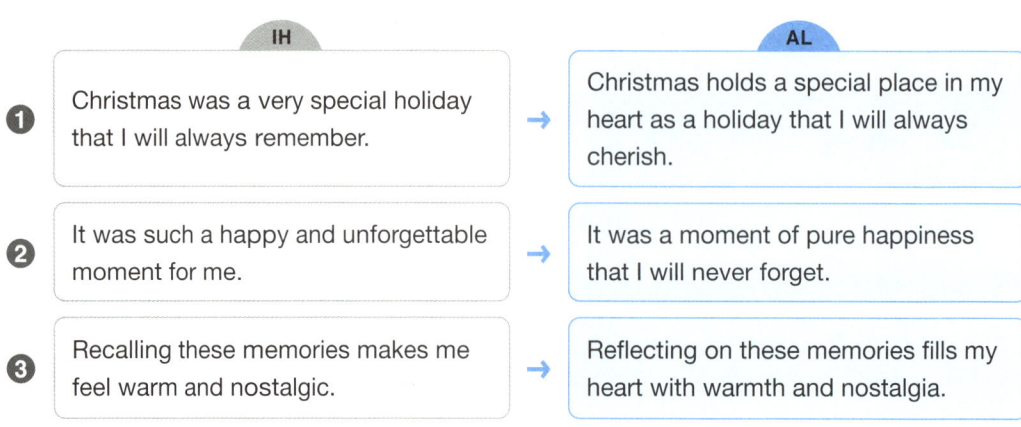

Chapter 15 Holiday·Gathering 명절·모임

Unit 30 Combo Set (2)

출제 가능성 ★★★★☆

Q1 Talk about gatherings and celebrations in your country. What do people do when they get together or celebrate things?

Question Analysis 질문 분석

Answer the following questions and identify the key matter and the information to be included in your response.
다음 질문에 답하며 답변의 주제와 반드시 포함되어야 할 내용이 무엇인지 파악해 보세요.

1. What is going to be the key matter of your response?
2. What information should your response include?

Warm Your Brain Up 브레인스토밍

Answer the following questions for ideas.
다음 질문에 답하며 답변 소재를 발굴해 보세요.

Intro	What role do gatherings and celebrations play in your culture? What is the purpose of gatherings and celebrations in your country?
Body	• How do people typically prepare for these gatherings or celebrations? • What activities or rituals are commonly observed during these events? • What are some popular types of food or drinks that are enjoyed during these gatherings?
Conclusion	• How do these events foster a sense of community and unity among the people? • What is the overall impact of gatherings and celebrations on people's lives?

AL Booster

- How have modern influences affected gatherings and celebrations?

Useful Expressions

gathering 모임   celebration 축하   traditional event 전통적인 행사   bring families together 가족을 한데 모으다
ancestor 조상, 선조   special occasion 특별한 행사   do leisure activities 여가 활동을 하다   no matter what 무엇이든
take place 일어나다   strengthen 강화하다   family bonds 가족 간의 유대감   a sense of unity 단결심   generation 세대
modern influence 현대적인 영향   value 소중히 여기다   respect for elders 어른에 대한 존경   preserve 보존하다
cultural heritage 문화 유산   a sense of belonging 소속감

Pattern Drills 패턴 학습

Practice using the given sentence patterns to help you deliver your response clearly.
주어진 문장 패턴을 익혀 답변이 명확하게 전달될 수 있도록 연습해 보세요.

1
Traditional events bring families together to _____.
- honor their ancestors
- strengthen their bonds
- share delicious meals

2
During these special occasions, we engage in activities like _____.
- cooking traditional dishes together
- playing traditional games
- exchanging gifts

3
While some things have changed, we still value _____.
- our traditions and cultural customs
- the respect for our elders and their wisdom
- the importance of family and togetherness

4
Korean gatherings and celebrations teach us about _____.
- the significance of community
- the spirit of unity
- generosity and the joy of sharing

Mini Actual Test 연습 문제

🎧 30_1.mp3

Respond to the following question while keeping in mind what you have learned.
앞서 배운 내용을 떠올리면서 다음 질문에 답변해 보세요.

Describe the gatherings and celebrations in your country. How do people come together and celebrate?

Model Answer 모범 답안

 30_2.mp3

Enhance your response by referring to the model answer.
다음 모범 답안을 참고하여 여러분의 답변을 발전시켜 보세요.

> In Korea, gatherings and celebrations are an important part of our culture. Traditional events like Seollal(the Korean Lunar New Year) and Chuseok(the Harvest Moon Festival) bring families together to celebrate and show respect to our ancestors. During these special occasions, we engage in activities like cleaning our homes, preparing delicious traditional food, and playing games together. Nowadays, people have more options and preferences, such as traveling or doing leisure activities with their families during holidays. No matter what activities take place during these gatherings, they strengthen family bonds and create a sense of unity among generations. While some things have changed with modern influences, we still value our traditions and customs. Korean gatherings and celebrations teach us the importance of family, respect for elders, and preserving our cultural heritage. They bring joy, happiness, and a sense of belonging to our lives.

Level Up to AL AL 공략하기

Read the examples below and see how IH-level sentences can be rephrased at the AL level.
다음 예시를 읽고 IH 수준의 문장을 어떻게 AL 수준으로 바꾸어 말할 수 있는지 살펴보세요.

IH → **AL**

❶ In Korea, gatherings and celebrations are an important part of our culture. → In Korea, gatherings and celebrations hold a significant place in our culture.

❷ Nowadays, people have more options and preferences, such as traveling or doing leisure activities with their families during holidays. → In recent times, people have embraced more diverse options and preferences, such as traveling or engaging in leisure activities with their families during holidays.

출제 가능성 ★★★★☆

Q2 What did you do at your last gathering or celebration? What was the occasion? Give me all the details about it.

❯ Question Analysis 질문 분석

Answer the following questions and identify the key matter and the information to be included in your response.
다음 질문에 답하며 답변의 주제와 반드시 포함되어야 할 내용이 무엇인지 파악해 보세요.

1. What is going to be the key matter of your response?
2. What information should your response include?

❯ Warm Your Brain Up 브레인스토밍

Answer the following questions for ideas.
다음 질문에 답하며 답변 소재를 발굴해 보세요.

Intro	• What recent gathering or celebration did you participate in? • What was the occasion or reason for the event?
Body	• What activities or traditions did you engage in during the event? • Did you enjoy any memorable moments or experiences during the gathering? • Were there any special decorations, food, or cultural elements that added to the experience?
Conclusion	• What did you learn or gain from the experience? • How did the event contribute to a sense of unity and belonging?

AL Booster
• How did the gathering or celebration strengthen your relationships with others?

Useful Expressions
family gathering 가족 모임   decoration 장식   purpose 목적   show love 사랑을 표현하다   milestone 이정표   heartfelt 마음을 담은   speech 연설   be prepared 준비되다   with care 주의를 기울여   atmosphere 분위기   be full of ~로 가득하다   laughter 웃음   togetherness 결속감   stand out 두드러지다   bring … closer …를 가깝게 하다   remind A of B A에게 B를 상기시키다   gratitude 감사   meaningful 의미 있는   lasting 지속되는, 지속적인   treasure 소중히 여기다

Pattern Drills 패턴 학습

Practice using the given sentence patterns to help you deliver your response clearly.
주어진 문장 패턴을 익혀 답변이 명확하게 전달될 수 있도록 연습해 보세요.

Recently, I had the chance to _____.

❶
- attend special family gathering to celebrate my sister's graduation
- see my favorite band in concert
- meet a renowned author

The purpose of the event was to _____.

❷
- celebrate my cousin's college acceptance
- raise awareness about environmental conservation
- honor the achievements of outstanding students

The atmosphere was full of _____.

❸
- joy and laughter
- enthusiasm and energy
- excitement and anticipation

One moment that stood out was when _____.

❹
- my grandfather gave all of us an allowance
- my friend surprised me with a thoughtful birthday gift
- my favorite artist took the stage and started singing my favorite song

Mini Actual Test 연습 문제 🎧 30_3.mp3

Respond to the following question while keeping in mind what you have learned.
앞서 배운 내용을 떠올리면서 다음 질문에 답변해 보세요.

> Tell me about your most recent gathering or celebration. What was it for? What did you do during that event?

Model Answer 모범 답안

Enhance your response by referring to the model answer.
다음 모범 답안을 참고하여 여러분의 답변을 발전시켜 보세요.

> Recently, I had the chance to attend a special family gathering to celebrate my grandmother's 80th birthday. We gathered at a beautiful place with pretty decorations and flowers. The purpose of the event was to show love and celebrate this important milestone in my grandmother's life. During the celebration, we did many things together. We listened to heartfelt speeches, shared stories and memories, and enjoyed a delicious meal that we prepared with care. The atmosphere was one of happiness and laughter with a strong feeling of togetherness. One moment that stood out was when we surprised my grandmother with a special video showing her life's journey. This gathering brought us closer as a family and reminded us of the values of love, respect, and gratitude. It was a meaningful experience that created lasting memories for all of us to treasure.

Level Up to AL AL 공략하기

Read the examples below and see how IH-level sentences can be rephrased at the AL level.
다음 예시를 읽고 IH 수준의 문장을 어떻게 AL 수준으로 바꾸어 말할 수 있는지 살펴보세요.

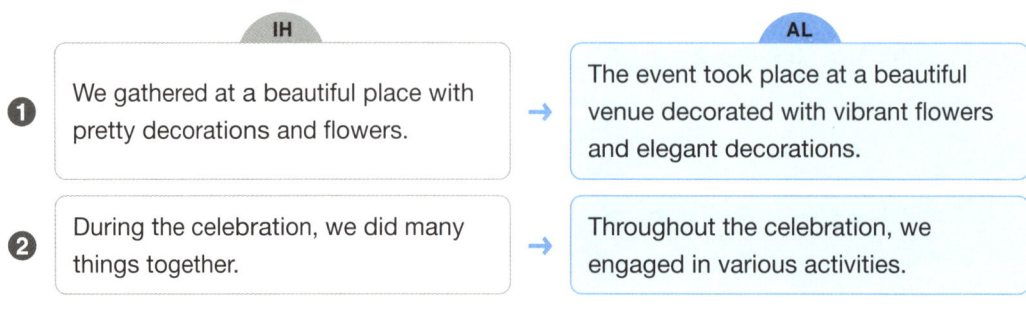

출제 가능성 ★★★★☆

Q3 Tell me about a memorable event that happened at a gathering or a celebration. Why was it memorable?

Question Analysis 질문 분석

Answer the following questions and identify the key matter and the information to be included in your response.
다음 질문에 답하며 답변의 주제와 반드시 포함되어야 할 내용이 무엇인지 파악해 보세요.

1. What is going to be the key matter of your response?
2. What information should your response include?

Warm Your Brain Up 브레인스토밍

Answer the following questions for ideas.
다음 질문에 답하며 답변 소재를 발굴해 보세요.

Intro	• Can you think of a special gathering or celebration where something unforgettable happened? • Why were you and others gathered?
Body	• What made the event so special that it remains unforgettable in your memory? • Did anything surprising or unexpected occur during the event? • How did people react and what emotions did they experience during the event?
Conclusion	• Did you learn any important lessons or gain any insights from this event?

AL Booster

- How did the event affect the overall atmosphere and mood of the gathering or celebration?

Useful Expressions

incredible 멋진　truly 정말로　as usual 평소처럼　unaware of ~에 대해 알지 못한　awaiting 기다리는　to one's surprise (~에게) 놀랍게도　something unexpected 예상치 못한 일　occur 발생하다　colleague 동료　surprise party 깜짝 파티　suddenly 갑자기　come alive 살아나다　clapping sound 박수 소리　join in 참여하다　fill A with B A를 B로 가득 채우다　heartwarming 따뜻한 마음을 불어넣는　unforgettable 잊지 못할　atmosphere 분위기　carefully planned 신중하게 계획된　care about 소중히 여기다

Pattern Drills 패턴 학습

Practice using the given sentence patterns to help you deliver your response clearly.
주어진 문장 패턴을 익혀 답변이 명확하게 전달될 수 있도록 연습해 보세요.

① On _____, something incredible happened.
- my birthday
- my graduation day
- my 5th wedding anniversary

② I was _____ as usual, unaware of the surprises awaiting me.
- studying in my room
- working at the office
- cooking dinner at home

③ The surprise performance created _____.
- goosebumps all over my body
- a heartwarming and emotional atmosphere
- a buzz of excitement and enthusiasm among the crowd

④ _____ made this event truly memorable.
- The kind words and moral support from my family
- The unexpected and heartfelt speeches
- The meaningful interactions and heartfelt conversations

Mini Actual Test 연습 문제

🎧 30_5.mp3

Respond to the following question while keeping in mind what you have learned.
앞서 배운 내용을 떠올리면서 다음 질문에 답변해 보세요.

> Can you share an unforgettable event that took place during a gathering or celebration? What made it memorable?

Model Answer 모범 답안

 30_6.mp3

Enhance your response by referring to the model answer.
다음 모범 답안을 참고하여 여러분의 답변을 발전시켜 보세요.

> On my 30th birthday, something incredible happened that made it a truly special celebration. I was working in the office as usual, unaware of the surprises awaiting me. But then, something unexpected occurred: my colleagues organized a surprise party! Suddenly, the office came alive with birthday singing and clapping. Everyone joined in, filling the space with happiness and laughter. The party created a heartwarming and unforgettable atmosphere, bringing us closer together. The carefully planned birthday song routine and the genuine joy on everyone's faces made this event truly memorable. It reminded me of the love and support I have in my life and how important it is to celebrate special moments with the people I care about. I will always hold this memory of my 30th birthday, filled with laughter and togetherness, close to my heart.

Level Up to AL AL 공략하기

Read the examples below and see how IH-level sentences can be rephrased at the AL level.
다음 예시를 읽고 IH 수준의 문장을 어떻게 AL 수준으로 바꾸어 말할 수 있는지 살펴보세요.

IH → **AL**

❶ Suddenly, the office came alive with birthday singing and clapping. → Suddenly, the office burst into life with the sounds of birthday singing and joyful clapping.

❷ It reminded me of the love and support I have in my life and how important it is to celebrate special moments with the people I care about. → It reminded me of the love and support I have in my life and the significance of celebrating special moments with the people around me.

Appendix 부록

ACTUAL TEST 1

ACTUAL TEST 2

ACTUAL TEST 1

Take this actual test as an opportunity for a final self-assessment. Since the real test doesn't display text on the screen, it's strongly advised that you focus on listening to the audio and refrain from reading the questions below.
실전 모의고사를 통해 여러분의 실력을 최종 점검해 보세요. 실제 시험에서 문제 텍스트는 화면에 나타나지 않으므로 가급적 음원만 듣는 것을 권장합니다.

#	Question
1	Let's start the interview now. Tell me something about yourself.
2	Tell me about the recycling system in your country. How is it done?
3	Now, tell me how you personally recycle. When, where, and how often do you recycle?
4	Tell me about a recent incident that happened related to recycling. What exactly happened? How did you deal with the situation?
5	Tell me about the things you do when you visit a friend's house. How often do you visit your friend's house? What do you usually do?
6	Talk about a time when you visited your friend's house when you were a child. Who did you visit? What did you do there? Tell me everything you remember.
7	Tell me about a memorable experience when you visited your friend's house. What happened? Why is it so memorable? Tell me everything from the beginning to the end.
8	What are some holidays in your country? What do people do during these holidays?
9	Have holidays in your country changed over the years? Are they different from what they used to be? Tell me about the changes in detail.
10	Tell me about a special holiday from your childhood. Where were you on that day? What do you remember doing? What made it so special?
11	I'll give you a situation and ask you to act it out. You want to watch a concert with your friends. Call the ticket office and ask three to four questions in order to gather detailed information about the concert.
12	Unfortunately, you have a problem which you need to resolve. You are ill on the day of the concert. Call one of your friends and explain your situation. Then offer two alternatives to handle this situation.
13	That's the end of the situation. Have you ever had tickets for a concert or other events, but you couldn't go? What was the problem? How did it affect your plan?
14	Please compare the activities that children and adults engage in at the park. Describe the facilities that cater to both age groups within the park.
15	Let's talk about some issues related to today's parks. What are the biggest challenges public parks are faced with these days? Discuss what has caused these issues. Which steps need to be taken to address these issues?

ACTUAL TEST ❷

Take this actual test as an opportunity for a final self-assessment. Since the real test doesn't display text on the screen, it's strongly advised that you focus on listening to the audio and refrain from reading the questions below.
실전 모의고사를 통해 여러분의 실력을 최종 점검해 보세요. 실제 시험에서 문제 텍스트는 화면에 나타나지 않으므로 가급적 음원만 듣는 것을 권장합니다.

#	Question
1	Let's start the interview now. Tell me something about yourself.
2	You indicated in the survey that you enjoy going to the park. Which park do you like to go to? Who do you usually go to the park with? Please describe your favorite park in detail.
3	What do you usually do at the park? How often do you go? Tell me about the routine on a typical day at the park.
4	Tell me about a memorable incident that happened at the park. What exactly happened, and how did you deal with the situation? What made that incident so memorable? Give me all the details.
5	Explain where and when you usually listen to music. Do you go to concerts, or do you enjoy listening to music on the radio? Explain how you enjoy music.
6	Can you talk about when you initially gained an interest in music? What types of music did you initially enjoy? Trace and discuss your musical interests from childhood until the present.
7	Tell me about a memorable experience when you attended a live music event, whether it was a concert or a street performance. Describe the atmosphere and your thoughts on the music you heard during the event.
8	What piece of technology do people use every day? How do people use it? Why is it so widely used?
9	Explain how technology has transformed our lives over the years. What are the similarities and differences between the past and the present? Share your perspective on whether you believe these changes have been beneficial.
10	Tell me about a time when you had trouble using a piece of technology or an electronic device. What happened? How did you deal with the situation? Tell me about the incident in detail.
11	I'm going to give you a situation and ask you to act it out. You want to buy a piece of furniture. Call the store and ask three to four questions about the furniture you would like to buy.
12	I'm sorry, but there is a problem I need you to resolve. You have received the new furniture, but there is a problem. Call the store and explain the situation. Propose two or three ways to resolve this problem.
13	That's the end of the situation. Have you ever had an unsatisfactory experience with a piece of furniture you bought? What was the problem? Tell me how you dealt with the situation.
14	Compare the movies today to the movies that you watched when you were young. How have movies changed over the years?
15	What are some issues that the movie industry is facing these days? What makes them so important? Tell me about some recent issues in the movie industry.

memo

memo

memo